The
Railroaders

The Railroaders

by Stuart Leuthner

Foreword by Oliver Jensen

Photographs by Lawson Little

Random House New York

ACKNOWLEDGMENTS

After ten years of work on one project, there are quite a few people to thank. Without their help and support, it might have taken another ten, or worse, not gotten done at all. The Brotherhood of Locomotive Engineers, especially their president, John F. Sytsma, and Richard Cook, public relations, require a special mention. Dick helped me find the engineers, dug out their records, sent me issues of the brotherhood's newspaper, *Locomotive Engineer,* provided some of his own railroad photographs, read manuscripts, and sometimes just dropped me a line of encouragement.

At the United Transportation Union, Lou Corsi, director of public relations, suggested when I first contacted him in 1972 that the men I was interested in were all gone. However, on his own, he began to contact local chairmen, and a few months later I started receiving lists of names in the mail. That was the real beginning.

"Edited by Oliver Jensen" doesn't even come close. It should be "Guided by." A twelve-hour editing session with him is not to be believed. Oliver is one of those rare people who not only understand history but can make it alive and interesting. He also appreciates the beauty of a New York Central Hudson.

Bob Loomis, my editor at Random House, with his gentle and sometimes not so gentle suggestions. Bob helped turn what was at one time a "design project" into a real book. Also at Random House, Marilyn Doof, Bernie Klein, Bob Aulicino, Barbara Willson and Calvin Curtis for their special skills and extreme patience.

Susan Attaway was there for the worst times. She had to spend one night in the basement of a church meeting hall with our year-old daughter because there was no place else to stay. Somehow we made it through and I appreciate her financial support in those rather trying times.

The railroad artifacts which appear throughout the book were photographed by Benn Mitchell and Peter Nicholas. The objects and photographs were supplied by the Depot Attic of Ardsley, New York, the Valley Railroad Museum and the railroaders themselves.

I felt that it was very important to have a photograph of the person who is "talking" to us. The old photographs are fine, but what does the man or woman look like today? Where did they work or live? Lawson Little combines the artist with a very realistic attitude toward life. He has given us an image that is exciting visually and helps us understand the person a little better. There must have been times—in fact, I know there were times—when he thought this whole project was some pipe dream of mine, but he stayed with it. I find it hard to put into words how I feel about his contribution, so I will simply say, again, thank you.

Everybody else. I wish there was space to give each one a paragraph because they deserve it. Peter Tilp, Ron Ziel, Carolyn M. Jensen, Don Janney, Aubrey B. Seigler, Garnell Brown, W. Graham Claytor, Jr., James Bistline, Raymond Delano, Bill Withuhn, Robert Jones, Association of American Railroads, Raymond Loewy, Bryant A. Long, Lenny Moffetone, William Sprinkle, Griff Teller, Bernie Morits, Alice Muller, Joe Bux, John Ryan, Mel Ost, Fred Furminger, Amtrak, Harold K. Vollrath, Albert Brown, Robert Collins, John Krause, Nancy Dolansek, Jean Marie Lynn, Paul Krot, Ernest Pellington, R. H. Ochiltree, Henry Horenstein, Lee Post, Rogers Whitaker, Dan McKinney, J. M. Roche, J. W. McDonald, Harry Allerton, Russell Sturgis, Ann Higginbotham, Katy Wern, Robert Barbera, Peter Cornwall, C. R. Wilburne, George A. Day, Jim Lyons, J. W. Hodges, W. B. Hopkins, Nellie Kelch Brock, Gwendolyn Knight Donmachie, H. A. MacMorran, John McMahon, William Wilcox, T. J. Smith, Marion and Douglas Attaway, Robert Parke, G. P. Sheahan, Joanne V. Matejov, Margaret Bennett Possamato, Steve Brown, Jon Lopez, Loren Breck, Joe Lassiter, Ed Robinson, Arthur Thomasson and Charles Whitten.

S.L.

Library of Congress Cataloging in Publication Data
Leuthner, Stuart.
The railroaders.

1. Railroads—United States—Employees—History.
2. Locomotive engineers—United States—History.
I. Title.
HD8039.R12U647   1983   331.7'61385'0973   81-40236
ISBN 0-394-51861-6

Manufactured in the United States of America
98765432
First Edition

CONTENTS

IRON FIREMAN

FOREWORD

When he was fourteen, and an ardent reader of Horatio Alger, Carl Peterson knew exactly what he wanted to be, which was a locomotive engineer, riding high in the cab of one of the steam monsters that hauled America on its journeys. It was not just any locomotive, however, that figured in his dreams, but one that pulled the most famous train in the land, the *Twentieth Century Limited*. To his surprise, he eventually got that job. The life Peterson led, and the experiences the other thirty-two old-time railroaders describe here in their own vivid words, is scarcely imaginable today. It was dangerous, back-breaking work, rewarding less to the pocketbook than to the soul.

"Railroad men," said another veteran engineer, Chester Geaslen of the Louisville & Nashville, "come to the railroad in the spring of their lives, and somehow remain to their autumn years, working while other people sleep, and trying to sleep while other people are working, but then, I'll tell you something . . . without exception, they would want it no other way."

For most of the men in this remarkable book the spring of their lives was the early years of this century, when railroads were the greatest industry in the country and commanded its largest work force. In 1910 there were 1.7 million of them, roughly four times the number working on the railroads today. If you went to work then, you are in your nineties today, and a rare survivor of a lost tribe. And it is a fortunate thing that Stuart Leuthner undertook in the last ten years to track down and record the memories of this proud, curious, vanishing breed. Criss-crossing the country, pursuing as many as five hundred leads, sometimes arriving too late, painstakingly interviewing his old gentlemen—and two ladies besides—he managed to rescue a slice of history that might well have disappeared unrecorded. Making this book was a job that had to be done now, or never.

He began with the aristocrats of blue-collar America, the engineers, who should rate beside the plainsmen, the cowboys, the sea captains, and the early aeronauts as folk heroes, but he soon realized that a truer picture also required the supporting actors in the drama. There was no engineer without a fireman and his scoop shovel, at least in the great age of steam: you graduated from one job to the other. And no train moved without track layers and section crews, without engine shops ringing with the clangor of machinists, blacksmiths and boilermakers, or, for that matter, without dispatchers in towers and crew callers rousing the men at all hours. On the train in those days rode also the lordly conductor, and the brakemen swaying perilously along the tops of freight cars, not to forget the dignified dining-car crews, sleeping-car porters and such special constant riders as the RPO man. For those with long memories, the RPO was the railway post office, rolling along with the rest of the "var-

At the Valley Railroad's Essex, Connecticut, station, Oliver Jensen (right) shakes hands with John Sheldon, volunteer trainman. It was July 29, 1971, and the newly reopened railroad's first train was just about to depart from the depot.

nish," or passenger cars. The mail was sorted en route, for next-day delivery at distant destinations, by men like Frank Lundy, possessors of fast fingers and encyclopedic memories for streets and routes and zones. Behind the men in the cab, tending the inferno in the firebox, chanting signals to each other, watching gauges and the shining rails ahead, rode many lost arts and skills.

It was often not easy for Leuthner to get this reticent company to talk freely to his tape recorder; railroad men tend to keep to themselves; their modesty is strong and their humor quiet. Considerable deeds of heroism or endurance are mentioned casually; much past injustice is allowed to slide away. Railroading was once stratified by race. Consider, for example, the changes related here by John Tibbs, retired Pullman porter, and Oswald Thorne, once a redcap, in days when both these jobs were occupied solely by black men. From that era, in which millions (mostly white) saw nothing wrong with the system, they preserve not only humor but forgiving natures. There is no black engineer, because there weren't any. There were black firemen, to be sure. It is also true that engineers and experienced firemen generally spelled each other at the throttle, but it never seems to have occurred to the companies or the unions to match the title and the pay to the actual job. War, which is an equalizing as well as a destructive force, brought changes not only for blacks but for women, like the two who appear in these pages, although it is still a little surprising to encounter the gentler sex working on Amtrak trains, like the young woman brakeman ("TRAINMAN" her badge read)

I saw swaying up an aisle with her pageboy hairdo bobbing under her cap.

Railroading is no longer the father-and-son business it once was. Steam has given way to the diesel, which the old-timers regarded with mixed emotions. Your clothes stay clean, but the thrill, and the sense of controlling a majestic piece of machinery, is gone. Henry Williamson of the Kansas City Southern is reconciled after a fashion, but still thinks a diesel locomotive "smells like a bus." What is perhaps more significant is the fact, noticed to their sorrow by many railroad men, that the American people, who for over a century waved at the passing of any steam locomotive, don't seem to wave anymore. An era has ended.

One of the great advantages of electronic tape recording is that it preserves exact language; its disadvantage is that it will ramble and repeat when the interviewer asks questions to make sure he understands a point or a story. In the editing, the author and I have intervened mainly to remove repetition or to shift passages around to make the narratives or the chronology clearer. These are nevertheless authentic voices, a part of the unknown history of America.

OLIVER JENSEN

INTRODUCTION

This is not a railroad book. It is a *railroaders* book. It is about the people who worked for the railroads. The engineers, brakemen, chefs, executives, the people who made it work. With few exceptions, books dealing with the railroads have become cavalcades of iron. Page after page of locomotives leaning into curves, in the roundhouse, at the coaling dock. You name it, it's been photographed. A typical caption: "Rods flashing, high-drivered Pennsy K-4s No. 5404 wheels the varnish as she hits her stride with the *Broadway Limited* near the Horseshoe Curve on a cold February afternoon, 1945." Or, "A Monon light Pacific, No. 411, with her characteristic flared stack passing through Dyer, Indiana, on the advertised with the *Hoosier* on a hot August day, 1947." The late Lucius Beebe went so far as to suggest that the only "classic" way to photograph a train was from the three-quarter head-on angle, the right side of course, to show the reverse gear, and the rods had to be down. In his book *Highliners,* he said, "The perfect railroad photograph—with its rural background, its clarity of definition of all moving parts, its indication of speed through smoke and steam exhaust, its full-length view of the entire train and its absence of any object or matter to distract the attention from the locomotive and consist themselves—is not easy to come by."

Evidently most railroad photographers and writers considered people among the objects that could distract us from the equipment. The only clue that there are two men in the cab of the locomotive usually is an elbow on the window sill. Sometimes the crew would spot the photographer standing in the weeds and two heads appear in the window, sometimes with an arm extended in greeting. These, however, were the exceptions. Why this happened is easy to understand. The steam engine is a very photogenic machine, especially when going fast. If there was a choice, who would want to take a photograph of a brakeman throwing a switch or mechanic working on a lathe when all those locomotives were just waiting to have their pictures taken? What writer would want to bother talking to a Pullman porter or trackman when he could compile a roster on every engine that the Pennsylvania Railroad ever owned or even thought of owning?

Don't get me wrong, there's nothing wrong with these books. I've got a wall of them. They are historically important and just plain fun to look at. If only the authors would have a retoucher get rid of the dust spots on the photographs. If there's anything you wanted to know about an engine, it's been written or will be soon. Did you know that the Burlington Class M-4 Texas types' operating speed increased but their tractive force was reduced to 83,300 lbs. when they were rebuilt in the thirties and their cylinder bore was reduced from 31″ to 28″? What about the man who made that M-4 get up and go? Or the man who kept it running? The railroaders have been neglected.

There have been exceptions. Don Ball's *The Decade of the Trains* has some wonderful photographs of men and women working on the railroads during World War II. These photographs are just as interesting, if not more so, than the motive power. For once the people become the focal point and the machinery the background. In his book *The New Haven Railroad: A Fond Look Back,* Andrew Pavlucik took a few pages away from the iron and included photographs of New Haven railroad men. A great deal of the text is based on his conversations with New Haven men. Some fine first-person stories are also included in Robert Jones's two-volume series, *Two Feet Between the Rails.* It's about time we heard from the people who actually sat in the cabs, made up the berths, threw the switches, and spiked the rails.

The railroads were one of the most important industries in this country when these people were on the job. Even

Writing railroad books is hard work. Dirty, tired but obviously happy, this refugee from the seventies is the author after riding in the cab of ex–Nickel Plate 759 with engineer Andy Barbera. On a fan trip from Bellows Falls, Vermont, to Boston in the fall of 1973.

into the 1950s, they were complicated systems of machinery and people stretching over the entire country. It's an undisputed fact that without the railroads' superhuman effort, World War II might not have been won. The railroads worked the way they did because the people worked. Worked in the true meaning of the word. There was only one way to do the job, whether you were running an engine pulling the *Super Chief* or replacing a rail on a branch line. You did it the right way. Not because you were a company man, but because that was the way you had been taught. A railroad employee didn't give 100 percent, he usually gave more.

Today we see the decline of American industry. For instance, foreign competition has the automobile manufacturers in big trouble. I find it hard to blame somebody for buying a Japanese car if the American car he could buy instead includes a glove-compartment door that falls off after six months or a hood that doesn't fit. There are many reasons why this has happened, but I think one of the most important is that the worker who puts that door or hood on doesn't care about the job he has. The least important thing in his life is his job except for the paycheck. He or she would rather be out in the family boat, playing racquetball or battling spaceships on the TV. American industry is trying to turn this around, but it will take more than television commercials saying that we believe in quality. It is a big job to re-educate workers in a work ethic.

I don't want to create the impression that everything

about the "good old days" was wonderful and that we should somehow go back to shoveling twenty or thirty tons of coal and working sixteen hours a day. That is nothing to be nostalgic about; it was backbreaking work. In the nineteenth century and the early part of this one, a man belonged to the railroad. He went home when they told him he could. When the Brotherhood of Railroad Brakemen was organized by eight employees of the Delaware & Hudson Railroad in 1883, it was the first step toward making a railroad job what it was to become in this century. Even in the 1930s, this same D & H railroad didn't own an engine with an automatic stoker. When the firemen's union asked that they be installed, Leonor F. Loree, the president of the railroad, told them they had the best stokers $1.25 could buy, Red Edge shovels!

Even with conditions at times that you couldn't pay people today to work in, every one of the men and women I talked to said they'd go out and do it again. They enjoyed the work they did and took pride in it. The railroaders were the aristocrats of blue-collar labor, especially the engineers in the days of steam. Most people don't realize it, but the railroads are still operating in this country, some quite efficiently. They are hauling a lot of freight, if not people. There are still men and women who are putting in a full day's work and doing the best job they possibly can. As with many things, only the glory is lost. The trappings that went with the age of steam were as important as the locomotives themselves. A set of Oshkosh pinstriped overalls, a neckerchief, a pair of goggles—that's a hard act to follow, especially if you're in the cab of a diesel engine that's one step removed from a bus.

The people in this book were the railroaders from that overall era. Here are their words and pictures. The human side of the railroads. They do talk about the equipment, but they also talk about the men and women they worked with. The people who made the whole wonderful system work. They have something to say about another time and another way of thinking. A belief in the job, the equipment and most of all themselves. I hope you enjoy their words as much as I enjoyed gathering them.

Some final thoughts. I tried to make this work as complete as possible, but because of the reality of travel, time and publishing, only so many railroads could be included. If your personal favorite is missing, I hope you understand that I would have liked to include them all. Also, there are five people who worked in some way for the New York Central. I made no apology for that because I have always thought since I was old enough to realize what a railroad was that the Central was the best that ever ran. I would also like to give special thanks to the railroad men and women whom I taped, photographed and got to know over the last ten years. I feel privileged to have made their acquaintance and passed some time in their company, and as Clyde Redfield, an engineer on the Lehigh Valley, said, "If there are railroads in the next world, I hope the tracks are smooth and the engines are all good steamers."

S.L.

When you put in sixty years and over two million miles on the Kansas City Southern, there are bound to have been a lot of changes on the railroad. It's a long way from kerosene headlights to these diesel road switchers.

WILLIAM H. WILLIAMSON
Shreveport, Louisiana

Many of the men in this book are elderly and have the health problems that go with advancing age. Henry Williamson was on the "downgrade," as he put it. His health was failing and he was using a walker to get around his daughter's home in Shreveport. Every once in a while he would glare at it and declare, "It's a hell of a way for a man to get around." However, the complaints were few and far between. When he talked about his railroad career, you could almost see the years fade away. He was a physical man who worked hard, used his body and enjoyed doing it. He'd sometimes let the fireman run the engine so he could "throw a little coal around." That's one of the reasons a lot of men resented the diesels. You weren't really working your engine or yourself. Henry wasn't happy having his picture taken with a bunch of "cabbage cutters." At one point he turned around and looked at them. "They still smell like a bus," he said.

As a boy I worked for Chatfield-Burnham Hardware in Texarkana, in their sheet-metal shop, or tin shop, as they called it then. Well, they had a strike, the men trying to get a little raise, and I was out of a job. I went looking for a new job and couldn't find one no place. There was no work at all for a boy. One day my aunt sent me to the meat market to get a soup bone. I went to that market but walked right by because I heard there was some work being done at the old Pacific Railroad, and I decided I'd go down there and see if I couldn't get me a train out of there to go someplace else.

I went to the old Missouri Pacific yards; Ed McCallum was yardmaster there, and he knew me. He said, "Henry, what you doing down here?"

"Well," I says, "I'm trying to get out of town. I can't find a job here, and I'd like to get a ride someplace on a freight train." The conductor, a real nice fellow, came up and told me to go back down to the caboose and sit down. The train would be leaving there in about an hour. And so I went to Little Rock in it. I worked in different places all the way down Louisiana to New Orleans, crossed the river, and came back up into Texas, Oklahoma and Arkansas. I'd been gone from home about eight months when I caught another freight train out of Little Rock to Texarkana. I'd accumulated a little money, had quite a lot of little wads of it in my pocket. I got back into Texarkana about four in the afternoon, got off the train and went back down to that meat market. The butcher was cutting meat in there and I says, "How about selling me a soup bone?"

"Why, Henry," he says, "you're a little late, we don't have no soup bone this time of day."

I says, "I don't care, they sent me after a soup bone, and that's what I'm going to take back."

He whacked me up some meat and wrapped it up. When I got home my aunt was sitting on the front porch. She greeted me with "Welcome home, red-head."

I said, "Here's your soup bone."

She said she was going in the house and cook it up right away, and how's I might not be the quickest boy in the world but I was dependable.

Then I had a job in Dennison, Texas, on the Katy Line, in the sheet-metal department. I worked out there for about eight months. Then they cut me off, part because there was a slack in business, and part because I was too young. I left there to come to Texarkana and got myself a job as a cashier, kind of a boomer job, on the Pittsburgh & Gulf Railroad, it was called then. Then I found there was

"Scrap Iron" in front of a KCS switcher in the early 1940s. His fireman is already in the cab of the engine, and Henry looks impatient to get up there himself and turn her loose.

another job on the Kansas City Southern as a hostler's helper and fire knocker. The hostler would put coal and water in the tender, and clean out the fire. He would get the engine ready for the crew and run it through the yard to the ready track. I hired out right away. That was 1903.

They was all coal burners then, and we had to clean the fires and dump the ash pans. The cinders and ashes would come down into what they called the ash pit. One day a crew came down with a caboose and an engine which needed its pan cleaned out. They didn't come in over the ash pit like they was supposed to, and the crew went over to get coffee while the pan was cleaned out. The old hostler told me to get my hoe and go over there and rake out the pan for them. They didn't want to take her over to the pit, wanted me to clean her out right there. By the time I got back with my hoe and crawled under the engine, I'd taken up a little time. The crew had come out of the restaurant and was ready to leave. The hostler, meantime, had gone back over to his little shanty. The crew came back and didn't see anybody around the engine, climbed up and got ready to go. I was still underneath there when the engineer started off. I jumped up on the wooden brake beam and started hollering as loud as I could. I wasn't sure he'd be able to hear me with all that machinery a-flopping around my head. After a little bit he finally heard me, set the brake and with the fireman came down off the engine. "Where's that hostler at?" he asked me.

I said, "I don't know, back at the shanty, I guess." For my safety he was supposed to stay up on the engine until I was finished. I came out from under the engine and said, "All right, let's go, you can highball out of here."

"No," he says, "you get up on this engine; we'll back up. I'm not finished with that fellow."

We backed up to the shanty, and the engineer got out. He gave that hostler a real dressing-down and a good punch in the nose. Railroading was a lot rougher in those days, and you could get hurt or killed if somebody didn't do his job.

I helped the hostler for eight or nine months, riding engines in the yard, learning how to fire. In 1903 I made out an application as fireman, and that is the year my seniority dates from.

In those days, all the engines were hand-fired. Some of them could break a man's back. We called some of the Baldwins "coldwater Baldwins" because it was so hard to keep any steam in them. That was a real job, hand-firing coal. When we converted from coal to oil, it was much easier. A steam pipe would run back into your oil tank. Put that steam pipe on, and it would heat the oil up, thinning it out. Then it went into the atomizer. That would pick the oil up and spray it around the firebox. You had to use the atomizer or the oil would drift, go out on the track raw and catch the track on fire. One day I was coming down on a slow freight with a new fireman. I'd told him a lot of times to keep that atomizer going. Before I got to the Red River Bridge, I looked back around the corner and seen some fire. We'd just been drifting down the hill, and the firebox was full of live oil. I just let that train coast down to a stop. We just was there on the bridge and waited until the fire was all burnt. The fireman got a lesson right there. He just about set the whole works on fire and he was a bit more careful after that.

When you were firing, each man would teach you, but you would study your books, too, on combustion, mechanical trouble, breakdowns, and things like that. You'd have to go before a pretty stiff examination to qualify. They wanted to put you out there to really run that engine. Some men never could get the job through their heads. They sometimes had to take two, three examinations before they could get passed.

You didn't just run the engine either. You had to make out your working reports. You had to report what you could or couldn't do on the road. Also make reports on what had to be done in the shop by the mechanic. If there was anything wrong with the engine, you were the only fella knew about it. A good man takes time to work on his report so he can pinpoint his trouble. Sometimes your valves were out of square, the staybolts could be loose, or your wedges need aligning. Same thing with the diesels, they didn't change that part of the job. With all those electrical parts, you needed to know what you were talking about. If you took five or six engines of the same kind, you wouldn't find the same parts on each, even though they were supposedly the same type. Especially with the steam engines. They were always making changes on them. Making them more modern. Each one was different. One would steam with plenty to spare, and another would kill a man trying to just keep her moving.

When I started they didn't have any electrical headlights for the engines or coaches. In the coaches we burnt fish oil. In the locomotives we had coal-oil headlights and marker lights. When you went on a passing track to get in the clear of another train, the fireman would have to go out in front and put a hood over the headlight so the other train would know you were in the clear. Next they went to carbon arc lights for headlights. They'd burn out right in the middle of nowhere while you were going along. You'd have to go out on the engine and light it on the run so you could meet the schedules.

Another thing in those days, the roadbed was so bad in some places you'd be limited to ten miles an hour. No ballast at all in some places. A few times I had engineers make me get off and look at the track before they'd go ahead. The brakes got a lot better, too, over the years. Finally got so dependable you didn't think about them not working. In the old days, you thought about them a lot and there were a lot of wrecks from brakes not holding. We had locomotives from every railroad in the country it seemed, when I started running. Company didn't have much money, I guess. Just taking what the other railroads had to sell. That was when we got the Baldwins,

Just married in 1911, Henry and his wife, Addie. The car was a photographer's prop because you couldn't afford one when you were making $3 a day on the railroad.

McQueens, Rogers, Grants, and all the rest. They made as many kinds of locomotives as they did automobiles.

In 1905 we had a yellow-fever epidemic in Louisiana. All the states were quarantined against Louisiana, so we had to cut off the division point from De Queen, Arkansas, to Ravenna, on the Texas-Oklahoma border. We'd go to the state line, and if you were going to Texarkana, you had to stay in the pesthouse until the time was up to go back. They were awfully short of engineers, so I was promoted up. At that time I was strictly on freight. Passenger trains take different qualifications. It affects your seniority, and so forth. You see, it's difficult to get a passenger train because that's the oldest job on the railroad. I mean, you have to be the oldest to hold the job. I done some passenger work about the 1920s, pinch-hitting for some men, but there were too many engineers ahead of me at the time. I passed my third-year examination in 1908, and that qualified me for anything, any kind of engine I wanted to run.

When I started as a hostler's helper, I made $1.50 a day. Firing paid $2, and when I was promoted to run, the rate was $3 a day. You know, that was for a sixteen-hour day! That was when I was promoted to run and was working on the extra board. Sometimes in those years, I'd be cut back to firing. That was before they had the sixteen-hour law. The government had made a law that you could only work sixteen hours. That was before World War I. During the war, though, they had to let it slide. Just needed the men and you didn't mind. Before that, whenever you got out there, you was going to be out there for a while. You worked twenty-four hours, thirty, anytime. You was just out there. Why, I've been on duty as much as thirty-six hours without sleep during World War I. In those days, labor laws weren't so strict. The wars were hard on the railroads, especially World War I. We were the only way to really move equipment and men. They had them troop trains, and they were pretty rough for both us and the troops. After the war things went back to normal.

The *Southern Belle* was one of the first trains on the

Kansas City Southern to use the diesels. At first I hated them. But once I got on them, I had to admit, they was easier and cleaner to run. I didn't get that old kick out of them that I got out of those old steam engines. In my heart, I'd rather have a steam engine any day. I wanted to stick my head out of the cab and watch those big drivers roll. My first trip in a diesel, I wouldn't have gotten it, but the other man had to lay off. The other fella was all worked up. He asked me, "How do you like my engine, how do you like my engine?" I told him, "I don't like diesels. If I wanted to run a streetcar, I'd go down and see old man Jacobs at the Shreveport City Transit."

I had my worst experience in a diesel, too. Coming down from De Queen to Shreveport. They had put that new train on. The *Southern Belle.* Trying to make a crack train out of her. It was August 1941. I left De Queen about ten minutes late that day. I made the time up coming into Texarkana and came in on time. I didn't know then, but my wife got on Number One, my train, at Texarkana to come back to Shreveport. She'd go up a lot of times when I was on the road to see her sister. I had heavy mail service at Texarkana, and it laid me out there fifteen minutes. I left late on account of that mail being sorted. By running at maximum speed I figured I could just bite off a little of that time I'd lost between each stop. We got out of our next stop five or six minutes late, and I said to my fireman, "We'll just take it nice and smooth, and we'll get to Shreveport on time." We were just south of Vivian, and when you come down from there you've got four miles of straight track. I was letting her run and we came down through there at about eighty miles an hour when the headlight of my engine showed on glass about a thousand feet ahead of me.

It was a "dodger" work train out there working the refineries. Picking up and dropping off cars. He was out there working and had forgotten about Number One. That was me! That work train got ready to leave and pulled on out on the main line. They hadn't lit up their markers on the old coach they were using for a caboose. They figured to light them when they got moving. If they'd been burning red, we'd probably have seen them earlier. But when I caught our headlight reflecting on that glass, I saw it was a train and "wiped the clock off"—that's railroad slang for using all your brakes. I put it into emergency and it looked for a second like I might be able to get pretty near stopped. On the end of the throttle there's a button. You shove that in, and it shuts the engine off, kills the whole works. When your engine's dead, there's less chance of it catching fire or anything. Kills the whole train, no lights in the coaches or anything. That's one good thing about the diesels. You smashed up with an old steam engine, and they kept right on steaming. Lot of men scalded to death by live steam.

The last thing I remember, I had the whistle pulled down and I saw the brakeman on the coach ahead come running out and jump off. It was an old Louisiana & Arkansas coach. I guess the thing must have been ninety years old. It had wooden sills in it which were supposed to be outlawed by all the railroads. However, it was just before we got in the war and the railroad was very busy. It had been putting all this old equipment on. It was pitiful. If it would roll they'd use it. When I hit it, the car buckled in the middle, threw up one of those sills and sent it through my locomotive's windshield. If that car had been steel, we would have made a hard coupling, that's all. In fact, the sill hit me in the head, curled my scalp back and knocked me out. Broke my arm, too.

Well, the conductor on my train knew something had happened and he started for the head end to see what was wrong. My wife got up and came down too. The conductor asked her not to come in case I was in bad shape. He said it was rough going on the tracks. She told him it was her husband down there and she was coming, and that was that. They were lifting me out of the wrecked cab and carrying me to the ambulance to take me off when they got there. Addie wanted to come with me in the ambulance, but the driver said it would be a rough ride. She'd heard me use the expression "take the bridle off" if you were late with a train. She told that driver to take the bridle off, and she would worry about the rough ride. She did tell me later that it was the wildest ride she ever had.

Nobody was really hurt in the wreck but me. My fireman had jumped off about the time we hit. He fell down the embankment and sprained his ankle. I was off work about six months. They had the same kind of wreck out on the Burlington just before that. The engineer ran into a passenger train that was on a block out there. He set his brakes, and he didn't have any. Ran into the hind end of this train with all-steel equipment. When it was all over, the engineer went with the fireman to the coffee shop across the street and got a cup of coffee. My trouble was all on account of that wood-frame outfit.

You asked me about my nickname, "Scrap Iron." A lot of railroad men end up with nicknames and I got mine from a dispatcher. I was going north one day, and the strap bolt broke on my main rod. I headed into Ashton and met another train. Then I went over to the section house where they had a lot of bolts and things. I didn't expect to find a bolt just like the broken one, but I reckoned to find one I could patch up with. The dispatcher wanted to know when I was going to get out of there with my train. The conductor told him I was over there in the scrap iron hunting for a bolt to repair my engine with. I found a bolt, made the repairs and got it all ready to go. Wasn't a first-class job, but it was one I could damn well live with. The next day, coming out of De Queen, I got some messages up there to do some work on the way down. The messages said, "Scrap Iron," do this or that. The conductor came down and told me I had got a new name. I didn't think anything of it, but it spread like anything and got all over the railroad. I don't know why something like that will hold on so long. I went down to the doctor's office not so long ago to get a little checkup, and he walks out and says, "How you been, Scrap Iron?"

The burned-out building behind Joseph Morits (right) and his son, Bernie, is all that's left of the Danbury machine shop. The roundhouse burned to the ground when a bum started a fire to keep warm.

JOSEPH A. MORITS
Brewster, New York

When the diesels first appeared in the 1920s, they were considered little more than curiosities. By the end of the 1950s, dieselization of the American railroads was almost complete. When the steam engines disappeared, so did the men who took care of them. Diesels didn't need armies of machinists, blacksmiths, boilermakers and their helpers. The huge roundhouses and shops they labored in are gone or lie in ruins. The skills men like Joseph Morits developed during their long careers were suddenly obsolete. You didn't need a valvesetter like Joe on a diesel; you needed an electrician. It was difficult to argue about the economic realities of the diesel engine. They needed less maintenance. Instead of "shopping," which is to say heavily overhauling, an engine, or adding modern refinements to it, which was the case with steam, railroads simply replaced diesels with new units. This was, however, one more of the changes in railroading that seemed to make it less human.

The New York New Haven and Hartford RAILROAD CO.

I always wanted to manufacture something and I'd always been interested in the railroads and I guess they just came together. I was always hanging around the railroad, even when I was growing up in Swanton, Vermont. There was a little railroad, the St. Johnsbury & Lake Champlain, and it ran right in back of our house. I was born and grew up in Swanton. That's only eight miles from the Canadian border. My father worked in a marble mill that was about a mile from our house. He worked right in the mill, grinding, shaping the marble. I've still got a table with a top that my father made.

I left school and went in as an apprentice machinist on the Central of Vermont at St. Albans. You signed a paper that you would put in the four years. St. Albans was only nine miles away from Swanton and I used to ride the trolley car to work. Cost a nickel then. When you first started in the shop they'd put you on simple things. You'd be handling machines; shapers, lathes, everything. The foreman would show you how to do the job and keep an eye on you. You'd do that for six months and then do something else for another six months. They would assign you to a regular mechanic and you'd help him and learn from him. You were always watching the other men working, how they did things. While you were working they'd follow you pretty close. Give you an examination every two or three months, see what you'd learned. If you did all right, they'd move you on to something else. Do another job.

We had school, too. Go one night a week on your own time. Taught us everything, even drafting, at those classes. How to read blueprints. I went to school all during the time I worked for the railroad. When they'd get a new engine, the railroad would send us to Schenectady, right up to the American Locomotive Works. They made a lot of our locomotives on the New Haven. We'd have a class in the morning, and in the afternoon we'd go right out to the shop. The Alco people would show us what was different or new with that engine and how to maintain it. In fact, when I was at St. Albans, the first electric generators for the headlights came. The CV sent me down to Pittsburgh to study them things. That must have been in the early twenties. When I got back another guy and myself went around and showed everybody else how it worked. That's how the railroad worked it. You'd come back from the schools and then hold classes for the other men.

I really liked the mechanical end of things and never found it too hard picking it up. If you were mechanically inclined it would rub off on you. Your apprenticeship was

for four years, but I took an extra one and learned welding. Electric welding was new then and I think I was about the third one in the shop to take it up. While I was up at St. Albans I saw what I really wanted, valve setting, and I nailed that down as soon as I could. It was a good thing to know because not too many could do it.

There was a Frenchman named Bernier. That's all he did, set valves. That man had built them right up from nothing. Assembled them on the engine. He dressed up as clean as anybody working in a store. Finished the day like that. He took a liking to me and I worked with him pretty close. Not many men tackled valve gear. Not only was it hard to do, but everybody who knew how to do it was holding out on how to do it. You had to remember a lot of things. Of course, the machine shop seemed more logical, they needed more men in there and you could always get a job, but I wanted that valve job. A lot of men didn't like working under the engine but that never bothered me.

When Joe Morits had his picture taken outside the round-house office with his new Dodge in 1948, he had fifty men working for him. Today his son has eight. He's lucky to have that many.

You had to be under the engine because we had the old Stephenson valve gear back then. Everything was under the engine and you had to get down in the pit. That was the disadvantage of that valve gear. It was one of the first they used but we had engines on the New Haven that used it until the end of the steam engines. Switchers, some small jobs. I think the Walschaerts was the best valve gear anybody ever had. Just the way it was designed and constructed. Heavier steel. It was simple and would stay in line longer. Another one we had was the Baker, but that was more complicated and had a lot of pieces that could go wrong in a hurry. Valve gear was like anything else, sometimes they'd get out of true, sometimes they would just break. What usually happened was that something got loose and moved some way or another. You looked after them so things weren't breaking that often. Might bend an eccentric rod, and you'd put it in the fire and lengthen or shorten it, whatever it needed.

The engineer would know that something was wrong. He could tell if the valve gear was out of square. He could tell by the sound of the exhaust. Once you got an engine going, you could tell if you had a nice clean exhaust or if the valves were out of time. If there was a problem, the engineer would put it in his report and that report would end up on my desk. If it was a boiler problem, I'd give it to the boilermaker foreman and he'd take care of it. Leaks, staybolts, things like that. Same with anything else, give it to the man who worked on that specific thing. If it was valves, I'd run the engine over myself and tell the machinist what was wrong. When you ran the engine over, you took another engine and moved the engine you were working on back and forth so you could watch the whole

It was 1920 when Joe, "The Cowboy," and his brother-in-law, Lewis Compano, had their picture taken at a circus sideshow.

valve action. I'd walk right next to the engine while it was moving. I'd take a scribe and make a mark on the valve stem when it got to the end of its travel. Do the same thing with the valve gear on the other side of the engine. By doing that you could get all four openings the same. Exhaust and intake. That's what you were trying to do. By adjusting the rods and links, you got things squared up. Everything was the same on each side of the engine, except the engineer's side had the reverse lever. That lifted the radius rod up and the engine could go in reverse. There was only one way to set the valves, the right way, but an engineer could use that reverse lever to shorten the stroke of the valve. What he was doing was actually changing the timing of that engine.

When the engineer was starting out he wanted the most power. He'd put that lever down in the corner and that would give him the most power in the cylinder. Then, as he started to pick up speed he'd move the lever towards the center, and the valve was leading the cylinder so the steam got into the cylinder early and you were using your steam more efficiently. That was what we called "cut off." A good engineer could use that lever to keep his speed and, at the same time, use the least fuel and water. That was the difference between one man and another. Some of them would be out of coal when they got in and another man would have coal to spare.

When I finished up my apprenticeship on the CV in 1920, I got a job on the Rock Island at Herrington, Kansas. You didn't have a job when you came out of that apprenticeship. You'd have to wait until a job opened up and then bid on it. The railroad would help you get a job by calling different roads to check for openings. Your best bet in those days was out west, because there was so much railroading going on, you didn't have any trouble getting a job. I'd gotten married in 1919, so my wife and I got on a train and headed out west to the Rock Island.

Herrington wasn't a very big town and it wasn't a very pretty town, either. Flat, hot and dusty. The engines were a lot different, too. I was used to the little power they had on the CV and when I got out there they had some big engines. The first job I took on the Rock Island was a welding job and I did that for six months and quit it. Welding was a good thing to know, but I didn't want to do it steady. Then I went to Dallas and worked for the Texas & Pacific. Stayed there for six months or so and quit right in the middle of the afternoon. Had a black guy who didn't want to work, so I turned him in to the boss. The boss told me I didn't know how to handle them. Told me to take a sledge hammer to the S.O.B. I told him I wouldn't do that and went back to Herrington. Six months later I went back to St. Albans. I was a boomer, I guess. I never was out of a job and I loved to travel. My wife didn't say much about it, but she traveled with me. I worked for the CV five different times; the Boston & Maine; the Lackawanna; the Texas & Pacific; and ended up on the New Haven Railroad.

My first job on the New Haven was in Hartford, then I went to the Cedar Hill shops in New Haven as a general foreman. That was a big place. We had over three hundred men in there. You could get the work done because you had the men and machines to do it. In 1932 I came to Danbury and became the roundhouse foreman. We had about a hundred men here when I came. My son, Bernie, tells me there's nineteen over there now. Bernie took my job when I retired in 1963. He started with the New Haven as a caller before the war, and when he came back from the Navy he stayed with it. He's pretty good, pretty handy. Came up through the ranks like I did. It's a different job now. When you had the steam engines the only thing that was electric was the headlight. Everything was mechanical. Then you went to the diesels. That was a little more sophisticated, and now they have the electric cars and they're all electronics. Very complicated. The personnel of the railroad changed after the diesels came. In my day a master mechanic had worked his way up and knew what was going on. In steam days a master mechanic was a *real* mechanic. Knew how to handle machinery and men. Today they take these young kids out of college and put them out there and expect them to do the job. At Danbury we had our gang. They were good men to work with. Some of the locomotives had to be babied, and so did the engineers who ran them. The older men, they fussed over their engine. It was *my* engine in those days. They used to assign an engine to a man on some jobs. When those guys would take a siding to let another train go by, they'd work on their engines. Always doing a little something. Our union didn't like it and told them not to do it. Taking jobs away from the men in the shops, they said, but that didn't stop them. There was an old man, Seymour, who had the job running from South Norwalk to Danbury. His engine stayed right there at South Norwalk. There was just a serviceman for coal, water and sand. Nobody else there. We didn't have to do much for that man. Every Sunday he'd go over and spend three or four hours on that engine. Painting her, wiping her down. Those old men were something. The new men came in and that changed, bet your life. They wouldn't wipe the engine off, much less fix it. They'd even sit in the dirt.

I was sad to see the steam engines go. I liked them much better than the diesels. Never liked the diesels, even when they were in the shop, brand new. I don't really think that steam did a better job. Steam engines need more care, for one thing. There was just so much more to them. Everything was different on the railroad when we had the steam. There was an ICC inspector came through Danbury once a month. I never had much trouble with them but I knew people that did. You had a book of rules you had to live up to. Flat spots on the wheels, thickness of the tires, things like that. You could only have so much flat on a wheel before you had to turn it on a lathe to make it true again. The inspectors had gauges for all that stuff. No engine was perfect, and you could bet that most of those inspectors would find something wrong to show they were working. If they pinned an engine, you didn't use it until it was fixed. No fooling with Uncle Sam. There were a few inspectors you might try to get around, take them out to dinner, but most of them, they were tough.

I mentioned the tires being too thin. To show you how it's changed, you go out and talk to a guy working today about setting a tire on an engine; he won't even know what you're talking about. The tire went around the driving wheel, maybe three inches thick. You wore that tire out instead of the driver itself. Heat up the tire first on the ground in a fire and then when it was pretty hot, you'd lift it up in place with a crane and put a ring around it that had flames coming out all the way around. It would heat up and expand and you could slip it on to the driver. Then when it cooled off it would shrink tight. What happened a lot was tires coming loose on the road. It was hilly country and the engineer would put the brakes on and the tire would heat up and come loose. All that sort of thing is gone.

The steam engine lived for a long time. They got a lot of years of service out of engines before they had to gear them down. We did what we could at a place like Danbury, and we could actually do a lot. However, when it came to major rebuilding they would send them to Readville, Mass., which is near Boston. They'd take an engine down to nothing in those shops and put it back together, good as new. Maybe better than new. They kept putting new equipment and making improvements to those engines each time they went in. Every four or five years an engine would go in for that kind of service. I've also seen engines busted in pieces. Wrecked so bad you'd think the railroad would throw them away. There was one engine that went in Hatch's Pond. That's up in the Berkshires. It was a passenger train and they hit a curve where something had happened to the rails. The engine went right into the pond. Quite a ways out, too. There were two engineers on it and both of them were killed. One was the regular man and the other was showing him the road. The fireman was pinned

between the engine and the tender and was in the water for six hours with just his chin sticking out. They finally had to amputate his leg under water to get him out. The railroad had to build a raft to float the crane out there so they could pull that engine out. She was rebuilt good as new. They never threw those steam engines away.

The flags weren't standard equipment on this New Haven Pacific. An engineer was retiring and the locomotive was decorated for his last run. In steam days, this was a widespread tradition. The year was 1934.

When the first diesels came to the Long Island Railroad, Sylvester Doxsey was in charge of the tests. At a Brotherhood of Locomotive Engineers Convention in 1926 he told the members, "We've seen the writing on the wall."

SYLVESTER P. DOXSEY
Lynbrook, New York

In the preparation of this volume, finding the "right" engineer for each railroad was often a problem. There's no book available with a title such as "Railroad Engineers of America." Friends, rail enthusiasts, railroad employees past and present, all were enlisted in the search. Finding Sylvester Doxsey, however, was very easy. Everybody who really knows the Long Island Rail Road said, "Go to Lynbrook and you'll find your man." His stories go back to a time when the Long Island was a great railroad and the Cannon Ball Express *ran to Montauk at ninety miles an hour. He remembers when they opened Pennsylvania Station, appropriately called "the Temple of Transportation." He also remembers when they tore it down. Sylvester had something to say about that. He summed it up best when he said simply, "The damn fools."*

When I was twelve years old I got a job with the Long Island News Company. There were agents called news butchers that used to ride the commuter trains. They had newspapers, magazines, candies, cigars, and so forth, that they carried around in a large hamper. That was 1896. Of course, I was going to school, but all I cared about was getting on the railroad in some kind of job. My father couldn't do anything with me and he decided, with the principal of the school, that I wasn't going to do much in school because I more or less refused. I was a stubborn kid. I bought my own first long pants. I had to have long pants in order to get the job with the news company. I remember it was during the Spanish-American War that I used to make the trip from Long Island City to Patchogue on Train 67 or 11. Then I would work a train at five o'clock in the evening as far as Freeport and back to Lynbrook. That was the job. I felt it was practically a railroad job because I had a company pass, and I felt pretty proud about that.

I guess I was only about fourteen when the superintendent of the railroad, a man by the name of W. F. Potter, was riding my train. I really wanted to get on an engine in the worst way, and I hit him up for a job as a fireman. Mr. Potter laughed and he says, "How old are you?" I told him I was eighteen. "Well," he says, "you talk to me in a couple years from now, and maybe we can do something for you." Then I got a job as an engine wiper at Lynbrook, from June 1900 until May 1901. Taking care of engines, keeping things tidy, things like that. I got a letter to go breaking in as a fireman in May 1901. I liked it very much, even more than I thought I was going to. In 1902 I fell off a locomotive and was hurt. I misstepped on the engine and fell off and hit a fence. The engine was going about fifteen miles an hour, and I got a broken leg out of the deal. It's bothered me ever since, and I was off until somewheres around March 1, 1903. I came back to work as a fireman. I worked from then until 1906 firing, and then I was promoted to running.

The first summer I fired, we used to run from Far Rockaway to Valley Stream, make a turn at Valley Stream, and then go to the Brooklyn Bridge. We'd go up on the elevated at Carlton Avenue in Brooklyn and right to the bridge. Then we'd lay up and make the trip back to Far Rockaway at night, during the rush hour. After I put in the first summer on that job, I got a freight that used to run at that time to Wading River. The Long Island doesn't even run there anymore. They don't run a lot of places we went in those days. At that time, you might say there wasn't much more than the station on Long Island. This town here, Lyn-

brook, was never heard of in those days. In 1900 it was just a railroad station, and there was, oh, I imagine, fifteen hundred people living here. It used to be called Pearsalls in those days. They wanted a new name and I knew the man who named it. He was the station agent at that time, and he said, "Turn Brooklyn around and make it Lynbrook."

Things were a lot different in those days. I was firing a job that went to Montauk when a fellow with an automobile raced us to Southampton one day. He beat us. He was there with his automobile before we made it in with the train. But, remember, we had a number of stops to make. Automobiles were new in those days and they were always trying to race with the trains. That was 1903, and I remember that auto quite well.

It was on that train that I had the only wreck I was involved in. It happened at Center Moriches when I was firing the westbound Amagansett train. We were supposed

Fireman Howard Owens came over to the engineer's side to get in on this photograph. He and Sylvester Doxsey were at Jamaica, in Queens, New York, in 1933 and just about to leave for Montauk.

to take the side for a superior train at Center Moriches. We failed to stop where we should and I noticed it when we kicked over the switch that went to the side track. Nothing for me to do because the engineer's hand went on the brakes as quick as he could. I also knew it was no place for me on that engine because anything could happen at any minute. I unloaded as quick as I could. I was going to make a run for it if I could and grab a red light to stop the train I knew should be coming the other way any minute. We had missed that switch to get into the siding and were sitting out on that main line.

The engineer was doing his best to back that train up because he knew what was up same as I did. But when he tried to back up he loosened up the brake lines and that allowed some of the air to escape and his quick move didn't work. It held him up because he couldn't release the brakes and the train wouldn't move. I scrambled up on top of the station platform when here comes this other train I'm speaking of and slammed into us. He had the right of way, and about two train lengths to go yet before he was supposed to stop. Even so, he must have hit at more than fifteen miles an hour. Well, of course, I was right alongside when they ran into each other and they both went right up into the air. I don't know how far, but both engines came off the rails, I could see light under those wheels. There was no derailment, they came down the way they went up, but that was a lucky shot. The conductor on the eastbound train was throwed up the aisle, and the same thing happened to one of the passengers on my train, but it wasn't more serious than that. A little metal bent, that's all.

As I said, I was promoted in 1906, in the month of May. When I first went running, we had the camelbacks. They were wonderful, for that time. Some locomotives were much nicer riding engines than others. Some were very hard riders. Hard on the engineer's backside, if you want to put it that way. Those camelback locomotives were always good riding. No severe jolts. A bad rider would tire you out in no time. Camelbacks had wide fireboxes and two firedoors instead of one. The firebox was much wider. That was the idea of the camelback really—to get that wide firebox. Then you could burn hard coal. The greatest locomotive that I ever had anything to do with was what was known as the D-16B. The last of my firing and the first of my running, they had those locomotives on the Long Island. They came here in 1905, and they were built in the Altoona shops for the Pennsylvania. They built them themselves, and we had about thirty-one of them here. They were, I think, about a seventy-ton engine, but they were just as light running, just wonderful.

That Pennsylvania K-4 locomotive was a great one too. The last year that I put in running, 1937, I had a K-4 on a Montauk job running out of Jamaica. Made the round trip every day. At that time, six days on and four days off was the way you worked a job. A few times I got those engines up to forty-five seconds to a mile, but that's when conditions were really good and it was the right spot to do it, because that railroad was never built for real high speed. All Pennsylvania engines were good steamers. The Long Island never used stokers, so it was good that they were. We didn't have to have the heavy equipment that they did on the other roads. No heavy freight hauling. No heavy hills. It was up to the engineer the way the engine was handled and as to what the fireman had to do. The heavier the train, the heavier the work for the fireman as far as that goes. With the steam locomotives, you had a lot to contend with, firing or running them.

I was assistant road foreman of engines when the first diesel came to Long Island for a trial. It was only a 600-horsepower switcher built by the Ingersoll-Rand people. I was in charge of tests when that locomotive came here. I was put on that engine, to try it out, and make my report on different jobs that it could do. That was 1926, and I can remember my report. I attended the Brotherhood of Engineers Convention in 1926 or 1927, and I had to make a little talk there in Chicago. I said, "Fellows, this is it!" It was such a saving in the way they were built and ran. It looked, even then, that it had steam beat by a mile. I can remember what I had to say at that time: "It's going to be way ahead of steam." Old-timers like myself liked steam best, but for no really good reason, when I knew they weren't the best for the railroad. Steam was just something that we had grown up with, I guess. With the diesel engine, it was just a case of opening the throttle, that was all. With steam you had to have water in the boiler and you controlled that engine yourself. You would try to get the best out of it, because there was always a little something more you could do to make the engine run better. The diesel would go just so, and that's all. It was the handling of the steam locomotive I liked. You couldn't handle the diesel. The diesel was a kid-glove job, where the steam locomotive was a work-glove job to make blisters on your hands.

We had so many grade crossings on the Long Island that there was bound to be incidents all the time. Once I was heading in on the doubleheader known as the *Cannon Ball;* I know you've heard of the *Cannon Ball.* Well, I was on the head engine that day, two engines, D-56s, a full-car train. We were making a good sixty-five or seventy miles an hour easy enough. Then I saw a truck. He could see me and I could see him plainly at least half a mile before he would get to the crossing. Surprisingly, to me—when I thought surely he would be putting his brakes on and starting to stop for the crossing, he didn't even start to slow down. The train and truck are getting much closer, and as

It looks like everybody in the yard got into this one, taken sometime in the 1930s. Sylvester Doxsey is the second from the right.

12

I say, I was looking right at him. He must have known that I couldn't stop at the speed I was coming. He didn't seem to be paying attention at all; he just kept on coming. And what was it I saw but he had a full load of brick. Well, of course, we slammed that load of brick head-on. All I could see was bricks flying, and I thought to myself, That driver's done for. I couldn't think of anything else, especially at that rate of speed we were going. We put the brakes on and stopped as quick as we could. We went back to see what we could do. He was a colored fellow, lived in Jamaica, I remember. He was seriously hurt, but he lived to come out of it if you can believe that. I don't know how anybody could come out alive from something like that. There was no damage to the train except a few dents, but his truck must have been thirty feet away from the track. It was upside down and in an open field, west of the little station at Pinelawn. I can still see that cloud of bricks.

Another time stands out in my mind, due to the fact that the fellow we hit said I didn't blow the whistle. I'll explain why this stands out in my mind. In 1907, I was running a Babylon job and I'd made a trip around Jamaica Bay, "over the horn," as we used to call it. The trains used to run from Long Island City out and over the bay trestle and around to Valley Stream. The Long Island gave up that trestle to the city subway system finally. It was made of wood and always catching on fire. Then we'd go back to Jamaica and Long Island City.

We made the trip around the bay that day at four-forty in the afternoon, over the horn, and then we started to highball it from Jamaica to Long Island City. The running ground in those days was good going. Good roadbed. There was a little grade to give you a start and about halfway between Richmond Hill and Glendale, there was a switch tower at the Glendale Junction. I was starting to get some speed up—possibly I was at fifty-five or sixty miles per hour—heading for Long Island City without a stop. You could really make up time out there. There was a block operator at West Richmond Hill and I came to the distant signal, which was just to the east of the crossing that I'm getting to. The home signal was at the crossing. If that distant signal was against you when you passed her, you had to have your brake on in order to stop at the home signal. If you didn't, you'd be going right by the home signal. Well, this day, this distant signal was against me and I didn't want to stop because I was a couple minutes off. I didn't want to take away time I wasn't able to make up, so I'm pulling the whistle for the towerman to get on the job and clear that signal. I was blowing the whistle extra hard and screeching it, in fact, for all I could because I wanted that thing cleared and he didn't do it. I rounded the curve and was just starting to put the brake on. There at the crossing was a truck that carried all kinds of soft drinks. It had boxes of twelve-quart bottles. It had a big team of gray horses, a beautiful team. This is before automobile trucks. Well, I was rounding that curve and come on to this crossing. The horses just cleared me, but the pilot of my engine went right between his wheels. It was a good square shot and I hit that truck a good one.

The view I had that instant was that the truck seemed to fall to pieces. Every seam on the whole truck came open and it just seemed to fall apart. The driver was on the seat, whipping the horses. The picture of the driver that I can still see in my mind, he was clear of everything, with a whip in his hand, at least twenty feet in the air. There was nothing anywheres near him, he was all alone. Then, of course, I couldn't see him anymore. His horses were clear, I was thankful for that. They went running up the road where they were bound.

I stopped, and after waiting several minutes, I started to walk back to see what it was all about. I got halfway back,

No. 93 was a brand-new engine, and Sylvester Doxsey was a very young fireman when he posed with his engineer and conductor in the early 1900s.

and I saw this driver coming with the whip in his hand, just like I saw him in the air. I couldn't believe he was alive, much less walking up the track. I thought the best thing I could do was get out of the way, which I did. I quickly ducked under the cars to the opposite side of the train. I made it to the switch tower, and I hid in the bottom. He came over to that tower and opened that door and hollered up to the operator, "Is that engineer in here?" He was cursing and really going on. He decided I wasn't in there because I was hiding good. I don't know what he would have done to me with that whip still in his hand. Looking for the engineer, me! He kept saying, "He never blew the whistle!" but I knew better. I had screeched that whistle, extra loud, on account of that signal being against me. He didn't find the engineer, 'cause the engineer happened to see him coming.

On the Pullman car *Lotos Club*, John Tibbs looks like he's ready to go to work. Built in 1913, the *Lotos Club* was owned and restored by Peter Tilp of Short Hills, New Jersey, who recently donated it to the Railroad Museum of Pennsylvania, located at Strasburg.

JOHN E. TIBBS
Cambria Heights, New York

In the 1920s there were 9,000 Pullman porters. With few exceptions they were black, and in a rather peculiar situation. On the one hand, they were trained professionals operating a complicated railroad car and serving passengers according to standards that seem almost unbelievably high today. (For instance, two entire pages of the Pullman service manual were needed to explain the proper procedure for serving a bottle of beer.) On the other hand, men like John Tibbs were called "George" (after George Pullman, the founder of the company), not by their names. It was only after the Brotherhood of Sleeping Car Porters pressed the Pullman Company in the 1930s that it gave the men name tags. It seems like a small token today, but it helped make people realize that the porter was an individual and not just a fixture that happened to come along with the car.

Well, I started off this way. I was a night bellman in a hotel in Baltimore, and the employment agent who did the hiring for The Pullman Company, Mr. Geohegan, used to stay there. He'd spoken to me a couple times and said, "Why don't you fill out an application and come to work for me? I could use a man like you." My father worked for the Pennsylvania Railroad, so I asked him about it and he said, "I think you would be better off on that job. You'd be away from home, but you get used to that very easily." So I filled out the application, Mr. Geohegan sent it in, and four or five days later I got a letter to go to the railroad doctor in Baltimore. I passed his examination and they sent me to classes in the New York Central yards in the Bronx. They instructed you on making beds, taking care of the car and how you were supposed to look after the passengers. How you were supposed to stock your linen and your supplies, cups, soap, that sort of thing. It was interesting and was something that every man who started with The Pullman Company had to go through before he could get himself a set of keys—to become a porter, in other words.

There was no fooling around on that job. When I started they had just stopped charging the porters for any shortage of linen. A car was allowed 180 sheets, 180 slips and 200 face towels. When you went out they were in bags and you had to put them in your locker. You're supposed to take all of your old linen and put your fresh linen on the bottom. Little things like that you had to learn. We had instructions for six days in the yard, and then we put in two night trips on the road to try out what we'd learned on a real train. I went up to Syracuse two nights straight. Made that trip up and back twice and I was given my keys.

Then I went to Montreal. They needed men in Montreal and I stayed there until the Florida season started, out of Penn Station in New York. I ran down to Florida during that season, and then came back to New York and just worked extra. That is, you got a job when a job showed up. You were on that list and the list revolved around until your time to go out. The Pullman Company operated the cars, you know; and if the railroad needed extra cars, say, for the *Broadway* or the *Century*, they would call and order them. The regular men knew their operations on their trains, but the extra men were likely to go to Florida one day, and when they came back they might go to Montreal, St. Louis, Chicago, or anyplace where a car was going. It was real tough to plan anything when you were working like that. I did that for, I guess, a year.

The next year after that I went into buffet-car service

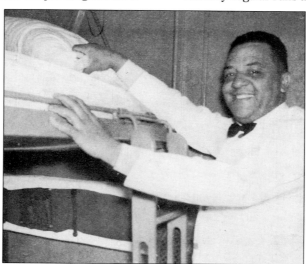

A passenger photographed John making up this upper berth on the *Orange Blossom Special* in 1950. The Pullman Company wouldn't use it in the company magazine. Bow ties weren't allowed.

and ran between New York and Philadelphia from 1929 until 1939, when I started running to Miami again. Then, around 1946, they started putting on through sleeping cars running all the way to California. That was the time that Mr. Robert R. Young was the president of Chesapeake & Ohio Railroad. I don't think you'd recall the advertisements they had in the papers about traveling all the way from coast to coast without changing cars? He was the one who really put through that service. Before that, the passengers had to change at Chicago. They really made a big thing of it and I ran to California for a couple of years. Those were good trains and I liked that run. Later I came back and started running to Venice, Florida. You were really going to Sarasota with the passengers, but the cars would go on further to Dennis because there were no facilities to hold them over in Sarasota.

With my regular runs and the extra work, I guess I went to every place in the United States, Canada and Mexico. I did some private car work, too. The private cars I liked better than anything they had. There weren't too many people renting private cars anymore because the charge on them was tremendous, but there were still quite a few of them operating. I had one man I used to work for, Mr. Bingham. He was an invalid, and he had a doctor, two nurses and a secretary that traveled with him every place he went. He would start the trip from his home up in Maine, stop in Boston and spend a couple weeks in a hospital. Then he would come down to Princeton, New Jersey. From Princeton he would go on to Hot Springs or White Sulphur Springs—spend some time there. Then we'd go to Sea Island; that's in Georgia. From there it was Palm Beach or Miami. That's the way that man traveled. It was almost like a regular job because you made five or six moves each time.

They liked their service on those cars; you had to take care of those folks. His doctor, Dr. Farnsworth, he was a man who loved the service on the private car. He was pretty well off, himself. He had a three-masted schooner up at Christmas Cove, and he bought an old railroad caboose and had it fixed up for a hunting lodge—he was something. But Mr. Bingham outlived that doctor; outlived the next one too, Dr. Smith. Then the third doctor he had, he got on the car one time and didn't like the idea of anyone getting close to Mr. Bingham, whatsoever. He stopped using the private car, so that job went out the window. It was some experience.

I went up to Quebec at the time of one of the wartime conferences and brought Mr. Roosevelt down. Took him and Mr. Churchill to Washington. We didn't know who we were going to get until we pulled in and found it was Mr.

Roosevelt and Mr. Churchill. I think the regular private car ran out as a dummy on one train, and we came down with another. It was a nice trip and Mr. Roosevelt was a very even-minded person, I would say. He respected everybody and he expected everybody to respect him.

Speaking of this, I'm reminded of Mrs. Roosevelt. One morning out of Philadelphia, I was on the nine o'clock train and she came to New York with us. Mrs. Roosevelt was an individual all by herself. Nobody couldn't tell her anything. We got into New York at eleven o'clock, and the superintendent of The Pullman Company, Mr. Burr at the time, he's waiting there and wants to make sure we have the car clean, put on extra cleaners—this, that and the other thing. "You're going to bring Mrs. Roosevelt back on the next trip from Philadelphia to New York." That's what he tells me. Said they were going to change all the chops and steaks on the car. Really do it up. Finally I said, "How is she going to get back to Philadelphia when we just brought her in on a trip from there?" He just said, "What?" I told him she just came in on the nine o'clock train, just her and her companion. So he looked and said, "Well, I'll be damned, how in the hell did she get in that train?" I said, "I don't know, she didn't have anything to say. Mrs. Roosevelt just had breakfast and got off the train and went on about her business."

One time I was going West and I had a man named Green and his wife in my car. They had a concession for Carnation Milk Company out there. They grew all of the carnations used in the advertising for Carnation Milk. They'd been to Europe and he told me all about his trip. He'd been all over. The first morning on the train he comes to me and tells me he's in bad shape. I asked him, "What's the matter?" He said he took his teeth out and dumped them out on the railroad track. I said, "You did what?" He told me he had his teeth on the fold-up sink and when he let the water out, the teeth went out too. "Doesn't the water go out on the track?" he asked. I told him, "Yeah, it goes out on the track." Then I told him he could go to the dining car and have some oatmeal, milk, toast . . . soft food. I said, "You can make it for a couple of days." This was a man who liked his ham and steaks and such. So after they go out of their room to the dining car, I took the screen out in the bottom of the sink—they all had screens in the bottom for just that reason—and got his teeth and washed them off. A little while later I carried them up to the dining car and said, "Mr. Green, I thought

you might want some ham or something, would you like to try my teeth and see if they fit?" He looked at them and said how they looked just about his size. I told him I got this extra set and you could use them for the rest of the trip, they're my good ones. He said, "I don't know, but I'll try them. I'm not eating oatmeal for this whole trip." He put them in and his wife was sitting there, almost falling out of her seat. I had told her in the meantime what was going on and I had to keep from laughing myself. He put them in and he had his breakfast and came back to the car. He said, "These teeth feel better than mine. You look a whole lot larger than me, what dentist made those teeth for you?" I said, "I forget, but you can keep them since they fit you so good . . . Those are your teeth, Mr. Green." I showed him the basin and how the screen was there to catch things. He thought that was the greatest thing in the world, how I'd kidded him.

So—we went to California and he gave me a nice tip when we got there; he got off the train and went on about his business and I forgot about him. But when I got back home my wife said to me, "What did you do, hit the double or something?" I told her, "No—why?" She told me to look in the living room. Mr. Green had sent a box of carnations, there must have been fifteen dozen long-stemmed carnations—just beautiful. Every color you could think of. He sent a note saying that anytime you want carnations, all you have to do is come out to the ranch. I told my wife the story; well, she started laughing and could hardly stop. Little things like that happened to you on the railroad. You remember them. The good ones, they're in your mind forever; the bum ones you try to forget real quick.

The Pullman Company as a whole was a very good company to work for. The only people you had trouble with were the small men like yard superintendents and district supers who thought they were going to be big shots by pushing around the men under them. We had one inspector I remember, in Charleston, and I'll never forget this fellow. He'd get up at two, three, four o'clock in the morning and come out to the water tank. In those days, of course, we had the steam engines on the train. We'd have to stop and take water several times

A typical heavyweight Pullman car. These cars were personal favorites of John Tibbs and had eight sections and five bedrooms. The Pullman section consisted of seats in the day, which converted to upper and lower berths at night. The bedrooms were private, and more expensive. Washrooms were located at each end of the car.

during the night. He'd get out there and jump on the train and try to catch the porter sleeping. If he did, he'd write you up. At that time in the morning there wasn't anybody on that train up but

John (left) with his brother and sisters in front of their home in Baltimore, 1914. Elmira is in the back, with George and Lilly Mae in front.

him, but he would write you up in spite of it, just trying to be a big shot. The Pullman Company finally demoted him to a linen clerk, and the last time I heard, he was stationed in Philadelphia handling piles of soiled linen.

The porters were congenial men as a whole. You could take a group of porters, you'd be liable to meet guys from New Orleans, Altoona, Montreal. You'd get to Chicago and we'd all go somewhere together. We'd have a great old time. But the porters and the cooks and waiters couldn't get along. The cooks and waiters always thought that their job was a whole lot better than ours, or something. I don't know what it was. The last few years that I worked, they began to get some common sense in their heads and we all began to get along better. Once upon a time, though, we used to stay in a hotel and they had to actually separate the groups, with the cooks and waiters on one floor and the Pullman porters on another. Otherwise there would be some damn argument or a fistfight soon enough. Men sitting up and there would be a poker game or crap game and the trouble would start.

The Pullman Company furnished quarters, but I never stayed in them. You couldn't get a good night's sleep— they were like a bunch of kids. I always stayed with somebody that had a little rooming house where we would get our dinner, breakfast and room. On Sarasota trips, I stayed right on the car. Most of the towns had those company quarters, but not for me, no sir. Too much noise and crazy kid stuff. They're still divided up, you know. The porters and coach attendants belong to one organization; waiters and cooks have another. Even the redcaps have their own. Some years ago Mr. A. Philip Randolph, our president, tried to get them all to join the same union, but they couldn't see it. They wanted to go their own way. When the railroads began to go downhill they all began to see that if they had all joined the same union, they might have had some strength.

I joined the Brotherhood of Sleeping Car Porters in 1929. They started negotiatng with the company in 1925, but they didn't get their first contract until 1938. When I started out I was getting $67.50 a month—that is, if I did thirty days or 11,000 miles in a month. In those days you had to be on thirty days to make that kind of mileage. After the Brotherhood became effective, the wages went up to around $240 a month. We got rates in the dining cars too. In other words, we got fifty percent off the price. You could eat anything but steaks and chops. If the cooks were running short there wasn't any for us. Every time you went into the dining car and sat down and ordered something halfway decent, there wasn't any more!

Until you were ten years in service you had to buy your own uniforms. Then they gave you two uniforms a year, later they cut it down to one uniform and two pair of pants. Then they cut it down to whenever you needed a pair of pants; you went in and told them. If you had a pair of pants that was getting thin, you'd take them in and show the boss. "Oh," he'd say, "they'll last another three or four months." You'd end up just as ragged as a jaybird. They gave you one cap a year. I still have one; I'll show it to you. On the *Broadway, Century*, an extra man who went in had to take his uniform and have it inspected by the superintendent to see that there were no patches on it. In those days they had regular men, like I said, and a lot of regular-extra men who only worked those trains. You had to have twelve years of service before you could get on the *Broadway Limited*. That was the sign-out clerk's idea. Actually a man who worked for a year for the Pullman Company those days could operate as an extra man on the *Broadway, Orange Blossom* or *The Panhandle*, or anything, you could work them all.

Now I don't know what the railroads are doing out there. I don't think they want passenger service, even Amtrak, and what's that other thing they have now—Conrail? The cars are not cleaned properly, the service on them is just about the worst I've ever seen. We were going to Montreal a while back on these special cars. They belong to this rail fan who runs trips and gets us retired men to work the cars. One of the special cars developed some trouble and had to be left behind. That meant an overload in the two remaining cars we had, so the fellow running the trip, Mr. Ost, got the other porter and myself a bedroom going to Montreal in the regular part of the train. When we went in the room, the beds weren't made. It was about one in the morning, and we wanted to sleep. We rang the bell for the porter and we told him we're supposed to have two beds in here. Then I told him that if he was busy, I'd make up the beds, and help him out. So he gave me the berth key and I broke down the chair, a chair that folds up and goes under the bed. He's standing there, looking. Just looking and asks me, "Is that where the chair goes?" I asked him if he wasn't the porter and he said, "Yeah, but it's the first time I've ever been on one of these cars and I didn't know how those worked." I mean, that's the kind of service that Amtrak is putting out for the people. I don't know how in the heck those fellows expect people to come back the second time. How in the hell are you going to sleep if the fellow that's the porter doesn't even know how to make the bed?

Union Terminal's magnificent Art Deco façade makes a fitting background for Homer Lewis. What look like steps are actually fountains that have been restored, with the rest of the building, to their original beauty.

HOMER D. LEWIS
Covington, Kentucky

Some of the great railroad stations have fallen, like New York's classic Pennsylvania Station, to so-called urban renewal. The city's other great railroad architectural monument, Grand Central, escaped the same fate because of the efforts of people who realized its worth. Others have become restaurants, museums and community centers. Most, however, wait in a state of limbo—for renovation or the wrecker's ball. That was the status of Cincinnati's Union Terminal when Homer Lewis had his photograph taken. As his footsteps echoed in the magnificent Art Deco interior, Homer described how it had once been filled with the excitement of people coming and going. The great adventure of train travel. Soon after that, the terminal was converted into a shopping mall and has been struggling with its identity. Amtrak has announced that it is considering routing the Cardinal, *a train which resumed service recently, through the great terminal, and if that happens, Homer Lewis may feel at home again.*

The first pay that I drew on the Chesapeake & Ohio was on the section gang, June 1915. I started as a water boy, but I carried ties when I wasn't carrying water. I remember the first pay I drew was up there in a county that was named after my people, Lewis County, Kentucky. I could show you within two telephone-pole lengths where that pay car, that little one-coach pay train out of Richmond stood. When I drew that first month's pay, two twenty-dollar gold pieces, two silver dollars, and the rest in silver change. Them twenty-dollar gold pieces! It was a pretty good payday for a kid in the country. Boy, I sure hated to bust them gold pieces. They got a ring to them, they ain't like silver clanging together. I was only seventeen years old but I thought I was a rich man.

All the education I got was from two years of high school and reading, and that's not too much. I grew up in Black Oak, which is four miles east from Vanceburg on the Ohio River. Two of my brothers went railroading before me. One brother, Gilbert Lewis, he went to work in 1909; he passed away in '66. The other brother, John, he's still living. He went to work in 1914. I'll be eighty-four on October 4. A lot of people tell me that they think I'm in awful good shape for a man that put in fifty years on the railroad. Icy days, in winter, and terrible heat in summer, and working Sundays, holidays and every other day.

My first real job was in the steel mill in Portsmouth, Ohio, making shells . . . I was charging the furnace. I knew it wasn't going to last after the war was over. The war was kind of winding down then, anyway. My brother John hunted me out a job firing on the railroad in June 1917. The boss hired me before he ever saw me, which was a good thing because I wasn't too big then. I done all right, though. I was promoted to running in '22. Then we had to fire five years. I was working out of Covington, Kentucky, on the Cincinnati Division. I stayed with it and then they opened that Northern Division from Russell, Kentucky, to Columbus, Ohio. Freight division, hauling coal. They was getting everybody they could on the extra board when they opened up there, and put, I believe, twenty crews on. Stripped our division of engineers and firemen and everything else. They made you do four round trips to Russell "on the bridge," that's what we called firing. They wanted you to be able to do business when you got out there, but I made it, all right. I was lucky, I was never cut off. I got twelve deep on the fireman's list, and that was as close as I ever got to being cut.

I got my nickname from an engineer I made a student trip with. I told him my name was Homer D. Lewis. He

The year was 1919, and Homer Lewis was at Maysville, Kentucky, with engineer Max Wilson. They were headed for Huntington, West Virginia, on eastbound No. 16.

said, "Homer Dick?" I said, "Yeah, that's as good as any." And I went by that ever since. When my boy was born, I named him Homer Dick 'cause he was born on my birthday, and we didn't want a junior. My real name was Homer Dewey. I was born in '97 when old Admiral Dewey whipped hell out of them Spaniards over in Manila Bay in the Spanish-American War. My mother told me I named myself. She said I would strut around the house and say, "I'm Dewey, I'm Admiral Dewey."

I didn't try to be the best engineer, but I did try to be second to none. And I just about proved to myself that I was. Just change one notch on the reverse bar during a 128-mile freight trip, it'd be surprising how many tons of coal and how many gallons of water you'd save. And if you knew how to save coal and water, you became a pretty good engineer. A lot of science to it. You didn't have to be educated because that was just horse sense, or whatever you call it. When the diesel came along, one of those diesel fellows, one of them smooth guys, said to me, "Dick, how do you like the diesels?" I says, "Well, there's one good thing about them. They make me just as good an engineer as you are. I can go just as far on a gallon of water on them as you can." All the water they used on a diesel was the cooling water.

Some of the steam engineers would brag what they could do with an engine. They'd tell you they'd gone so far on so much coal and water and all that. This one fellow I remember, Old Mitch, tried to show me up. I had taken a hundred loads of manifest freight and never stopped from Silver Grove to Russell, Kentucky. Mitch had 106 cars, six more than I did. I made it in. I didn't know how much water I had in the tank, but I had a boiler full of water. That's all that was required. Just so the hostler could get it to the pits. Old Mitch, he had to stop and get water before he pulled in the yard. Somebody told me that. I acted innocent about it the next time I saw him. I said, "Somebody told me that you had to stop to take water to get No. 90 in the yard the other day." He said, "Aw, go to hell."

When you got one of them big engines, you had to know how to handle it. We were never allowed more than eighty miles an hour on the Huntington, West Virginia, division. It might have been engine 491 or 492, I'm not sure which, that I had on a run between Portsmouth and Russell. I felt that engine trembling, just trembling like a little fox terrier. To myself I said, What's the matter? I looked up at the speedometer and it was sitting on ninety-two miles per hour. I thought, you better get down to eighty or your butt will be on the carpet. They had speed recorders on those engines. The office would read the tape. The needle would point at seventy or eighty, or whatever you were doing. I know an engineer, I wouldn't even mention his name, who asked me if I wanted a key to the recorder boxes. He said that you could open it up and stick that needle where you wanted it. Now, what the hell would I want with that?

Whoever said those steam engines were temperamental as women knew what he was talking about. Some of them would get cross and mean. We'd name them, you know. The firemen would name them. We had one of them old K-1s. We called her "Old Maude." She just wouldn't steam. One of them was fast, good steamer and everything; we called her Rachel. Steam engines, like ships, always females . . . You wouldn't believe the people that I've talked to when I ran passenger trains. When you run passenger, you talk to people. The old people over there at Cincinnati Depot, they'd always walk up to the engine and talk to me. It was amazing how people loved them.

When I hired out in '17, they had what you'd call the Mikado-type engine and we had some of them in here. They had the first stoker that was invented. The Street Stoker. The coal went up in a chute and then down into the firebox. You'd get some of that fine coal, and get out there on the road and down would come a hard rain. That rain hitting the tank and just running in rivers of water, just a stream of water down in that stoker. It would get just like mush. Then they got some old Hanna Stokers, Duplex Standards, and they finally got the improved Standards.

Homer had only been firing for two months when this photograph was taken in July 1917. The work must have agreed with him.

I never ran that old turbine locomotive, the Chessie. It was the most useless, wasteful no-account thing that they built or had, and they knew it when they got it. The railroad had three of them built, and sold them for junk just a few years later. Coal and water ahead of you, and the machinery behind you. You sat there looking at gauges and everything was behind you. I was running engines at the time, but I gave up my passenger rights because I didn't want to be called for that thing. Nobody did. It burned more coal standing still than it did running. That's a fact. You had to keep that stoker going. It was that powdered coal and it was like dust and it burned—oh, did it burn! You was always fighting smoke, you know. All the time, you was fighting smoke in the terminals. Over in Cincinnati, if you made a certain amount of black smoke—boy, they hauled you in. You'd just stand around the depot with that turbine, you had to keep that stoker running and the blower on, blowing those cinders and smoke. The city ordinance said no black smoke.

I was firing for an old fellow, C. Bagby. He was a great fisherman, he and I went fishing a lot together. We got along real good. We got a letter from the smoke man over there at Cincinnati, and he was complimenting us. Said he watched us all the way out of the yard up there across the C&O Bridge, and never saw anything but gray smoke. The smoke man worked for the railroad and would write you up if you made too much black smoke. You know what old Bagby said? "I looked over there and I saw you sitting over there and I thought you were asleep . . . that's the reason you didn't make any smoke."

Most of the men were congenial and liked to kid you. But when you were first hired, they'd make it rough for you. They'd try to make you think that you didn't know nothing, that you was just a country hick. A Baltimore & Ohio man asked me, after the merger, How do you like your new brothers? He says, "You're an old B&O man now, just the same as I am." I told him that I don't think the C&O can upgrade the B&O, but I know damn well the B&O can downgrade the C&O, and that's what they did. I never did think much of the B&O. They always had some old rattle-trap engines, and the fellows over there, they'd make black smoke for five minutes getting out of the yard.

The Kanawhas, those 2700s, they were the finest freight engines ever built for that size. Of course, the H-8s and the other big engines, they had more power. But that old Kanawha, they'd take 160 loads of coal down from Russell to Cincinnati, and you were doing a steady fifty miles an hour. Those 400 Pacifics, they were good engines on passenger. I'd want to mention the L-2s, too. They were the fastest and the most powerful. They streamlined a couple of them. It helped a little and made them pretty. They came to the Cincinnati Division in the forties. The C&O didn't build them from scratch, they made them from older engines. Anyway, they just used them eight years. The oldest one only lasted eight years. They were like new and they cut them up for junk. They put some of them engines around the places like White Sulphur Springs or Louisville, for display. Some of them were vandalized and anything loose was stolen or broken off. Someone said they saw bums sleeping in the tender of one of those engines. Finally they moved some of them back on the track and took them down to be cut up. People just didn't seem satisfied until they had destroyed them.

An engine blew up on me way back in March 1919. I was firing the engine when the boiler let go at Frost, Ken-

Typical of the Kanawha-class engines of the C&O, engine No. 2737 slows for a station in West Virginia. They were named for the river along whose banks they ran for so many miles; they were among the most modern steam engines ever built.

RICHARD COOK

tucky, about ten miles east of Portsmouth, Ohio, about five in the morning. The engineer—we called him "Daffy Dan"—went shooting out of the cab, over a fence and into a cornfield, and I landed out in the middle of the westbound track. It didn't knock me out; just knocked me crazy. People rushed to the wreck and found me a-wandering around the track in a daze. I told them I was hunting for Dan, I was afraid he'd been really hurt. Turned out he wasn't hurt as bad as I was. He just inhaled some steam and smoke.

Afterwards I was crazy as a June bug. A train took us down to Portsmouth, to old Hempstead Hospital. The nurse said they were trying to get my clothes off and put a nightgown on me and I broke away from them and run down the hall raising hell! The doctor caught me and knocked me out with a shot. He told me later that the trouble started when they tried to cut my hair so they could sew me up. I asked if they had a union barber; no nonunion barber was going to cut my hair! When I came to they'd hung my watch on the head of the bed. That thing was ticking and sounding just like that old engine. It seemed so loud that I thought I was right back up in the cab. Then I just floated down the bed there, and I remember the last thing Dan said to me before the explosion. He called me "Little One" because there was three of us named Lewis and I was the youngest. He said, "Pull your gun on, Little One, and put some water in the boiler." He meant the injectors when he said "gun." I pulled the gun, and *bang!* It went when that cold water hit the red-hot crown sheet.

Later on, the C&O installed a low-water alarm, and other safety stuff, but a couple of engines blew up, anyway. A fellow exploded one of those Texas engines, they called them T-1s, up on our Northern Division. Blew him clean out of his shoes. The brakeman lived for a while, but the rest of the crew, they never knew what happened.

It wasn't any play running an engine. Keep your mind on what you're doing, that's what you had to do. You'd run all night in the fog and you wouldn't see the track under you for a whole 128 miles. You'd pass them signals just that

quick. You had to see it to believe it. If you'd run one of those red signals, why, you were in a lot of trouble. You might go right through a caboose. The dispatchers tried to keep trains a mile apart and give you a chance, but you still had to keep your mind on what you were doing.

Road foremen could give you a hard time. Once I was on a hot-shot manifest freight, No. 90. They had a caboose in the middle of the train with two special cars. This foreman says to me, "Now, be careful, them two cars are worth two million dollars. That's secret government equipment." It was during World War II. I said, "What in the hell do you expect me to do with it, try to turn it over in the Ohio River somewhere up there? I'm going just like I always do."

The worst thing was when the railroad went to putting trainees on them engines. I went out there one night; there was five of them. They took boys out of high school, some of them; they didn't even wait for college; and they put them on the engines. I'm speaking of the diesel days now. Well, there were five of them on there and they'd put an extra diesel unit on. The road foreman told me, "Now, Homer, don't exceed the speed limit. Use two hours and a half on the hundred-and-twenty-eight-mile run." Well, them five boys got on, and they was just all up my cab asking questions and looking at this and that. So when I finished the air test and was all ready to go, I says, "Now, you fellows listen. There's room back in those other units back there for twelve men. There's three seats in each unit, so you fellows get back there. There's only one of you gonna ride up here with me. The rest of you get back there and get settled down 'cause when I whistle off here, I'm going rough." Boy, they scattered. You couldn't handle it, running along at sixty to sixty-five miles an hour, and looking behind you talking to a convention like that.

The railroads, it's altogether different now. I got my fifty years in. I call them the golden years of the railroads. They were the best, those fifty that I was on the iron, from June 1915 until December 29, 1965. I was lucky that's when I served my time.

21

Section gangs used motorcars like this one rusting in Paterson, New Jersey, to get from job to job. Motorcars replaced the handcars, and they in turn were sent to the scrap yard when many railroads switched to trucks.

ALEX A. RAMICCIO
Pompton Lakes, New Jersey

Every occupation has its "stars" and its supporting players. The railroad engineer was very visible in the cab of his engine, especially during the steam age, and so was the conductor in his immaculate uniform—even the brakeman riding in the caboose cupola as a train roared by. That train would not have been passing by, however, if it were not for the work of the track gangs, less visible on stage but all-important. Today much of the work on the roadbed is done by one man in a machine that looks like a moon buggy. In Alex Ramiccio's time you did it with muscle and a sledge hammer. He probably knew his stretch of railroad better than his front yard. When trains like the Erie Limited *were traveling at eighty miles an hour, the stony roadbed had to be in the best possible condition. The Erie even praised its roadbed in advertisements. "You ride better because of the rocks" was a headline in a 1941 ad.*

I'll never forget this as long as I live. I was working in Ridgewood, New Jersey, on the main line and I had a habit of always sticking my hands in my pockets. I got out of the car, shoved my hands down in the tight pockets of my overalls and started across the track. The train was coming. Then in the middle of the track I fell. I wiggled and wiggled, but it was no good—I couldn't get my hands out of those pockets. I could see that engine leaving the station, so finally I started to roll. And rolled right over that rail and off the side of the track. I'd been warned about keeping my hands in my pockets, but it didn't seem important at the time. You learned quick on the railroad that mistakes could cost you your life.

A lot of people figure, oh, he's only a trackman. If it wasn't for us working on the track, those conductors and engineers they wouldn't have a job. No road to ride on. Like everything else, it was a job. In the beginning it was fun, but towards the end it was just work. Times change, you're working with a different class of people. It wasn't like when you had all the old-timers. Then you had good men. They were conscientious. What you told them to do, they did. You could take a gang of four, five men and say, "Boys, this is what we're going to do today." You could go home and go back to bed if you'd wanted, because the job would be done and done right.

You couldn't do that today. I hear from some of the fellows who are still on the job. You got to be right there and watch every move. Today you get a bunch of those fellas and I don't care if they're white, black or what have you, and here's how they talk to you: "You're not my boss, you can't tell me what to do. If you want it done, you go do it yourself." That's what you put up with today.

You wouldn't hear that in the old days. Everybody took pride in their work. You wanted the job. Today they figure they got it made. You can't fire a man. The unions protect them too much, even the bad ones. I was always gruff, but I like to think I was fair: "Never mind fooling around, we got our work to do."

I was born in Italy. Came over here with my mother when I was three and a half years old. That was in 1909. My father had already come over. Like everybody else, looking for better things. He came to Caldwell, New Jersey, and got a job on the Erie. He was a foreman on the Caldwell branch. When I got older I used to like to go by the station to see the trains and watch my father work. In 1912 he went to work for a gravel company on Long Island. When they dug the sand banks back, he'd extend the company's pit tracks to the new bank. In 1918 they sold

out and the new outfit had crews of their own, so my father was out of a job. We moved to New York City and it was rough. I was the oldest and we ended up with eleven kids. We lived on the East Side. You were always getting in trouble in my neighborhood. Fights. My father used to raise hell with me, tell me to stay in. How can you stay in the house? I never had any high school; I just managed to get through grammar school.

Then one day some fellow called up and told my father he could have another job on the Erie out here. We came out to Ridgewood in 1922. Probably the best thing for me that we came back to Jersey and I went on the railroad. I thought it was a big thrill, and seeing that my father worked there, I figured if it was all right for him, it was all right for me. I wasn't quite seventeen when I went on and I stuck it out. What the hell, I was only a young fellow and I had never seen steam engines like that. Only thing I'd seen before was a trolley car going up and down the road when I lived in the city.

I had my ups and downs, changing jobs all the time. Got promoted, got demoted, seniority changes, that's how it was. I worked with my father when I started. It was a little rough with him as boss because I had to lead the way all the time. He didn't want the men to think that because he was my father I didn't have to work. I got the dirty end of it. Started as a trackman. I watched those trains go by and listened to the guys talk. That's where I learned to chew tobacco.

The trackmen are the forgotten men of railroading until there's trouble. Underpaid, that's for sure. In those days we made thirty cents an hour. Then we went to thirty-two. We got a penny now and then. They told me the job was temporary when I first started. Maybe work three days a week. That got to be four, then five. Finally we were working seven days.

From trackman I went to lamp man. It didn't pay no more money, but it was an easier job. I had to keep the signal lights working, and clean. Fill them up with kerosene every other day and clean the globes so they would shine. I'd be all full of soot and stuff after a day of that. Then I got a job as assistant foreman. First foreman job I had was when we built a new railroad line around the reservoir in 1927. Went from Midvale to Greenwood Lake. We had all these fellows from New York City living in camp cars. Took quite a while to build it. We used to call those guys the hobos. Every day they was drunk. They got paid every two weeks and the commissary took care of everything. They never saw their check. By the time they took their room and board out, what little money was left, they drank it up. What a crew!

Today they still do maintenance, but it's not like it used

It doesn't look like Alex Ramiccio is very happy with what he's hearing on the phone. As he puts it, "I was gruff, but fair." Alex was working at Fairlawn, New Jersey, in 1959.

to be when we worked on this Greenwood Lake branch. It was forty-four miles long, from Jersey City to Greenwood Lake. When we split it up, I think there were fourteen foremen. There were two branch lines off that, and they each had separate foremen, too. If you had a double track, they'd try to equal it out with the men who had single track. I had to run from Pompton Plains to Mile Post 32, which is six miles of single track. You'd have fifteen to twenty men in the summer. Down to maybe three in the winter. Seasonal work. Used to hire a lot of college kids. You maintained it year round. Every day you had something to do. Starting in the spring, we'd be putting in new ties. Raising the surface of the track. Getting rid of low spots. We'd also be cutting brush, pulling weeds around the station platforms, a little bit of everything. Try and get your section of track in the best possible shape.

Before they got the machines, it was all done with a pick and hammer. Hard work. Backbreaking work. Today they've got a machine that pulls the ties out and inserts the new ones in the same hole. Them days you had to dig it out on the side. Then you had to break up the old bed, put the new tie in and raise it up so the track was level. All by hand. You'd have whatever you needed in the way of men. After you'd raised the track you had to sight it. Make sure it was level. You had to do all that by eye. I'm amazed that we could do that track by eye as well as they do by machine today. Can't believe it, but the human eye is great. We used a spotting board. It was eight or nine feet long and about ten inches high with different marks. Lay it across two rails and you had another board with a peephole on legs above it. You'd get down on your knees and sight through that hole at another man holding another board. The men would raise the track until it was level. Did a beautiful job.

Now they've got what they call the electromatic tamper. A man sits on there with an electric eye, and that tells him how much to raise the track. All by machine. All you need is a foreman on the job to keep track of the timetable so a train doesn't hit you. Does away with a lot of labor. The first machines came in 1952 or so. That was the first I seen of them. Real antiques compared with what they have today. The machines were a help. We could pull spikes with an air gun. Put them in with it, too. They have something better than that today, but we thought that was some progress in those days.

Laying rail was the hardest work. They were heavy, let me tell you. They were thirty-nine feet long. Carry them, lift them. Remember, too, a lot of times when you were working on single track you'd have to make your repairs under traffic. Every time a train was due you'd have to have that track closed up. This was a commuter line. At one time we had fifteen to eighteen trains running out of here in the morning. Even during the middle of the day you didn't have a lot of time if you wanted to do any work. Maybe thirty-five to forty minutes at the most. You could change a rail in five minutes if you had the men. You had

everything ready. Pull the spikes on three ties, leave one, pull the next three, and so on. Leave one bolt in the joint on each side. You wouldn't be finished in five minutes, but you could let the train over that rail. Take you ten or fifteen minutes to close it up. You didn't have to worry about the train because you had your flag out and you knew when they were due. They'd told the engineer where we were before he left so we wouldn't surprise him. Everybody knew his job. We'd have that rail in before you knew it.

Today I don't think they would know how to change a rail. I really mean that. When they wanted to change to heavier steel on the main lines, we got the old stuff on the branches. Trains were getting heavier, especially the bigger engines. They went from ninety pounds to one hundred per yard. That's how we measured rail. It was good steel we were getting. They didn't let it wear out. Then in 1927 we laid all-new steel. Brand-new hundred pound. Started using welded rail in the later years, in quarter-mile lengths. Very easy to lay. They have a whole trainload. They anchor one end of the rail and then the train moves slowly out. The rail is on rollers on the cars and comes off real nice. It gets rid of the joints which caused trouble.

A lot of times the old rail would break in the joint. Diesels would pull out real smooth, but steam engines on a downstroke would hit a joint and after a few months you'd have a broken rail. Steam engines would burn holes in the rail starting at the station. I've seen them start out of Midvale on a frosty morning. First thing they are slipping and they open the sand, and they keep that throttle open. Grinding away at that rail and pretty soon you've got some real grooves. They'd all have a different excuse, making up time, stuff like that. Some of those guys wanted to get home in a hurry and some of them were just plain rough.

We used to have rail inspection once a year. Regular work train with this machine in one car. It was called the Sperry Rail Service car. An x-ray kind of thing. They'd go along and it would make a line like a cardiogram. When it saw something wrong a bell would go off in the car and they'd stop. Find fissures and fractures in the rail. The kinds of things you couldn't see with your eyes. But we did get so we could tell by the sound: go over that crack with the motorcar and you knew you hit something wrong. Just sounded different.

Today the ties come already drilled from the plant. We had to make our own holes. Beat 'em in by hand. I was proud of the way I could pound a spike. I won a contest one time in Port Jervis driving spikes. The railroad used to have outings and they had these contests for the trackmen. I don't remember my exact time, but I did pretty good. The other guy said I had a soft tie. I don't know how soft it was, but I had to belt it a hell of a lot of times. I liked to hit my own spikes. You alternate with two guys and you make too much contact. You hit each other's hammers and you don't know which way the hammer's going. You might really end up getting hurt. I used to tell them to hit theirs and I would hit mine. My legs had marks on them, you wouldn't believe it. When those spikes fly, they hurt. You learned how to hang a hammer. Fit the handle in the hand and hit it on top of a rail that was solid. Hit it in nice and easy and make sure it was straight. If it went in crooked, forget about it. The handles were all standard size until later on they started making little shorties. I liked them because I was short and I got a better grip, more pressure coming down on the spike.

When your regular maintenance was done for the season, you'd do patch-up work. Picking up low joints, oiling up the joints. Take oil with a brush and paint them. Had the whole gang doing it. Easier to keep things tight, and it looked nice. We'd line up the stone ballast with a board. Lay the first stones along the bottom and then rake the other stones up to it. I haven't seen a piece of track like that in a long time. When they had track inspection we'd dressed everything up for a month. They gave a prize for the best piece of track, $100 first prize. Then they'd put up a sign at your headquarters, Banner Section. They want quantity today, not quality. When we did our work we were proud of it. We'd stand and look at it and say, "Doesn't it look terrific!"

When I first came we had handcars. You couldn't get enough men on them. Some of those guys used to lean on those handles and I want to tell you, they could make those things fly. That was fun on those things. I had them seven or eight years. Then we got the gas cars in 1929. Just like driving a car except you didn't have to steer. Had auto engines in them. Today they have what we call high-railers: trucks with railroad wheels besides the regular tires. Drive the truck up on the tracks at a crossing and drop the train wheels on the rails. Lock the steering wheel, give her the gas, that's all there is to it. Great.

One day I had a handcar up here and I thought the train was gone. In them days they weren't too strict about getting a schedule. I put the car on the track and all of a sudden I hear this whistle blowing. That train had gone by, but this was a light engine coming down, going in for repairs. I just got one end off because I didn't have too much clearance. Then I got out of there. It was wood and it was demolished. I was scared to death that day and I really caught hell for that one.

Another time I was coming back from Greenwood Lake at night with some fellows in an automobile. It was late and we were just out for the evening, having fun. There was this guy going up Ringwood Avenue and he made a right turn onto the tracks and went along until he got stuck on the bridge. He opened the door and dropped down about thirty feet into the water. Of course, I was working on the railroad at that time and my first thought was that I knew there was a train due. I went up to the wigwag signal at the crossing, took down the lamp that was on top and flagged the train. They put a chain on the car and pulled it off. Caught the guy trying to take the license plates off the car so they wouldn't know who the owner was. We figured he was drunk and the fall sobered him up in a hurry. If you did a good job, they didn't hand out medals, but I got a letter of commendation for that.

Winters were rough out there. We had a supervisor, years ago, if he saw a flake of snow or he got a report that there was going to be snow in the area, he'd have us at our stations. We all had stations to go to in case it snowed. Mine was near the Hackensack River where they had all the automatic switches. Keep them clear if it started snowing. Many a night I slept right there. The foreman never got paid for overtime. You got nothing for it and at

A "steel-driving man." It was all pick and hammer in 1934. Even though he was a foreman at the time, that didn't stop Alex from grabbing a hammer and working with his men.

eight o'clock you had to be on your regular job. We were twenty-four-hour men. If you worked fifty hours a week, you still got the same pay. It didn't make any difference, they called you. No matter what it was, wrecks, anything. If you were going someplace, they wanted to know where you were in case they had to get hold of you. You got the devil if you didn't. If you got a report at four-thirty in the afternoon that something was wrong, you'd go down and look at it. Had to take a crew with you. If it was serious, you'd want to fix it.

I knew my railroad. I'd walked it many a time. A lot of times the engineers would tell you that this or that place was riding rough. You'd get up on the engine with him and feel it. Go out and fix it. If they saw you before they went on their run, they'd tell you to "Check that spot over there. Looks a little rough." If they didn't see you, they'd turn it in. Then you'd get a phone call, big rigmarole, lots of red tape. The red tape was eliminated if you saw it first. I didn't see I got a big reward, but I made a living on the railroad. I used to take the job home with me, but in later years I left it there. Sometimes, though, you'd think, Did I leave that all right? I remember a couple cases when I went back. Halfway home but I went back just to see that everything was okay.

These dreary cars at the Syracuse station are a far cry from the Pullmans of the *Twentieth Century Limited* that Carl Peterson used to run. To its credit, Amtrak has been upgrading its equipment, and service is improving.

CARL A. PETERSON
Dewitt, New York

Since she worked for the Delaware & Hudson Railroad herself for ten years, Alice Peterson must have known what to expect when she married a railroad engineer. When your husband worked off the extra board, the hours were long and irregular. He might go to work at four in the morning one day, and four in the afternoon the next. When business got slow, he might be lucky to get one or two days' work a week. Holidays usually found your husband on the road. Carl is the first to admit it was rough: "A railroad wife really brings up the family because the husband is away from home a lot." It wasn't all bad, though. An engineer's wife was proud of the job her husband did, and of his position in the community. They were, as one man put it, "the blue-collar aristocrats." A woman does have her limits, however, and when one of the Peterson children wanted to go railroading she talked him out of it: "One in the family is enough."

I used to read many Horatio Alger books when I was a kid. When I was fourteen years old, I knew what I wanted to be. A lot of books in those days were about railroads. They were the ones I loved to get hold of. I used to read in the papers about the *Twentieth Century Limited* and what a great train it was, so I told everybody, I told my folks, I wanted to go on the railroad, I wanted to be an engineer on the *Twentieth Century Limited.* That was a wild dream at that time, of course, but that's the way it turned out.

I grew up in Hartford, Connecticut, born August 20, 1892. Went to work for the railroad in 1911. I started in New York, and worked on the subway for a year because the Central wasn't hiring then. I was lying about my age; I was over six foot and I was saying I was twenty-one. I was just getting ready to qualify as a motorman on the subway when I got a notice that if I came up to Albany, they were hiring firemen on the Mohawk Division. So right away I got on the night boat—it cost me $1 to ride from New York to Albany—and looked up a friend of mine who lived up there. He took me to his rooming house. Then I went over to West Albany and got a job and stayed with the NYC until 1957. I never was laid off, like a lot of fellows who were, in 1921, and again after the crash of 1929. I got knocked back, but not laid off. In 1929 I had a regular run as an engineer in passenger service, but in 1932 I was back firing, which lasted until 1936.

When I began, it was only the scoop shovel; that was it. And not only that, no automatic doors. Chain doors, where the chain hung from the top of the cab, then down onto the doors. You would pull the door open and kick it closed every time you shoveled. With every exhaust, the chain doors would go slightly in and out. I used to get a kick out of watching those trains go by in the night. There would be just enough light coming out around the chain doors to light up all of the steam and smoke going overhead—it was quite a sight. Even when we got the stokers, the fireman was still busy because he had the stoker engine to watch all the time and you had to know how to handle it. The Hudsons and the 6000s were good. They had the latest stokers on them and they were easy to fire. Not like in the beginning when we had all saturates. There were no superheaters and of course saturated steam was nothing like that superheated steam for running well. I think it was 1911 or 1912 when we got the first superheaters and the automatic firedoor. You stepped on the pedal and the door opened. You would throw in a scoop full of coal and take your foot off. Reach for another scoop full of coal and put your foot on the pedal again.

Looking pretty happy after forty-six years with the NYC, Carl Peterson waves from the window of the engine of Train No. 40 leaving Syracuse depot on his final trip, August 30, 1957.

SYRACUSE HERALD-JOURNAL

You can't imagine what a difference those two things made in the job. When I look back now, I wonder how our backs stood up to it. When I first qualified, they put me on switching around the yards like West Albany. The yard engineers were a nice bunch of guys and they would try to teach you. You learned the biggest part of your firing there. I had been up the road a couple of times, I guess. It was about three months after I had gone firing when I got on with this engineer, Danny Schneider. I'll never forget his name, he got to be a passenger engineer afterwards. He was a nice guy, but I got him out of West Albany with an old 2900. I think we had seventy empty cars going west. A helper engine would push you out of the yard at West Albany, up as far as Karner, and then you were on your own. We weren't doing too hot, but we staggered along until we finally got to St. Johnsville, where freight engines went on the pit and got a clean fire and a fresh tender of coal. Well, we started out of St. Johnsville and the ten miles to Little Falls where you go upgrade through the rock cuts. By that time the steam pressure was low and we stalled. Danny Schneider's nerves were getting the best of him by then. He hadn't had a very good fireman that day. After I got steam enough up we were able to pull out of the rocks, slacking back three or four times, and just before I got off at Little Falls, he looked over and said to me, "How long you been firing?"

I told him less than three months, this was my third trip on the road.

He says, "You'll never make a good fireman—when you get up to Little Falls, get washed up, get on the next train, deadhead back to Albany and quit." He says, "You'll never be any good."

Well, me being only a kid, that broke my heart right there. He took it right out of me. But I didn't quit.

A lot of people thought that railroad men were a tough, rotten bunch. We did have plenty of brakemen who were more floaters than anything and they weren't the nicest guys in the world. But the engineers—95 percent of them—were perfect gentlemen. A lot of them were smart men too. They had started their days in the 1890s and they'd learned the hard way. A fine bunch, but they expected you to make steam, and firing took some doing. In the old days the grates were higher than when we got the superheaters, and you had to build it up in the back and then just spread the coals so they would roll down near the front of the crown sheet and keep a good fire going everywhere. If it would begin to get a little dead anywhere, then you would grab one of your big long rakes and move the coals around to get any dead spots burning. Sometimes you'd be getting leaky flues and then they didn't steam good at all. For that, in the earlier days, you would gener-

Carl helps his wife up into the engine before his last trip. Many engineers took members of their families along with them on the final run. Alice Peterson has the gloves on, and it may be that she is planning on doing some running.

ally have a bag of corn meal or something like it. You put that in the water in the tank and when it drained through and got up through the injectors into the boiler, it would seal the flues up. Of course, once in a while one of them would blow. Then the seam would split and the fire would go out, and there was nothing else you could do until they towed you in.

They wouldn't let you on the *Century* to fire or run it until you had a lot of experience. That had to be passenger-train experience, too. The engines only ran to Syracuse then. They cut them off at Syracuse because they didn't have the big tenders yet. Later on they ran from New York to Chicago without a change of engines. By the time I got to Verona, which is about three miles east of Oneida, and a little bit downgrade going in there, I would be done. I could climb right up on the seat and ride the last twenty-eight miles into Syracuse, and up through Washington Street, and the fire would just about be finished. There wasn't too many of them dared to do anything like that. When I first tried to do it with Irv Chapman, he said, "You're not going to make it, Carl." I said, "Well, we're going to try it anyway." He was afraid for the train we had behind us, the *Twentieth Century*, but we made it.

We had track pans on the Central. You'd scoop water from the pans on the fly and then you wouldn't have to stop at a water tank. It was a two-man job. The first one out of Syracuse going east was at Rome. Then the next one was east of Herkimer. That was a good many years ago. The next one was at Yost's after we rounded Big Nose Curve. The last one on the Mohawk Division was at Scotia, just west of the Mohawk River going into Schenectady. On the fireman's side on the front end of the tender, there was a place where we used to store oil cans and things. There was also a big valve in there, the air valve that operated the scoop. The fireman couldn't see the start or finish of the pan; that was up to the engineer. The engineer sitting on the right side could see markers at each end of the pan. In the winter and at night, there was a blue light on one end and an amber light on the other. When we would go onto the pan and he could see the light easy, he would yell "Down!" and put his left arm down. The fireman would push the scoop valve, and the scoop would go down into the pan. Then at the other end you'd get to the other light and he'd yell "Up!" and raise his left arm. The fireman had to be watching that engineer all the time. It would happen once in a while, but not too often, that they'd miss. At the end of the pan there was a slope—all steel sheets, welded together, and all smoothed off. Then there was a guardrail beyond the pan that ran about two hundred to two hundred and fifty feet or something like that right in the center of the rails so the scoop wouldn't dig up the ties. If that scoop didn't come up fast enough, that guardrail, boy! what a crease it would put in the bottom of those scoops.

People marveled at water pans in the days of the steam locomotives, and it was quite a sight. I've been asked one question many times: How did they keep the water pans from freezing up during the winter time? There was a pump house at each water pan, and men on duty twenty-four hours. When the weather got cold, they had operating valves in the pump house to send little jets of steam into the pans so they would never freeze up.

In this Mohawk Valley we had fogs of all kinds. People used to wonder why we didn't run locomotives and crews a lot further, Buffalo to New York, or something like that. If they had to run up and down through those fogs and snowstorms, they'd know why. You had to know where you were all the time. Road crossings, you had to know them all, and we had a lot of them between Syracuse and Albany. You had to know where the slowdowns were. Now, heading east out of Syracuse, we didn't have a slowdown until we got to Utica. If you didn't have to stop at Utica you had to slow down to fifty miles an hour going through the city. The next slowdown, before they took Gulf Curve out, was at Little Falls. That was a reduction to forty-five miles an hour.

Once in a while you would get a couple of sections on the *Century*. During the war they ran many, of course. Years before that, when I was firing the *Century*, they would often run two or three sections. We were always in the lead—we were the regular crew. Going through those fogs at night, and snow and thunderstorms, at seventy-five, eighty miles an hour, you begin to think about the trains behind you. Only five-minute intervals. At eighty miles an hour it doesn't leave much room. You always had to watch the signals, but by that time they had the signal situation in pretty good shape. It used to be when I was firing, those signal bridges were only about seven eighths of a mile apart. However, a third signal back on a signal bridge would give you the first indication so you had a chance to react. A while back I took a ride in the cab of a Turbo and the darn signal bridges are over two miles apart. They've got a lot more room today than when we were going faster.

I was promoted to engineer in 1916, and I was running engines until they promoted me to road foreman in 1940. Transferred me to Syracuse, that was in 1941. That year the war broke out, oil and gas supplies got short, and a year later the rails were moving everything. Of course, in those days most freight had still moved by rail. It was a busy time. In 1942 they created two new jobs called chief road foreman. Tommy Hanes was assigned west of Syracuse and they assigned me east of Syracuse and we both had our offices right here in Syracuse itself. He covered the line to Buffalo and beyond and up to Niagara Falls, Watertown, all those places. I went towards Albany and New York, Boston, Montreal, and the West Shore lines into Weehawken, and to Camp Kilmer down in New Jersey. Yes sir, during World War II, we ran a train out of that camp every thirty minutes with about twelve or fifteen cars on each one. Taking troops from there down to the port of Weehawken in New Jersey.

That was all steam too. Around the country they began to switch to diesels before we did. We had some, but steam did it during the war. Our job was to keep things moving, and we had all these traveling engineers, road foremen and firemen to keep track of. Tommy and I each had a secretary and we would give them orders as to where we wanted our men placed, and which trains we wanted ridden. Maybe a train was losing a little time, or something was going wrong, and you'd get your men placed in different spots to try and find out what the problem was and correct it. We got in a lot of tight spots during the war. We weren't getting a very good grade of coal, for one thing; they were taking the best for the steamships.

Many a time we would be at the Syracuse station all night long helping the fellows. You couldn't work those men all the time. So, as I said, Tommy and I put in many a night getting those trains through and even poking our share of ash pans. My immediate supervisor was the master mechanic. Next in line was the superintendent of motive power, Archie Bingham. His office was at Grand Central on Lexington Avenue. All of the locomotives were under his supervision. As a general rule, master mechanics came out of some big terminal where they had been terminal engine house foremen. There they had charge of locomotives, or they came out of the engineering department where they built locomotives. They really had to know the power. When Hanes and I got to be chief road foremen, they told us right off, "You've got an unlimited expense account." Of course, during those years I would be all over the railroad. I'd be down at Camp Kilmer, maybe moving troops out one day. The next, I'd go into Grand Central, and see about something there. The suitcase I carried with me, I had overalls and everything right with me, and I'd ride those engines many a time to see how crews were doing. I rode a lot up to Montreal, up that way

When this photograph was taken on his front-porch hammock in Hartford, Carl was sixteen years old and high-button shoes were the style.

because we were operating a lot of passenger trains up over the Adirondack Division at that time. They would have big meetings once in a while; they would get our opinions, and they wanted to learn what we heard from the crews. One time they wanted to change the book of rules a little bit and we were called into Buffalo on three or four different meetings. They would take our suggestions or they could throw them out. Tommy and I had an awful battle there for a while because they wanted to keep those locomotives running steadily. Some of them were falling apart at the time, just too many miles and not enough service, but they insisted. You had to do the best you could. Sometimes we'd run out of supplies. Tommy and I got them to put coal cars in the Syracuse station and we had a crane up there and bucket to save time. They'd send in men to grease the locomotive rods, right there in the station. It was one thing right after the other, all the time. We were on call twenty-four hours a day.

I never had any wrecks of any kind when I was running, but I had to cover a lot of that stuff as road foreman. A *Twentieth Century* locomotive blew up here in Canastota in 1943. It was about four in the morning. I was there from four-thirty that morning until two the next morning and then somebody brought me home; I was only in bed about four hours when I had to go out there again and stayed all day and all night, straight through. We had to save everything we could, all the parts of the locomotive that were left. The injectors, the water pumps, were all knocked to pieces, but we did find what we could.

The cause was a burned crown sheet that's at the back end of the boiler. What had happened, she had come from Buffalo, and the crew had been having trouble with the water pump and the injector. No. 5453 was the regular engine on that train and they hated to take her off and put another one on. If I had been down at the station, I might have done differently, but I'm not sure. This assistant of mine, another road foreman, and two traveling firemen had been there; they looked the situation over, talked it over with the crew, and decided they could make it. But by the time they hit Kirkville, twelve or thirteen miles east of Syracuse, they were running into trouble. We went back and questioned the towerman at Kirkville who was on duty that night, and he said he heard the low-water alarm screeching when they went by there. The crew apparently were just getting ready to dump the fire. When we reconstructed everything afterwards, we figured that the fireman, Jack Larson, was on the deck with the shaker bar ready to drop the fire—you understand, through the grates, down on the tracks, so the boiler wouldn't blow up. But it was too late by then; they had burned out the crown sheet. She blew, and boy! it was a mess. The traveling fireman had been sitting on the fireman's seat—his body was lying way over near the canal east of Canastota. The fireman was all torn apart, and the engineer blown out on the other side. They just didn't want to quit.

I was at Little Falls three days in 1940 when they had that big wreck on No. 19, the *Lake Shore Limited*. That investigation went on for years, and I don't mind telling you, it was a long time before I found out what we thought happened. The speed limit at Gulf Curve was forty-five miles an hour and had a terrific high elevation. If you tried

A lot of people, including Carl Peterson, think that this was America's finest steam engine. Among the last locomotives to be built, the Niagaras fought the final battle for steam against the diesel on the New York Central.

to walk around that curve, you'd slide off. Andy Bayreuther was a road foreman and he had orders to ride No. 19 that night. He got on at Albany with Jess Earl, one heck of a nice guy. They came into Gulf Curve and they were going too fast. We think he must have reached right up and shut the throttle off. Well, he had all those cars behind him and we didn't have those tight lock couplers in those days. There was slack in there, and when he shut the throttle off, the rear end with all its momentum came right up, hit the tender and drove the engine right off the track at Gulf Curve into a solid-rock wall. It was awful: thirty-one killed and fifty-one injured. Jess and the fireman were killed and Bayreuther was in the hospital for months. Last I heard, he's still alive down in Florida.

A funny thing happened to the baggage car. It was on the head end, of course, and in the wreck got uncoupled from the cars behind. It had already hit the tender and pushed the locomotive over the bank. The car then kept going around the curve until the air pipes burst, so that the brakes went into emergency. It stopped about halfway between Gulf Curve and Tower No. 24 at Little Falls. Just the baggageman was inside; he opened the side door and looked out into a cold, rainy and horrible night. There he was, all alone, nothing ahead of him and nothing behind him. That guy aged twenty years right there. He walked up to the tower and the operator asked him, "Where's your locomotive and the rest of your train?" That's when they went to Gulf Curve and found out.

I never went after an engineer when I was road foreman. If I thought they needed criticism, I'd let some higher official do it. Tommy Hanes is dead and gone now, a few years ago, but we both left those jobs, and as far as I know, we never had an enemy. I used to ride the locomo-

tives a lot even when I was chief road foreman. When I would be down in Albany on business and getting ready to come back home, instead of riding in the train, I would climb on the engine and ride with the crew. I often did that with engineer Johnny Mahoney. When Johnny saw me coming he'd go over and sit by the fireman. "Carl," he'd say, "she's all yours." I'll never forget one night, coming up on No. 15, the *Ohio State Limited*, it was drizzly and rotten outside, and the rail was lousy too. The sand had quit running on one side, the driving wheels were slipping and sliding, and I was easing off on the throttle all night. We did keep going, but Johnny Mahoney sat over there and just laughed. The son-of-a-gun wouldn't come over and help me a bit.

They talk a lot about those Hudsons and the Niagaras that ran on the Central. They were wonderful, but the Mohawks were also very good engines. They could do double duty, freight and passenger service. We could use them on heavy passenger trains and on those long-distance mail trains. I ran a mail train, No. 3, coming out of New York. All mail cars for Chicago. That train would run seventeen, eighteen, nineteen cars. One of those Mohawks, and you'd usually get two helpers out of Albany to push you over the hill and then you'd just sail along. That train ran on a passenger schedule. The Mohawks could do a job, let me tell you.

As far as I'm concerned, though, there was no engine like a 6000, the Niagara. They were big and so high! If you put a Hudson on one track and a 6000 on the next track, you would look down into the cab of the Hudson. The height even scared a lot of the engineers. We had straight track through Amsterdam, and just west of Amsterdam beyond the depot there was a reverse curve set for seventy miles an hour because of the elevation. Even so, a few of our men would slow down to around fifty or fifty-five through there. But I never did. I never got scared. You'd feel them pick themselves up and get their drivers back

The herald behind Carl and conductor Louie Van Eppe has disappeared from the American railroads. It is, however, far from forgotten, and many people still remember the finest fleet of trains to ever run in this country.

down on the rails and haul through that curve. When I got over that little unfamiliar feeling after we first got those engines, I used to roll them right by Midler Avenue in Syracuse and head right towards the station at eighty miles an hour. Then I had about a mile and a half to slow down for the stop. Of course, the 6000s came late in the game and we didn't have them too many years. It's too bad. They were good from beginning to end and the wear and tear on them wasn't bad, because they were completely fitted with roller bearing—rods, driving boxes, even the engine leading and trailing trucks, tender wheels, everything. The railroad ran them right through from Harmon to Chicago without a change. Coming out of Little Falls, boy! they would get those cars up to eighty in no time at all. Sixteen or seventeen heavyweight steel Pullman cars. I'd ease that throttle right down to about the third notch or so, and they'd charge along. You'd hit a little grade after you got through Rome and give it a notch or two more, but after that you'd just ease her off all the way to Syracuse.

Starting in the mid-thirties, we began to get speedometers and recording tapes on all our locomotives. The tapes were all sealed and when they took them out they sent them to Buffalo. The Central had mostly girls working there, men supervisors, and they would run those tapes out on a long board and every bit of the railroad was right there to be seen. If your speed showed a variation in any curve—say Big Nose Curve was supposed to be fifty miles

an hour and you had done fifty-three—well, only a day or two later you'd hear all about it and have to answer for it. If you got caught in two or three violations, especially in passenger service, they took you right out. They'd discipline you, maybe send you to the yard engines. A little ahead and a little back, that's all that switching is, and I hated them. Boy, after I got married and I ever got called for yard engines, my wife used to get a kick out of me. I would be broken-hearted every time. I wanted to get out on the road and go!

I think the scheduled time on the *Century* was two hours and fifteen minutes from Albany to Syracuse and vice versa. You couldn't make up much time there, but you could get a little bit if you needed it. I have taken sixteen cars on the *Century* and gone from Syracuse right into Albany station in two hours and one minute, and that's fourteen minutes faster than the scheduled time. Of course, the towers reported you by at the exact times, and if something happened—a wet rail or something, and you lost a minute or two, even though you picked that up before you got into your terminal—by the next morning they were right after you. The office

wanted to know the reason you lost the time. I know people down through the Mohawk Valley, farmers and others, would say they set their kitchen clocks by the trains. I've seen some of the fellows that are running the trains out there today; practically all of them fired for me at one time or another. They tell me they lose forty-five or fifty minutes between Syracuse and Albany because the track is so bad. Lately, they've started to fix it up.

They had the diesels on when I finished up. It wasn't like running a steam locomotive at all. Why, you could hang your head out of the window on steam locomotives and watch those drivers turning over underneath you. The diesels just carried you along, but they didn't talk back to you. They were cleaner and in the winter time they were a lot more comfortable, but the thrill was gone.

I got on the *Century* after I quit the road foreman's job. After the war was over, my wife and kids said I was getting grouchy and miserable, probably because I had so

What appears to be scrap steel is part of the boiler of engine No. 5450. She blew up at Canastota, New York, in 1943, killing the entire crew. Standing (left to right) are: Howard Palmer, traveling fireman; Carl Peterson, chief foreman of engines; Charlie Stuart, road foreman; and Elgie Rath, traveling fireman.

much responsibility on my mind. There was a lot of pressure in that job. The railroad wanted to transfer me again (it was another promotion), and I said I'd talk it over with my wife. She said, "It's up to you. I'll go, but let's talk it over with the kids." They said, "Pop, we're not going this time." That's all I needed. I didn't want the job anymore, anyway. I held my seniority and went back running until I retired in August 1957. We were still going eight-five miles an hour in 1957. The *Twentieth Century Limited* was still running and running good when I quit. All this is long before Amtrak. It was eleven years later before they killed the *Century* and I'm glad I missed that.

My wife tells this better than I do, but on my last run, I went down with No. 40, the *Mohawk,* and back with No. 39, the *North Shore Limited.* The assistant superintendent and chief clerk took us out for a big lunch at our arrival in Albany. My wife made the round trip with me in the cab.

They always put a road foreman on with a fellow making his last trip—this one was Billy Donlan—and my regular fireman, Barney Kelly, another nice Irishman, he was with me too. I had sixteen cars and two big diesel locomotives. Coming into Little Falls, I eased off instead of putting on the brakes, and one of the engines in the head unit caught on fire. The cab doors were good and tight, but a little smoke was beginning to seep underneath the doors and we knew right away what had happened. Billy and Barney each grabbed a fire extinguisher and put out the fire. The cause was an accumulation of oil between the exhaust stack and apron up at the top of the engine, and it got hot pretty fast with the load we were putting on that engine with those sixteen cars pulling behind us. Billy came back into the cab and in his Irish brogue he said to my wife, " 'Tis a damn good thing he's quitting. He's a hell of an engineer but he's burning them up!"

Don't let this ex-Marine fool you. Underneath that tough expression is one of the nicest guys you'd want to know. His first "locomotive" was a "made-it-yourself" creation of junkyard parts with garden hose for tires.

CHESTER F. GEASLEN
Fort Wright, Kentucky

Writer, historian, athlete, soldier and railroad engineer. All of these describe Chester Geaslen. He has written four books about the history of northern Kentucky and contributed articles to the Cincinnati Post *and the L&N Magazine. Chester played just about every sport he could try, including football, basketball and golf, and several seasons of baseball in the Bluegrass League. He also worked on a newspaper and served as Marine in World War I. That's quite a list of accomplishments, but when he was asked which he enjoyed the most, Chester wrote the following: "Railroad men come to the railroad in the spring of their lives, and somehow remain to their autumn years, working while other people sleep, and trying to sleep while other people are working, but then, I'll tell you something . . . without exception, they would want it no other way."*

Through the years I used to think that there was a lot of romance in working on a railroad engine. You see trains flit by and the fireman and the engineer waving out the windows to everybody. Well, I think I was railroading for a year and I never had occasion to wave at anybody out of the window. I was too busy feeding a firebox. Hell of a job feeding those fireboxes.

I was born in Cincinnati, Ohio. In 1902 my family moved to Kentucky and when I got out of eighth grade I got my first job driving a grocery wagon. I've been working ever since. I entered a shorthand and typing school, and then got a job in an insurance office, where I perfected my typing, which I wasn't too keen about anyway. One year later I chucked that and got a job learning the blacksmith trade on the Chesapeake & Ohio Railroad at Covington, Kentucky. I was raised with a great bunch of fellows and we were all athletes. We played basketball, football and baseball. Then, when President Woodrow Wilson declared war against Kaiser Bill's Germany, our whole group volunteered for service in the Marine Corps. Four of us were accepted and we were ordered to the Marine base at Parris Island, where we were torn down and rebuilt to Marine specifications. We became part of the 74th Company, 2nd Division, U.S. Marines. At St. Nazaire we used to unload ships at the docks and stand MP duty in the town. St. Patrick's Day, 1917, we were en route toward the front in the Vosges region. On Easter Sunday, we were in the trenches at Verdun, where we were serenaded by whistling shells screeching over our heads. Sirens were set up throughout the trenches to warn us of an approaching gas wave. We had already come under the shellfire of the *boches* before, and lost three horses, but no men. Not so lucky at Verdun, where we lost a number of our men and I was wounded. We were hospitalized at Souilly. Those of us who could move about were transferred south to Chaumont, then to Vichy. We had all heard of Vichy water back home. We all found it to be a pleasant soft drink and took healthy gulps, one after another. The French people stared at us in amazement. First there were stomach growls like thunder, then Mother Nature stepped in and we were *hors de combat*. We were a mess. Later we were assigned to light duty in the record department in the headquarters at Blois. The war ended November 11, 1918, at 11 A.M., and what a celebration we had—amid tears of joy.

We came back in May of 1919. We landed at Hoboken with 123 Marines in our group. Our traveling orders told us to report to Quantico. I think we took a ferryboat to

In the 1940s, brakeman Glen Browning (left) put his camera on the ground and pulled the shutter with a string, catching "Chick" Geaslen (center) and engineer "Little Daddy" Bryant.

Manhattan and then a streetcar to Grand Central Station. The station had wide marble banisters. Well, we put our luggage on this banister and down it went, *pssssss!* Here we were with hobnailed boots walking on those marble steps, and hell, half of the squad landed on their tails clear out in the middle of the station. Whenever I hear about Grand Central Station, I get a funny feeling in my rear end to this day.

After I was back for a while, I played baseball in the Bluegrass League. We only played three games a week. One day there was a Texas Leaguer hit into the infield. Shallow for me and deep for the infielders. When I first looked at it I thought I had a chance for it, so the closer I got, the more I yelled, "Let me have it, let me have it!" Then there was a three-way collision. The shortstop and the second baseman had spiked each other, they had to be taken out of the game, and I had the wind knocked out of me. I'm trying to compose myself, picking a clover blossom or something, and I hear this raspy voice from the stands yelling, "God damn you, are you trying to kill the whole ball club? Why in the hell don't you stay in center field where you belong?"

Well, I looked at him and I picked up my cap and shouted, "Boy, why don't you come out here and kiss my ass!"

Suddenly there was one of those quiet times you sometimes get in a crowd and you could hear my voice coming off those hills—gee, it even caused me to cringe. I looked up to see if the game was about to be resumed, but it wasn't. The manager, the umpire and a minister got out there, and the manager, old George, says I insulted every woman in the grandstand, and "I got to get you out of this ball park before the game is over, because the menfolks will thrash you." So out I came and I had to walk all the way to the hotel. Walking in those spike shoes, that was some ordeal. I packed up my things and went to the station to wait for the train. A conductor told me the Louisville & Nashville was looking for men to hand-fire their steam engines. I had a friend that had got a job as a fireman and I figured I'd try it too.

That was the spring of 1922. I had to put in ten days breaking in. They wanted to see if you could stand the gaff, shoveling coal for six, eight, ten hours a day. It was hard keeping the maximum amount of steam up in a locomotive in steam days. You'd put your foot on the foot pedal and the door would fly open. It would look just like red flames to most people, but a keen, experienced eye could perceive burnt-out areas. There would be areas that were different colors and you knew what each one meant. You'd hit those burnt-out areas to keep your fire even so you wouldn't have any cold spots. It was an art to know when and how to do it. You'd look at your smokestack to make sure it had cleared thoroughly before you put any more coal in the firebox. You'd always have a "heel"—what we called the mound of coal inside your firedoor. If you had that heel there, your fire wouldn't be vulnerable. You wouldn't get holes in your fire if you kept that heel, so you put the third scoop of coal there each time.

What you'd try to do when you were hand-firing was hit the left sheet, and then the right sheet, and then put one right down the middle. If you hit the steel base on the firedoor with the shovel, you'd spray coal all over the whole fire. When we got the automatic stokers, you'd do the same thing with the spray that you had done with the shovel. You'd take your shovel—you still needed a shovel—and look under it. You can see the fire better looking under the shovel. If it was getting light on one side or the other, you'd increase your coal admission on that side. Sometimes you'd be running along and you'd hear a *clank, clank, clunk,* and you knew you were grinding up a piece of steel that had come along with your coal. Somewhere along the line someone had thrown it in the coal or it fell in, but however it got there, it would sometimes tear up the worm gear and then you were all through for the day. You just couldn't keep up steam in those big locomotives with a shovel. Like I told you, it was a hell of a job hand-firing.

Another thing I remember well was the extra board. Now, that extra board business is when the railroad says, "Now, son, you go home and sit right by your telephone, and when we need you, we'll call you." It may be one hour, one day, one week, one month. They just seemed to feel that you were in bondage to them, and if your phone rang, you'd better be there to answer it. No guarantee of income. You got paid for services rendered. It was the best I could find at the time, however, and there was something thrilling about working on those engines, after all. Through the years I used to think there was something special working for the railroads, no matter all the problems. The unions helped make railroading livable too. Before the unions they'd send you right out after coming in, you know. There wasn't any respect for federal law, about sixteen hours in service and no more—things like that. I've had some of the fellows say to me they'd be taking their overalls off after maybe twenty hours getting a train in, and the call boy would come, say they were out of men. That man would sit down to a pot of coffee and a couple of sandwiches and take off again. That kind of thing was stopped. It was enough of a challenge to run a steam locomotive, much less to be dead tired while you were doing it. We spent many hard hours learning how to do it well. Those engines were there to haul trains if you could make and use steam to do the job.

It was quite a pleasure and also a relief when you got all of your loose ends together. Read your fire, know how to use the throttle, make that engine do what you wanted it to do. It was quite satisfying to think that you could meet the challenge of those big robust locomotives. Our last and best were the M-1s. Emmas, we called them, and they were beautiful machines. When the diesels came they found they needed two or more diesel units to supplant one M-1. A train that an Emma had been running away with, a diesel couldn't do near as well. They used the M-1s

in freight service until it was noted that when one was used in freight it was making better time than some of the passenger locomotives, so they tried them in passenger service and found they just ran with those trains. They were ball-bearing engines. On smooth rails you'd give a locomotive steam, and then shut it off, you'd get a rumbling sound like a motorcycle going by. Not those M-1s! The bearings took up the slack in the connecting rods. Those engines would just glide along—no rumble, no noise.

The diesels were a step in the modernization of railroads. We were glad to get away from the heat and the cinders. You could make a trip and go to bed without having to scrub for an hour to get the grime and soot off your face and body. Some of the fellows even started to wear ties to work. We had some of the old-timers that would lament the fact that they could get clean in one washing, whereas they used to have to scrub two or three times and never get the black out of their ears. The diesel, though, just didn't have the romance or the challenge. After the diesel program had been adopted in the yard and road service, you would occasionally hear someone say, "Oh, look what's coming!" You would see that black smoke in the air, and then pretty soon you'd see that old steam engine plowing along. They were using them for reserves then. Once in a while you'd get one on a run and you'd complain loud enough for everyone to hear, but it was still a thrill, even when they were in bad condition. They just didn't keep them up at the end. I missed them when I realized they were gone forever. Diesels had some wonderful features, but they were vulnerable to breaking down. Not so much mechanical repairs, but electrical problems. The shock of starting and stopping would break the wires and connections. The company went back to using steam on the locals for a while for just that reason. Trains that were accustomed to stopping at every town and setting out cars and picking up empties and such. That was when we first got the diesels; I'm sure they've made a lot of improvements since those days.

I guess I wasn't an engineer for more than a month taking extra calls like handling troop trains from here to Corbin and Ravenna when I got a letter stating that there was twenty-five of us men being transferred to the Pensacola Division of the L&N. "Transportation will be afforded you," it also stated. We got into Mobile around midnight and we had to do a lot of doorbell ringing because railroad men were not what you would call desirable clientele for the hotels. We usually stayed in rooming houses when we were out on the road. So we woke up some old lady, and we had to sleep two, maybe three men in a room. The days were blistering hot and the nights were not much less down there. Then some of us were sent to New Orleans. That was a great treat because New Orleans was a romantic city and we walked around every bit of it. It made a lot of country boys feel like metropolitan gentlemen.

We came back home here to our home division and found ourselves on the extra board as firemen again. Things were kind of flat because John L. Lewis would call out his miners about three or four times a year. They had to reduce the forces on the railroad—with no mines working there were no loads to take away. It was tough, and my wife and I had three children. Everybody knew the De-

Not exactly the NFL, but Chester Geaslen (center) and his two teammates, G. Normile (left) and A. Reenan, look as if they took the game seriously. "Pros" with the champion Christ Church squad of Cincinnati, Ohio, in 1922.

pression was on except the damn stork. In my young days I had a paper route, so I walked into the office of the Cincinnati *Post* and asked if there was any danger of a fellow getting a job there. The circulation manager said he thought he'd heard everything, but that was the first time he'd heard that. I got a job hitting towns in Ohio, West Virginia and Kentucky making sketches of streets and numbers of houses. I had a crew that would then contact every home and talk to housewives about subscribing to the *Post*. Then I was put in charge of a division. I had this Covington Division and I had newsboys in every town. I worked at that for a good while, and then I got a letter from the L&N that business was picking up, they were putting on ten crews, and I had thirty days in which to report. So I went to the newspaper and told them the railroad had contacted me. My boss said that just when I was getting so I was some use to them, I was going to quit. So I went back to the railroad and sailed on through.

I enjoyed my railroading days, and the people; by and large they were a great bunch of men to work with. I owe all my railroading ability to their intelligence. I had them tell me that they enjoyed working with a man like me who was doing the best he could to help them out on the job. Those men knew how to make a fellow feel at home in the cab of that engine. You can't help but like the guy you're working with when he has an attitude like that. Those old

engineers knew their jobs like no one else.

We had something happen one day that I think was humorous and showed how those old-timers worked. We had a coal-train wreck one morning in Kentucky, and all of the officials were down there. They had to get the main line cleared. Well, an old engineer named Stormy happened to be running that train and the superintendent was up ahead giving him a signal. Now, under the rules he had no right to give him a signal, but he could tell someone in the crew to give him one. "Come ahead, come ahead!" the superintendent was yelling.

Old Stormy gave her a head of steam, took up the slack, came right up to that point, and *crunch!*, tightened everything a half-inch further.

The superintendent's still out there calling, "Come ahead, goddamn you, can't you see this signal?"

Stormy looked out of the cab and said, "Yes, I can see your signal, but it's not safe to come ahead with this train."

"Well, I'm telling you to come ahead, goddamn it!"

Stormy didn't say another word, backed up and opened her up and jerked the whole end out of a car. The wheels had been on the ground and nobody had noticed it. That engineer knew something was wrong, but those officials wouldn't pay attention. He leaned out of the cab again, looked at the superintendent and said, "Well, there you are. She's ahead now."

In the East Syracuse yards of Conrail (at one time the New York Central), Irene Ingison stands next to one of the tools of her trade, a 184-ton locomotive. The thing she liked best about her job? "I liked being the boss."

IRENE M. INGISON
Syracuse, New York

Women's liberation is a very important issue today. In the early 1940s it wasn't an issue at all. The men had gone to war and they needed bodies on the railroad, any kind of bodies. Women like Irene Ingison found jobs they would never have gotten had it not been for that. Most of the women who went to work during that period went back to their homes or typewriters after the war ended, but Irene liked it out there and stayed. Good money, security, all of that went with the job. But most of all, she was a railroader! She had a job with responsibility, but it didn't come easy. The practical jokes, the hostility from the older men, the union problems. Irene fought for a job she really wanted and won. As she puts it, "I like to be where the action is."

I loved the outdoors, directing guys, throwing switches, tying up brakes. I loved it all. I got all my diplomas for office work and I hate it. All day in that office. Even went out and took a refresher course one time. You can keep it all. I got two diplomas for nursing. Didn't want that either. Who the hell wants to wash those dirty old men and all that crap? I never did like working indoors. I loved the railroad and that's what I wanted to do.

Before I went on the railroad, I was a dressmaker and tailor, at a factory making women's dresses and men's shirts. Worked at sewing on and off until the war came. This lady down the street who used to take care of my kid, her son was a railroad fireman on the New York Central, and he told me where to go down to hire out.

The trainmaster at Syracuse told me he had two jobs open. One for $4.98 a day as messenger, and another for $6.99 as switch tender. I told him, "You just hired yourself a switch tender."

He asked me how much I weighed and I told him 106 pounds. He said, "That's awful light for that type of work."

I said, "What the heck, dynamite comes in small packages." He told me that if that's the way I felt, get on down to the yard and qualify.

I qualified for three days on my own time. When you qualified you'd kind of get some idea what it's about. I went to work that same night at eleven o'clock. There were about twelve of us women working at that time. They couldn't get enough men because of the war. After the war all of them left except three of us. I was the last of the lot.

My dad came over here from Canada in a Model T Ford with two crates of chickens, one on each side of the car. He never paid the head tax on us kids, so when I got older I found out I wasn't an American citizen. I had to finally get six sets of witnesses to prove me of good character. I had a yardmaster, trainmaster, brakemen, all railroad people. My mother died when I was eight and my father couldn't take care of us. We were skipping school and such, and pretty soon the authorities put their feet down. My brother Bill and I were put in an orphanage in Oswego—St. Francis. My older brother and sister stayed with my dad.

After I was fifteen, I was sent to the Guardian Angel Home in Troy. There's so many children that they can't really give enough love or understanding to each child but I got as good an education as there was in the world for a girl then. Believe me, I learned a lot more than if I was at my mother's knee. Every educational opportunity was there if you had enough moxie to learn. I took everything: shorthand, typing, sewing. I used to make the nuns' habits and priests' cassocks and took beauty culture, cooking, nursing. When I was twenty I got out of there. You had to have somebody sponsor you. They wanted you to have a home to come out to. They didn't want you coming out into the world green, not knowing what it's all about. I went to work for a year for a lady in Schenectady.

Then I wanted to see my father and family and I came here to Syracuse. I worked at sewing for forty hours a week for $5. My dad was staying with this lady at a hotel. I used to clean all the rooms, mop them, make the beds and everything for my room and board. Besides the sewing. I had wanted a bike all my life. I bought a Western Auto bicycle. Rode that bike for years to work even when I was on the railroad. When they gave me a raise to $8 a week, sewing, I thought I was rich.

I met my husband in Syracuse and we were married in 1939. My son was born in 1940. My husband was what you'd call a fair-weather truck-driver. I used to go on the truck with him to New York, Scranton, or wherever. Eleven tons of loose cabbage, onions for the pickle factory. I'd help him unload. Grab a pitch-fork and away I'd go. I liked to see different places and it was better than sitting at home. When I got on the railroad he didn't like it a bit. He used to telephone the caller and mark me off duty, so that when I got there, somebody'd be in my place. Finally I had to put a stop to that. I said to the yardmaster, "You don't accept any call, only from me." My husband just didn't want me working with all those men. We ended up getting divorced and I let him off scot-free. No alimony, no support. If I had to scrub floors the rest of my life, I was going to make it on my own. I did, too.

Rose Card (left), Lee Gardner (right) and Irene Ingison on the job in the East Syracuse yards in 1949. Irene seems to be doing all the heavy work while the others hold the lanterns.

For twenty-one years I worked two jobs. Waiting on tables during the day and working on the railroad eight hours at night. It was rugged, but I was a lot younger then. I could take it. We were working seven days a week straight time on the railroad. No clause for "time-and-a-half after forty hours." We'd all try to see how long we could take it before we laid off. The longest I went was forty-one days in a row. In the winter up in Syracuse it was tough. They didn't have enough switch cleaners to take care of the switches, and in the book it says when there are no switch cleaners available, the brakemen and switch tenders will clean their own switches. Many a time I had a hard broom to clean them myself in order to get things moving. You couldn't just stand there like an idiot and not do it. Part of your job. You'd have to stay until your relief showed up. If I worked three to eleven, say, I'd have to stay until my man got there. Maybe the guy got stuck in a snow bank. You'd have to stay, that was a must! The jobs had to be protected. Those engines had to keep working.

When I was working as a switch tender, I'd get to work and make up my time slip. Then I'd talk to the yardmaster. He'd tell me the trains that we were doubling from one track to another. I'd throw the switch in order to make it a cross-over from one track to another. They'd take the two sections and make up the train. When we'd made up the train I'd put it in my book. What time, what the number of the train was, the conductor's name. I'd keep a log for the eight hours of moves we made.

I was an outdoors person and had to go out and actually throw the switches. Any kind of weather. The yardmaster would give me the dope on the outside speaker or on the phone. He'd tell me that the engines were there for such and such a train, maybe NY2. We'd get that train ready to go. When it was ready to depart, I'd call the yardmaster and he'd call down to the main car inspector and he'd put one or two men out to inspect each side of the train. They were called "car knockers." They checked journal boxes, and the air hoses for breaks, any leaks. Checked the brake rigging to see if any were down or had a brake shoe off, stuff like that. They were given maybe a minute a car, or just a little longer. If he called them at ten o'clock, he'd expect them to be off that train by at least eleven, maybe eleven-fifteen. If they ran into trouble they couldn't fix by themselves, they'd call the yardmaster and tell him. If it couldn't be repaired en route, they'd throw that car out of the train. Didn't want to send it down the track and possibly foul up the whole train. When the train was inspected and ready, I'd call the yardmaster and he'd highball the train out of there. That's more or less what a switch tender was involved with.

If we were flat-switching, we'd have a hard time making sure of the cars we had to switch. Had to keep track of the numbers. The tracks were numbered, too, and I'd have to throw the switches for the right ones as the conductor was pulling the pins on the cars. We'd have a list of what cars were going on what track and made up our trains from that. I didn't have to make the air-hose hookups or do the couplings. I didn't have to tie up the hand brakes, either, unless something started to run away. If a car was going to wreck or run into something, you didn't care what your duties were. You'd climb up on the deck—that's the roof—and grab that brake wheel. Turn it until you got the car stopped.

Today you're not allowed up on the deck. They've only got half ladders and there's the new Ajax brakes on the side of the car. You can put them on a lot faster. We used to jump boxcars. It was two feet between cars. Corrugated-roof walk and when you jumped you wouldn't slip. Now with the big new cars they've got those five-foot drawheads that stick out at each end and hold the couplers. Now it's ten feet between cars. Impossible to jump. At night you'd have your lamp on your arm. Put your arm through the handle. I know a few guys who hit the switch by mistake and jumped into a gondola full of coal or guts. Thought they were heading for another boxcar. Oh, gee, you could get hurt. That's one of the reasons they took those ladders off. They were always telling us, "Put your hands and feet in a safe position. Know where you are all the time."

You had to keep your feet in the best shape. Wear a shoe with a soft sole that would take the shock from that ballast. Thick soles with ridges. Give you a better grip. You couldn't go without gloves and you wouldn't want to. Steam engines, diesels, both got you filthy. Engineer fooling around with his dipstick, checking the oil on the diesels. They stunk from that fuel oil. Steamers weren't so bad until one of those guys decided to play a trick on you, especially if you had a nice white T-shirt on. He'd put the injector on and blow water and that soft coal out of the stack. You'd look like a speckled trout. All in fun. At the time I didn't think it was very funny.

When we started, we got a lot of heat—the women, that is. They used to play some dirty tricks on us. They'd nail my lantern to the floor, put pebbles and toilet paper in my gloves. I'd fall asleep, and they'd blacken my face with cork, give me a hotfoot, maybe burn waste under the bench. Another thing they'd do was lock me in the men's room and not let me out. I'd come home and cry. I'd say, "You can stick this job. I'm going home and not coming back." After a year of that, I said to myself, Hey, baby, if you can't lick 'em, join 'em. Ever since, it's been beautiful. They weren't mean men, just giving us women heat because we were out there working with them for the first time. More of the teasing kind of thing, needling us. Hell, we went with 'em all. I used to go with a guy, for cripes' sake, for thirty years. We all went with the railroad group. We were all young. I mean, if you left yourself open for comment, that was up to you.

They were teasers, but respectful at the same time, really. Like nobody'd come up and goose you, grab you from behind your back, anything like that. They knew they'd get belted, anyway, but they just don't do that fresh kind of stuff. There's one four-letter word they never said in front of me. If they did slip, they'd say, "Oh, Reenie, I'm so sorry," and turn forty shades of red. I'd say, "Forget it, kid, I didn't hear a word, let sleeping dogs lie." They'd pull those dirty tricks, but they'd never hurt you. Like the night they put the black on our faces and locked me in the men's room: I didn't own a car at the time and I would have had to take the bus home. One guy took Muriel and me home. All they had at that time was brown soap and cold water. No powder room for the ladies! Just a men's room.

The engineers were different. Mostly older men of the old school. Oh, they resented the women something terrible. A lot of them wouldn't even let us ride on the engine. I'd have to walk from switch to switch, where later I'd just hop on the engine and ride. There were a lot of them wouldn't have us in the cab. Not all, but a lot of those older men. Some of them wouldn't even talk to you, wanted no part of you. They figured a woman's place was in the home, not out in a railroad yard. The brakemen and conductors, they were very nice for the most part.

When I became a brakeman, I switched cars, made my own air hitches, released my own brakes. We had to throw

Irene gets a wave from the engineer. Things weren't always so friendly. When she started in 1941, some of the older engineers thought the last thing the railroad needed was women working in the yards.

Brakemen don't have to go up here anymore. The railroads have taken the roof walks off, cut the ladders in half, and moved the brakes to the side of the cars.

our own switches because they had done away with the switch tenders. The yardmaster would give me the numbers for the train. If you had a train heading west, you'd put the caboose east, then your Ohio cars next. Then your Chicago cars. Like that. As you'd go along the main line, you'd drop off the groups of cars. You can't just throw a train together. Got to be grouped according to destination. When they'd get there with the train, you'd cut off those cars and ask the yardmaster where he wanted them. He'd tell you and he might have a few cars for you to pick up and take with you. Okay, you'd bag your cars in there where he wanted them and pick up the ones he had for you. That's what conductor and braking work was about. Oh, you'd have to check your air hoses again after you made those pickups. Make sure you could get air into the train after you tied it back up.

We had a few switches that were so tough that even three men couldn't get them over. These section men used to be all pretty strong, heavyset Italian men and the bosses forgot that didn't mean that anybody could throw them. Now, you pit my 106 pounds against 230, where you going to go, right? So I'd try and get a couple of those guys to help me with the bad ones. Those switches could get out of whack, too. If one gets sprung, the next guy who goes to throw it is not going to make it even if he pulls his guts out. During the war they were too busy to take care of anything and since the war they don't have the men or the money, so the whole thing is in bad shape. Very, very bad shape. Not only that, the cars are wider and longer. This brakeman and I were working on Track 25 one day. There were some big Conrail cars on the next track and every time the trains came by I could hear them hitting each other, *tick, tick, tick*. I told that brakeman that

there'd be a lot of cripples on that train. You can't have cars hitting each other like that and have them stay in one piece for very long.

They've rebuilt a lot of the Syracuse yard. Took out tracks to make more room so that doesn't happen. They put millions of dollars into this new yard, modernizing it, everything new. Now they want to send the trains right through without stopping. This could be the hub of business with all the railroads coming in here. The government gave Conrail all the money to revamp the yard and then they pull everything out? I don't know who's doing the thinking, but that's what's happening. Fruit cars that belong at the market that's seven miles away. They'd let them lay in the yard and rot, finally throw all the stuff in the dump. Whole cars of melons, sweet potatoes, what have you. A guy is waiting for his lumber for two weeks. This is foolish management. I can't help it, this is the way I feel, and I used to blow my cork because it's so stupid. Years ago, you'd put a caboose on the tail end of those produce cars and take 'em right up to market. Clear sailing down the local track. There's nothing in your way. Grab that guy's lumber and get it up to him. No, it isn't the railroad it was. No way. There used to be seven hundred fifty people working in this yard back in 1944. Now there's fifty around the clock. It's one thing to modernize, but you got to produce, otherwise they go some place else. To trucks.

On my job you had to be alert. You'd become automatically on the lookout for any kind of sound or movement because you could get into trouble out there very easily. You had to watch everywhere, anytime, no matter where you were. Diesels can sneak up easier than the steamers could. That's not all. You've got to watch the track next to you. You'd be surprised how quiet a train can be. Anything can creep up on you, cars run away, or what have you. We used the walkie-talkies instead of hand signals when we could. Got them in 1974, thereabouts. They were good, but also good and heavy. You carried them from the right shoulder to the left with a strap. After a while they gave us ones that were lighter. Half the time you'd get out there and find out that the batteries weren't charged. You'd get into a bad position and get no signal. If an engineer had been one very long, he'd stop when he didn't hear anything. You can't hear the orders, you don't move.

With all the radios we used, you had to be careful when you gave orders. You had to do it according to engine number and job number. Mostly engine numbers if you could. If you called the engineers by their first name, there might be two Jacks or Joes, and you were going to tell some guy to move when he was not supposed to. There might have been a man in there opening a knuckle or making an air hitch. It could be very confusing sometimes because the engines all had radios and there were all kinds of trains out there and each engineer was trying to talk to the dispatcher. In order to avoid a crack-up, sometimes I've had to break in and somebody would say, "Oh, no, not Reenie again!" I'd say, "Sorry, fella, but I don't want to have a wreck." You tried to be kind of gracious about it.

They took the switch tenders off in '68. Then the union went to bat for the men. There were a lot of men who were switch tenders who had given up their braking rights so they could hold a day job and it was decided that they'd get the seniority. They were marked up as brakemen.

"So," I says, "what about us women?" There were two of us left at that time.

"Well," the railroad answered, "we got papers for you to sign: we want you to resign. Women can't go braking."

I told them no way: "You've gotta be kidding. Resign? After twenty-three and a half years? I'll see you in court."

As sure as shooting I wrote to Washington. They referred me to New York and they sent some people up here from the Human Resources Commission and the Equal Employment Opportunity Commission. The railroad and the union threw it back and forth, and they finally sent a judge and girl lawyer up from New York. The judge ruled in our favor and that afternoon we were posted. They realized they were beat. It took me two years to do it. Everybody said to me, "You'll never make it, kid." I told them as long as there was an ounce of breath in me I would. The railroad just wanted to get rid of us two women any way they could. They didn't want any part of us, and the worst part of it was we never caused any trouble. We never had any bad marks against either of us. If we had created any discipline problems or put cars in the ditch, I could have understood their attitude. But we never bothered anyone. We did our work and that was it. I didn't see where they had a grievance except we were women, that's all. We were okay during the war when they needed us. We got paid the same as a man and we paid our union dues the same as a man, but I had to fight for what I got.

Some of the new kids didn't like me particularly because I made them work, but that was fine with me. I'd hear, "My father works here, my uncle works here, my grandfather worked here and don't you know who you're talking to?" I'd say, "Yeah, you're about the fifth generation out here and your grandfather was probably the best of the lot." I'd try and watch everybody. I was like a mother hen, more or less, and I always took the safest course. I'll tell those kids, they can always make a new boxcar, they can't make a new you. One night this other brakeman and I were sitting and waiting for the engine to come by so we could hop on. Right in the middle of the train that had been inspected, or was supposed to have been inspected, there's this boxcar with its door off the track. Just hanging out there. The first breeze that hit it was going to take it off. Hit a car, brakeman, anything. It drove me crazy, I couldn't stand it, knowing it was there. I went in and told the boss about it. I couldn't just go home and know it was on there like that.

They laid a lot of brakeman off here in 1970 and 1971. I couldn't hold a job here, not even nights or on the extra board. I still wanted to work instead of drawing unemployment. So I went to Buffalo to work. I drove up there and stayed for a whole year. Lived in a convent with the sisters. One dollar a night. The guys got a big kick out of that, me living in a convent. The only thing I couldn't do was smoke. I'll tell you, they were surprised when I drove up to the Buffalo yard the first time. I went up there in a pair of pink shorts and my hair up in curlers. I walked into the caller's office and asked to see his seniority book as far back as 1944. The guy didn't give me a hard time. He had heard there were women brakemen in Syracuse, but he hadn't seen one. Evidently he must have figured I knew what I was talking about. Talking seniority, 1944. I looked over the book and then I asked him what jobs were up for bid. I looked those over and then told him to tell that guy, there, he's bumped Monday. You should have heard him. Here I was walking onto his railroad in my pink shorts and bumping one of his men. Oh, Christ, we had more laughs. The guys treated me great. They really did.

A rose among the thorns. Irene and the yard crew she was working with in Buffalo's Frontier yard.

Sitting in the backyard of his home, Bob Thomas remembers when a man wanted to be a "brag engineer." If you could get a train over the road and use the least coal and water, your crew would brag about you to the other crews.

ROBERT L. THOMAS
Wildwood, Florida

"I always wanted to work on the railroad. I wanted to be an engineer, so my cousin and me just worked our way to the Northwest looking for a railroad job." At an age when most children, today, are worrying about which new record album to buy, or college to apply to, R. L. Thomas left home and traveled across the country and found his railroad job. Starting as a fireman, he lived the American dream. Fifty years later he finished up his career as an engineer on one of the great trains of its time, the Orange Blossom Special. Bob was one of the countless boys who started at the bottom, and with a combination of hard work and seat-of-the-pants smarts, rose to the top of his profession. The president of the railroad rarely commanded the respect given a veteran railroad engineer.

I always wanted to work on the railroad, that was the only way you could get to be an engineer. Had to get some actual experience, get you a job firing. I didn't want no job in the shops. Didn't want no job braking. I wanted to be an engineer. You see, I just walked away from home when I was a little boy. I lived eleven years in Sampson City, Florida, and three years in Worthington Springs, that's north of Wildwood. Sampson City is six miles out on a spur track. The only things there was a sawmill and a small lake. When you're raised in a sawmill town, you don't know nothing. Thinking back, it was a darn pity. We are talking about a period of time just before World War I and it was hard times.

My cousin and me just worked our way right into the Northwest. First job I got on a main-line railroad was on the Northwest Pacific Railroad at Kootenia, Idaho. They had a pretty little old roundhouse there made out of brick. My first job was to clean fires, but I worked on a lot of logging roads before I went with the Northern Pacific. Just fired— never did run them. I fired both the Shay and the Climax geared locomotives. The Shay had the cylinders on the side. Odd-looking thing, but it would pull if you could keep any steam up. The Climax, that was a nice little piece of machinery. I thought it was a big improvement over the Shay locomotive. The Climax was slow but very powerful. Fired both oil-burning and coal-burning locomotives for those logging lines. I worked for the Three Lakes Lumber Company at Three Lakes, Washington, the Weyerhaeuser Logging Company near Tacoma, and the Eby Logging Company in Washington State. I didn't like dragging around in the woods with those geared locomotives, so I went with the NP.

I was up there in the Northwest for a while and my family didn't know where I was. After I'd been gone that long, I didn't think they would bother me and make me come back home. Besides, I had me a railroad job. Then they sent me a wire that my mother was sick and not expected to live. Found out where I was. You know a mother in them days, they was really a mother, they was the king. I had $100, and when I got home, I didn't have any money left. My railroad ticket was $96 to get to Jacksonville. I had no way in the world of getting back out to the Northwest. I'd never heard of or seen anybody that had anything like $100 before in my life.

So what was I going to do? I asked my mother's brothers—they were trainmen, conductors, on the Seaboard—where I could get a railroad job down here. They told me to go to Jacksonville and they might be hiring some fire-

men. Well, I went up there and there were no jobs there. I came back home and heard they was hiring some firemen in Tampa. I was about out of money and I had to get some sort of work. I'd never been to Tampa, but I heard that it was a big railroad crossing, and I knew that if you got to a railroad crossing, well, the train was going to stop. In them days, tramps, hobos, whatever you call them today, they didn't think too much about traveling at all. They just walked till they came to a water tank or railroad crossing and knew that a train would stop sooner or later. I went down to the depot and got a ride on a log train going to Hawthorne. I got off there, went along the Seaboard side, found me a boxcar and got in. I got along all right and nobody bothered me until I got down to Summerfield and the conductor came along and saw me and put me off. I built me a little fire. It was wintertime, cold as hell. Another train pulled in and the conductor on that train came walking along looking his train over and saw me and asked me what I was doing out there in the middle of nowhere and where was I going? I told him. He asked me where I had been working and then he told me, "You go back to the caboose and tell the flagman that I sent you back there, I'll take you to town." I laid down there on the cushions and went to sleep. He woke me up and told me that we were at Tampa Junction. That's where the shop was and all. He told me I could get off there and walk right down there into the shops. That's where I wanted to go, so that's what I did.

The derby hat wasn't official railroad gear, but Bob Thomas must have wanted to look like a successful young railroader at Kootenai, Idaho, sometime in the early 1900s.

Directly, I walked around and didn't see anybody. One little fellow came along and he says, "You looking for something?"

I said, "Yes, sir, I'm looking for the road foreman of engines. Would you know where I'd find him?"

He said, "Well, he ain't in town, did you want anything in particular? I'm the shop foreman."

I told him, "Yes, sir, I want to get me a job firing engines on this railroad."

He asked me if I was experienced and I told him I was, and where I'd been working. He said, "I'll give you a job, put you to work in the morning, brother. Are you ready to go to work?"

I said, "Yes, sir!"

So he gave me a nickel carfare and told me to go down to a boarding house and get me a room and make arrangements there for meals. The next morning they called me for a local Train No. 66, Tampa to Wildwood.

That morning I went to work, it was 1917 and I stayed until 1967 on the Seaboard. Mr. H. Y. Harris, shop foreman, was the man who gave me my job. I fired for five years on the Seaboard before I was promoted to engineer. In the thirties, in the Depression, I was cut off for five years and had to go back to firing. Whew! Back in them days firing wasn't work, it was just murder. In fact, when I went to work on this railroad, there were four white firemen and all the rest of them were black. White people wouldn't do those jobs. It wasn't so bad where I had just come from. There were good jobs up there on the NP and you got good coal. On the Seaboard, they didn't have no real coal, they were burning that old snake-eye, you know. You had to stir and scratch it and beg it to burn. You would do the job and like it, or they would get somebody else. It was up to you how much you could take physically.

The engines that I done most of my firing on was an 800 Pacific-type engine. They were good pullers. I liked them as much as any of them. Up on the NP there was bigger engines because they had to have power in them mountains. Down here on this level railroad, they didn't think much about power. You'd just drag along and get in when you could. Little eight-wheel standard locomotives, ten-wheel for freight service. Those 800s was what I was firing during the Depression. All summer long. Two or three months in the winter I would get on the engineer's extra board and make a little bit. From 1929 to 1939, I'd be working on and off. They were all hand-fired engines. The stoker came in too late for me as a fireman. The only firing I did was with a shovel, rake and hoe.

When we got the stokers it helped for faster running because you didn't have to depend on the speed of a man shoveling coal anymore. You didn't want to kill a man when he was doing his best. It took a while for a lot of men to learn how to fire stokers when they first come. They were awful tricky and delicate things. Most of the time the fireman would overload—put too much coal in and it would start to pile up. And then it wouldn't be getting enough air to burn all that green coal, and pretty soon you were out of steam—practically dead. You'd have to stop and the fireman would have to clean the coal out and get it going good again before you could move. In the beginning, it was too much of a good thing.

The steam engine was a remarkable piece of machinery. You know the valve gear distributing the power—well, setting that up wasn't like fastening a wire to a spark plug. A man had to have experience to do that. The power piston was underneath and the valve cylinder where the steam came in was on top connected to it, and that thing had to be set just right to swap the power end to end. Steam pushed on both sides of that piston. You had to use the valve gear to make the engine work. You regulated it with your reverse lever. That's where the skilled mechanics came in—setting the valves perfect so you could work in a little lead. The lead is just what it says, makes it a little quicker than it should be. Made a big difference in a steam engine. If you couldn't work any lead in it, it would just loaf along, but if the valves was set up just right you would use your reverse lever and cut it back, well, until it would really operate. The mechanics in those shops could take those steam engines apart and if they didn't have a part they would make one, put it on and make it work, and it would work right.

Everybody was a skilled man, no matter what his job was. To start with, a locomotive engineer had to have a good physical body and he had to stand a lot of punishment. Next, he had to learn how to fire and take a bad steaming engine and get over the road with it anyhow. We had no signals, you know. Never heard of things like CTC, centralized traffic control; we run by smoke, the flagman actually kept the trains apart in them days. It was run by train orders, routes, rights, direction and class. There were all different classes of trains. The first-class train, he had the right of way except for wrecker trains. The second-class train, he cleared out of the way for the first-class. The third-class, he had to clear both of them. Beyond that, you had to clear everything. You had to be a good train dispatcher yourself in that cab, because they didn't give you nothing but a time card. You had any slow orders, any special orders for extra trains. Other than that, you were just setting in the side of the yard down there, and if you could use a track for a few minutes, you'd start moving and go as far as you could. Every once in a while you'd hang your job out the window. You'd get on the road and then you could advance yourself one more station against the regular scheduled train. The scheduled train didn't know anything about you, he didn't pay any attention to a train running extra. It was up to you to stay out of his way. The rule required you to be there and be in the clear for at least five minutes before the other train was due. You'd better get there. They'd run you off the railroad if you weren't.

You had to do a lot of hard thinking and you had better be right. You can't realize now what it took out of you. Maybe you had a hill there somewhere, and if the fireman was good and could keep the steam up, you might get over that hill. If not, you might stall and then all hell would break loose. Like the hill at Dade City, for one. You had to figure out before you tried it whether it was going to work or not. Get up on that one with the steam going down and you're in a mess of trouble. An engineer out of Wildwood, he went up that old hill, fell down, stalled and had to double the hill. Had to take the train over the hill in two sections. The superintendent asked him how come he doubled the hill and he told him, to get to the other side. I thought it was a pretty good answer. There is no business in the world that had less supervision than railroading. A man just knew his job and went out and did it.

I don't know what they got in the shops now, I haven't been in them for a long time, but the old mechanics and people that were in there are all gone. Either cut off or died by now. At one time, this was a big railroad town. That's all changed. The people are gone and the steam engines are gone. Hauled them off for scrap. Oh, I was sad to see them go, hated to see them go. They were old friends. There was a little difference in each of them. My favorite, yes sir, No. 407, she talked. Would go right along talking back to you like an old friend. The 362, she was a good engine, too. Nobody knows what makes one better, maybe she happened to be set a little differently. One would pick up and pull a little better. You would notice that particularly on a hill. One would take it better than the other

Most of Bob Thomas' photographs were destroyed in a fire, but this one survived. A little out of focus, it shows Bob and his fireman, "Coffee" Rivers, next to the *Silver Meteor* about to leave Miami in the 1950s.

one. You'd run those steam engines a whole lot by sound. Listen to them and they'd help you run them if you'd let them. Change your valve setting and you could hear it, they'd change their tone for you. You just had to get so you could hear those changes and make them work for you. You don't have to listen to a diesel, you just put it on and that's that.

When the diesels came in, the instructors did all the talking and made it look pretty complicated. Then we come to find out there wasn't nothing to it. It was simply automatic—most of it was on automatic control. It took care of itself if anything happened. It was like a Christmas tree, you got the bulbs on there and if one goes out, they all go out. You learned how to put a fuse in different places, and it was that simple. There was things you could do, but if a generator flashed, or a head blew, you didn't even have to shut it down. It would shut itself. You could sometimes make temporary repairs, but not often. Steam engine, you were expected to know how to fix it. The best machine there is, after a while certain things would give, a pipe, mechanical things go out of alignment. Nothing's going to last forever. I don't care how good it is. You'd better know how to fix it. Now, the engines we had on the railroad down here, they wouldn't have let them run through

the yard on the Northern Pacific. They just couldn't have done the job right. When you came to work in the steam-engine days, and you looked at your engine on the Seaboard, and there wasn't no water running out of it, you'd be afraid to go up to it. If you couldn't see no leaks, you'd think she's about to blow up on you. No water in her. The Seaboard just didn't need the engines like they do on those big roads in Washington and Oregon.

I operated on the Florida Division, both steam and later on, when they came, the diesels. Local trains, local passenger trains. Mostly night trains. The name trains operated in the daytime, of course, like the Seaboard *Silver Star,* the Seaboard *Silver Meteor* and the *Orange Blossom Special.* I finally got seniority enough to hold a job on each of those trains, and the *Silver Meteor* was the train I was working on when I retired. I made the first trip when the *Orange Blossom Special* came into Florida. Operated from Baldwin to Waldo, Florida. Later, of course, occasionally I'd catch an extra trip on her. My seniority increased and I finally stood for her. She operated in the wintertime, of course, just about five months a year. Incidentally, I also brought her into Wildwood the last trip she made. That was a wonderful train.

It was a long time after the diesels came in that I ever had a job on one of them. They first came on the passenger trains, the diesels. It was a good while before we got any freight diesels. It was a much easier and nicer job in some ways. It was so much easier on your body physically, done away with them cinders and sand. A lot of people forget that along with the cinders, they had the old sand dome on top of that engine. You'd always be getting sand in your eyes. It was just easier to do, nothing to it, just sitting up there and thinking it out; I'd never had a job like that in my life. I was real proud of that job, but I soon discovered there was nothing I could do about it—the engine, that is. The thrill was gone. It didn't have no skill to it. A lady could run it, just sit up there like that. Couldn't blow the whistle no more on the diesel. The whistles on the steam locomotives was the most beautiful sound in the world. Nobody knows how many different kinds of whistles there were. Every railroad had its own and sometimes each kind of locomotive has its own special sound. I don't see why they made the old diesel horns like they was—they could have made a whistle. Those horns annoyed the people that lived along the railroads. They was too loud.

When you were going at low speed, you had to blow the horn at the same intensity as you did if you were going fast. I know people who would cuss at you. You didn't have the control you had with the old steam whistle. In the steam-engine days, folks would wave at you when you blew that old whistle. You could operate them steam engines, yes sir, make them do the job. That's right, it took more to run a steam locomotive—no comparison about it. At one time engineers on the railroad were highly skilled men and I know we didn't get any wages or money for the skill we had then. You're talking about a steam-locomotive engineer, you're talking about a skilled man. People nowadays don't realize, don't have the slightest idea what it took to run them engines. You could take the finest locomotive that had ever been made and it was no better than the man that was operating it.

When the mergers took place on the railroads, men like John Engelhardt found they had divided loyalties. "Working on the Erie for a good many years and then to turn around and come home with the Lackawanna."

JOHN W. ENGELHARDT
Wanaque, New Jersey

Standing with his feet wide apart, reaching for an imaginary foot pedal which would open the firedoor, John Engelhardt was shoveling coal in his kitchen. He was showing how you stood on the deck and held your shovel just so in case the engine hit a low spot. Demonstrating how a man made steam to run a locomotive before diesel electric made the scoop shovels as obsolete as the engines they were used on. Watching him standing there, swinging his whole body into the job, you could almost feel the heat from the imaginary firebox. John likes to tell you that railroading was interesting work, a good way to make a living and as good as anything else. And he is one of the few men who still have one of the shovels that helped him make that living for forty-eight years.

It all started while I was a water boy on the Lehigh Valley Railroad. We were working out at Aldene, New Jersey, putting in a bridge. The water boy was the helper in the gang, you had to carry tools on the job—a man wanted this or a man wanted that, a sledge hammer or a big crosscut saw . . . It was also my job to make the coffee for the lunchhour, and I made that coffee right out on the ground on the rocks. Every day we had to block up the track to let the *Black Diamond* express pass over. That train had a beautiful Pacific engine on it. Watching that engine—and getting the smell of it, the smoke and the smell of the oil from the lubricator, seeing the fireman up there, all that made me say, "That's what I've got to do instead of what I'm doing." So one day I took it upon myself to go down to the main office at Johnson Avenue and I asked them for a transfer, and said I wanted to go firing. They asked me how old I was. Well, at the time I was seventeen. I didn't dare tell them I was seventeen, so I told them nineteen. They said I had to be twenty-one. I could lie for two years, but I couldn't lie for four years. So, back I went to the railroad's Bridge and Building Department.

In Jersey City, where I lived, this guy who lived on my block says, "Hey, John, you want to go firing on the Erie? They're hiring firemen." I went down to the road foreman's office and told him I'd like to go firing. No trouble. I went through all the things you had to do—the physical and the IQ. At that time it wasn't exactly what you called an IQ test. It was only fifteen questions. Now they must have a hundred and fifty. Also, you have to have a high school diploma, which we didn't have in them days. Then I had to go out and get five signers so I could fire steam locomotives. I had to get five firemen to sign a paper that said they thought I could do the job. You had to ride with the crew on your own time and try your hand at firing. I hired out December 27, 1926, and spent my first year in yard service. They sent me to Secaucus in the Croxton yards. To tell the truth, I don't know whatever kept me from quitting that first year. You see, we had the pig farms up there in Secaucus in those days, and that smell used to come down to that lower end of the yards. When I worked those night jobs, I used to come home in the morning and I couldn't eat.

I put in one year out there and then said to myself, "That's enough of that, now I want to go to Jersey City and qualify for passenger trains." They give me a paper and told me to go out and get five signers on my own time. The fireman on the job would show me how to do the job. You made a trip up on one train and maybe you made a round

trip. Whatever you could get. Then they put me on the extra board and I worked as I was called. If it was wreckers, passenger trains, yard jobs, whatever job was next, that's the job I would go on. You had to take your turn on whatever job came up.

When the Depression hit us, I was laid off and went to work for the Federal Shipyards out in Kearney. When that job finished, I lived up in the mountains in Minnewaska for the winter months because it was bad. There was no work. I went back to the railroad looking for a job, any kind of job, when the good weather came back. Finally they had a job open up in Midvale, New Jersey, watching engines overnight. I would sweep coaches, put water in the boilers, take care of the fires, push coal ahead in the tenders, everything. Yes, I carried home many bags of coal for the stove. We were working for peanuts then, about $4 a day. It was rough sledding, but we managed. When I moved up here, I got a three-room bungalow with an outside toilet for $10 a month. I would rather be working for that little bit than be standing out somewhere waiting for a relief check. Relief wasn't so plentiful in them days, either.

After about six years a fellow told me about a job on the tug and ferry boats. So down I went and they hired me. It was with the Erie marine department and I learned how to fire the tugboats. I didn't like them. They was hot and dirty because they burned soft coal. The ferryboats wasn't bad, they weren't bad at all. They used to burn what they called big peat coal. You had two firemen. Two big boilers with three big doors for each. You had to pull all that fire, the dead ashes, right out in front of you when you cleaned that fire. It only took you about three, four minutes to clean the fire. After you knew how to do it, there was nothing to it. Push your live coal ahead, then let the rest burn out, as you were going across the river. The other two fires would do the work.

In the latter part of 1940, the Erie started calling the laid-off men back. I had my fill of boats. I was glad to be back on the railroad again doing what I really wanted to do. I fired until I was set up in April 1956 as engineer. I was quite lucky because within a couple of years I was able to hold some good passenger jobs. When I retired after forty-eight years in service I was number one in passenger service. When I went back to work on the road, my rights went on just the same. Didn't affect my roster position.

I fired all those years for different men, some real good men. That's when I got to know Levi Pellington. I used to have to go over to his house when he'd oversleep. When he was on that second engine out of here in the morning, they used to leave about five-thirty. I'd be watching over the fields to see if he was coming. If I didn't see him by five

Engine No. 2941 was on the ash pit in 1952 when a kid asked John if he could take his picture. "If you send me one." A few months later he got an envelope. An honorable rail fan.

DICK HORSTMANN

o'clock, I'd go over there to his house with my oil lamp. I'd pound on the door and get him out of bed. Levi would jump out, put on his overalls and over he'd come. I'd be gone back and be on the engine waiting for him. We kind of looked out for one another the best we could.

In those days they put the engineer's name on the engine if he really got the job done. I was a very proud man up there firing that passenger train with names on it like Dennis O'Brien on the Northern Division or James E. Cooney from Jersey City to Port Jervis. A man was given credit for his work. We had George Penfield, who had the best engine on the railroad, 2526. On any other locomotive of that type, you could open the throttle maybe three to four inches, where with his you'd open it one inch. It was true and square, because he kept it right up to standards. That engine was a beauty. If there was any work to be done in the roundhouse on his engine, he was there with it. He'd watch everything they did.

I got along with George, because I got to know his habits. He kept his engine nice and shiny. If we were going to make a station stop on a hill, the water would surge in the boiler and come back, and *wsssssh!*, out the pop valve it went. The water in the boiler had a compound in it to keep it from foaming, which would then get the boiler all speckled with white spots, but I became wise to that. When we did come to a station of that sort, like West Arlington, George would shut the throttle off, I'd grab the handle of the firedoor, and I'd open it a bit. That would let the cold air in the firebox and keep the pressure down. That prevented it from popping off. I was working with the man,

and he knew that. That engineer done anything I wanted. We had a different engine, for some reason, for a while. The injector handle wasn't right. Three times he put that engine in the roundhouse to have it fixed the way it should be. Other men couldn't work with George. They'd have arguments and one guy tried to hit him with the shaker bar. But I found out what the man was like, and we got along fine.

I was a young fireman in Secaucus, it was on a night job, and we were going through a low freight tunnel. We had to go to Weehawken that night and we had a double-cab engine. It was my first year out in Secaucus, and I was still a green sort of fireman. I was lucky just to make steam, much less know anything about it. The engineer, he hollers back, "Hey, kid, we're going to Weehawken, don't have her too hot going through the tunnel." Now, that tunnel's about a mile long, we're going through and the signal on the other end is red. So he shuts the throttle off, and we mope through the tunnel. But my fire is red-hot. I'm all ready for a big trip to Weehawken but don't know that we're going to get held up. We stop down there by the red light and she starts to sizzle *sssssssss!*—the pop valve, you know. The engineer's got a boiler full of water. He can't put any more in there to cool it because he had the injectors on while we were rolling through the tunnel. So we lie there inside and we lie there, and I have a nice big bright fire. All of a sudden she lets go—*pop!* She has a good two hundred pounds, and the steam goes all over. Now, we're in a double-cab engine, right? The engineer is halfway up there near the steam and I'm clear in the back. Steam,

The year was 1952 in the Erie's Midvale yard. By the shape those overalls are in, John looks like he's the only guy working. The engineer even has a tie on.

The Erie Railroad always seemed to be short of cash and they used their engines longer than most railroads. This K-5 Pacific was twenty-nine years old when this photograph was taken in 1952.

dirt, everything going all over him, not me. What that man doesn't call me! He's hollering, "Open them doors, open them doors!" Well, the pop valve finally closes and we get the green signal.

When we got out of the tunnel, he opened up that son-of-a-gun. He pulled that throttle all the way back and gave her the business all the way to Weehawken. I knew what he was doing. He was trying to knock my fire out and make me work harder. What I did in the tunnel, I didn't mean to do: I was just glad I had a nice bright fire. So I opened up both doors. Cool air! The steam went right on down, seventy-five, at most a hundred pounds. The air pumps were ready to stop, which meant we would stop short, so he eased off and I went back to work.

In July 1952 they gave us our first diesel. I felt sad in a way. It was easy and there wasn't that much to do on the diesel. It was also something of a curiosity for a while. But I hated losing steam, especially that last engine we had. It was originally on the Erie's Chicago run, but they got the big Alco diesels for that, and the old steam engines went wherever they could be used. Steam was more thrilling and interesting, but I said to myself, Well, the diesels are here for good, and all I have to do is sit over on the right side and look smart. Look straight ahead. Oh, yes, we had a few buttons to push, a few things we had to know about. Everything on the diesel was covered over. You couldn't see what was wrong even if you wanted to.

I want to tell you about the dead man's ashes. We were working what we call "The Midnight." It was a passenger train out of Jersey City and we left at a quarter to twelve at night. Just a few minutes before we pulled out, this young man came up the platform and showed the engineer a piece of paper. It said something like: "To the crew on Train 545, the Superintendent of the Railroad has given permission to this man to ride on your engine for the purpose of disposing his father's ashes to the wind, and it will be up to you, if you so desire, to let him ride." The young fellow told us his father was a commuter on that line from Arlington for about forty years, and it was his wish that his ashes be thrown to the wind from a train on that line.

It was all right with us, so we all got up in the engine. When we got out around Secaucus, I said, "Now, when we get on the other side of the Hackensack drawbridge, you have a long stretch there that would be a good place to throw them out." I told him the meadows would be a good place to unload the ashes because he was getting off at the first stop. I didn't say "the dumps" or anything, I just said "the meadows." It wasn't cold, and we didn't have the curtains pulled over. We're heading for the Hackensack River drawbridge, and I got down to put a few shovels of coal in the fire. Now, the young man saw the bridge, and I guess he got excited. He opened the bag and started to unload it out of the cab. But because of the bridge, the wind blew all those ashes back in the gangway. All over me, Mart, the engineer, the young man himself—ashes flying all over the cab! I didn't holler at the guy; what was done was done.

When we got to Arlington, the fellow thanked us and got off. Mart says to me, "Hey, John, did you get any of them ashes on you?" I said, "Did I get them on me? I not only got them on me, I got them in me." Mart's got a peacoat on and he's all covered gray. So we went along the next few stations. After a few stops, he says, "John, when we get to Midvale, I think we ought to have a drink."

As I said, I was set up as engineer in April 1956 and stayed right in passenger service until I finished. I was lucky and held some good passenger jobs. I think railroading's changed since I was a young man. The diesels had a lot to do with it. I remember, as a young fireman, I used to work nights, afternoons, all hours. I'd be coming through the roundhouse at midnight, and the machine shop and blacksmith shop, they were working full blast. They had full crews, twenty-four hours a day. Three shifts. After the diesels, I walked through the blacksmith shop and it was dead, just dead. I could stand there and reminisce, just by myself. I would remember Patty So-and-so, a little guy, he was a blacksmith boss, he was Irish. I could almost see the boys standing there, doing their work. One day I says to another Erie guy, "Let's take a walk over to the Erie Terminal to see what's happened." We went over there and the whole station was leveled. We came up to the roundhouse: nothing, by God, nothing. The roundhouse was there, but the pigeons were flying through. They were making their nests up there, you could see this old heavy chain . . .

It doesn't look very special today, but Garnell Brown (left) and Ozzie Thorne remember when the red carpet was rolled out and this platform in Grand Central Terminal was the center of all activity. The *Twentieth Century Limited* left from Track 34.

OSWALD S. THORNE
Bronx, New York

The numbers tell the story. In 1940 there were five hundred redcaps working in Grand Central Terminal. Today there are four. When Ozzie Thorne went to work in 1936, during the Depression, there weren't too many job opportunities, especially for a black man. As Ozzie puts it, "If you were black, you could sweep the floors or be a redcap in Grand Central." His father, a redcap since 1916, took him down to the terminal, and Ozzie ended up staying for forty-two years. He saw the long-haul trains like the Commodore Vanderbilt *and the* Twentieth Century *disappear and the redcaps with them. When he retired, there was a handful of men left at Grand Central, and Ozzie was glad to go. "Once we were busy. At the end we'd sit and wait for a train. Wait for someone to call a redcap. You could end up sitting all day."*

We used to call him the "Hard Rock" because he drove a hard bargain. Jim Williams came to work at Grand Central in 1900 and worked until he died in 1948. They called him Chief Williams and he had the power to hire and fire you. He was a big man at that time because there was over five hundred redcaps under that man. In fact, he was the one who started the redcap idea in the first place. They used to be known as porters and wore dark uniforms and dark hats. One day it was so busy and people were having so much trouble finding the porters that Jim Williams took a piece of red cloth and put it on his hat; that was the beginning of that. He was a light-skinned man, average height, and his uniform was always a little bit different than yours. It was tailored and more like a powder blue. His cap was special, too. And of course he always wore a fresh carnation or rose in his lapel every day.

Chief Williams, he wanted you to look immaculate. You had to have good shoes. Keep up the heels and soles. When we first hired out they would let you wear a pair of dark pants and you'd borrow a coat and cap. Work for two or three weeks until you could get the money for your uniform. When I started, a uniform cost $20.40. We had to go to Brooks Brothers because they had a contract with the railroad. I think it was 1946 or 1947, before they started giving us an allowance for our uniforms. We had an inspection once a month. Chief Williams would come around and see if you had any holes in your pants. If your shoes weren't shined, he'd send you home. You really looked good in your uniform. We even had our own barber. He was a redcap who also did barbering work on the side. Had a barber chair right there in our locker room. You didn't see no long hair, whiskers, none of that. Our locker room was on the lower level. It was big because we had five hundred men using it. It's still there but it's all cut up. A lot of different departments use it now. Then we had our own showers, bathrooms, and even a man who just kept that locker room clean.

You had to punch a clock when you came on duty and you had to be in full uniform. Jim Williams had a captain that worked in the stationmaster's office, and if you were five minutes late, this man had orders to send you home. Take your name, your card, send you home. You had to report to Jim Williams in the morning and tell him why you were five minutes late. On the other hand, he had his favorites, too. They could be an hour late and nobody would say a thing. Jim Williams had a staff of stool pigeons, too. Those pigeons would tell him everything. Even what you did on your own time in Harlem.

"Ozzie" Thorne and "Boo" Brown in front of the information booth in Grand Central. This photograph was taken for an article that appeared in the New York *Daily News* in 1975.

I never was one of his favorites, I'll tell you. So I made sure I got there on time. From the time my father brought me down to Grand Central, Jim resented me. I could take orders, don't get me wrong, but you had to give me orders that made sense and not just take advantage of me. He and I didn't hit it off from the time I was hired until he died. When the redcaps got the union, about 1935, things started to change. Without question, it was a fine thing when you could take the power away from a man who could hire you and fire you at will. Everything started to work on seniority. The Pullman porters started their union first and then we started ours at Grand Central. Then they got the men at Pennsylvania Station and later on they combined with the skycaps at the airports. It made the job a whole lot better. Conditions got better.

I started with the railroad on May 4, 1936. Grew up in New York City. My father was a redcap supervisor. He started at Grand Central Terminal in 1916 and worked until he was seventy-three years old. He didn't really retire, just got sick and never went back. At that time you could work until you were seventy-five years old. We had them drop dead on the job. One guy, he took sick and they took a leg off. Came back and wanted to work with a wooden leg. Oh, we had some men out there. Almost everybody had a nickname. Garnell Brown, he was "Honey Brown," and we had "West Point Johnson," "Rabbit Cummings," "Dry Bread," "Mickey Mouse," "Mush Mouth Mason," and I was always just plain "Ozzie."

When I went to work at Grand Central, work was not plentiful. I had been working as an elevator operator before that. The elevator operators had gone on strike, but my building wasn't union. These two union guys came in and said I'd have to close down. I'd seen what they had done to a fellow across the street that didn't shut down. Beat him up. I told my boss I was closing down and he told me that if I did that, I was fired. I told him I'd rather be fired than get my brains beat in. So my father took me down to Grand Central and I found out that you could make a livelihood at redcapping and I stuck with it. You could always make that fresh money. We used to call $5 a "hand." Some days you could make two hands. That was a lot of money in those days. Lots of men raised families, bought homes on a redcap's wages. If you were a married man you had to discipline yourself. If you made $7 or $8 in a day, you'd hold out $2 and take the rest home.

When I first started, we worked thirteen days and then got one off, but after the union came and got some power, they saw to it that we worked five days a week. The money got better too. The railroad didn't pay redcaps anything before the union. We just worked for tips. Management would have hired a thousand redcaps. Nothing out of their pockets. We carried four or five bags at a time for whatever the passenger wanted to give. You could work all day long and never make a dollar. We didn't get a salary until 1940. The Wagner wage and hour act came in and we got

The redcap locker room at Grand Central. One can just imagine the stories that were swapped here between the redcaps about their experiences with the traveling public.

thirty cents an hour. When I retired I think a redcap was making $175 a week, which isn't bad.

Around Christmas time they would run three or four sections of every train. You couldn't walk through the terminal because of the people. You had to carry the bags because you couldn't get a truck through the crowds. That's what killed a lot of the old redcaps. Two golf bags, two big suitcases in each arm. You had to—excuse the term— "jack-ass" them. You wouldn't believe the business in

those days. The *Century*, that was *the* train. Anybody who ever rode a train, that was the one they wanted to get on. Used to have all sorts of stars on that train. They had a list of everybody who was riding the train that day and they would relay it to the news photographers. Put that red carpet down when the train came in and when it left. The sweepers put that carpet down and we weren't supposed to walk on it. Had to walk on the side. I didn't. I was sort of hateful in my day. We had *some* people in those days—I wouldn't call them Uncle Toms exactly, but they would bow and scrape a bit. I was as good as the next man.

We had some great movie stars on the *Century*. Jimmy Durante for one. I always said he was one of the best tippers there ever was. Always had a $10 bill in his hand no matter how many bags he had. Joan Crawford, Marlene Dietrich, they always needed two or three redcaps because they had so many bags. They were both good tippers. Mae West, she always had six men trailing after her and they'd take care of the redcaps. Perry Como—but I could go on and on and the majority of them were very nice people. The cheapest of them all were Franchot Tone and Rudy Vallée. And old man Rockefeller. You could carry five or six bags for him and he'd look you right in the eye and give you a dime. If you asked him what that was for, you were out of a job. You got so you could prejudge a person—if they were going to be a good, a mediocre or just a plain bad tipper. Those who smoked pipes, they were usually more conservative and they never gave you too much. Somebody smoking a cigarette or carrying an attaché case that looked like it might have some whiskey in it, they were good tippers. You got so you could tell by the luggage. If they had expensive bags or a lot of tags, you knew they'd been around. They were traveling people, and they knew how to tip.

I had people I'd take care of specially when they came into Grand Central. They'd call ahead and ask for me. Some people only wanted a supervisor to wait on them. A man by the name of Crump was one of them. His father was a senator from Tennessee and every time he came in I'd put him and his wife on the *Century*. There was another one, Mr. Ross. He was a big race-horse man from Delaware. He'd always come into Pennsylvania Station, then go over to Grand Central in a couple of cabs. Have a cab just for the bags. He'd call ahead and I'd know when he would be there, and would take his bags and put them away for him until the train left that night. He'd be going up to Montreal to do a little hunting. Have his friends with him and they'd have a whole car reserved. A man like that wanted service and he got it. He paid for it, too.

There were others you wanted to stay away from. Prophet Jones, the preacher from Detroit, was one. He'd step off that train in his minks and diamonds. Medallions of gold around his neck with diamonds all around them. He would reserve the whole train for his disciples and what not. Maybe ten cars. They might have four or five hundred bags. We had to carry those bags up to Vanderbilt Avenue where he would have ten, maybe more limousines and buses for his people. He loved police officers. He had a fellow who traveled with him who had a suitcase full of money and those cops would line up and he'd give each of them $5. Some of them would go back and get in line again.

Four generations of Williamses. Jim Williams, chief of redcaps, is on the left. Next to him is his father, John. Jim's son, Wesley, also known as Chief Williams, is next to him. Wesley Williams was the first black fireman in the city of New York. Standing in front is James Williams II, Wesley's son. Taken in the 1920s.

When it came to paying off the redcaps he was very cheap. Give you only what the going rate was for each bag, fifteen cents in those days. I complained one time and he said he didn't get his money from black people. He ended up poor.

We had a tel-Autograph machine near Track 26. That's one of those machines where you write in one place and it writes the same thing someplace else. The people who were in the tower would write on this thing—say, for instance, that the *Commodore Vanderbilt* was coming in. They'd write: Train No. 67 on Track 28. That would let a captain know he had to get hold of the redcaps and line them up. They had whistles and they'd start blowing them to let us know we were needed. When you heard those whistles you'd move. The captain would cut off six or seven men at each opening. That was where the doors of the train would be. In about seven minutes the train would come in. Captain would be first in line and he'd say to you, "Take the next one." When the pretty bags came out, he'd make his move. Captain was assured that way to get somebody with money. If you ran out of passengers by the time it got to you, you came back empty-handed and had to wait for the next train.

On the evening shift you could load two or three trains at the same time (they weren't all going out at the same time). I was doing that one night and they had one train on Track 28 and another was on 27. One train was going to Chicago and the other was going to Detroit. On the curtain at the gate it said the *Wolverine* was going from Track 27 and I had the bags for a group of people loaded on that train. I'm inside looking out what was supposed to be their window when I see what I think is the train next to us leaving. I looked at my watch and asked the conductor what the hell was happening. The *Wolverine* didn't leave until six-fifteen and it's just a little after five. He said, "We're the train that's leaving and we're going to Chicago." They'd made a mistake at the gate and changed tracks without telling us. They used to pull off so easy with those trains, you wouldn't know you were moving until it was too late. Now, here I had these people's bags on the wrong train and I had to ride to Harmon, where they changed the electric engines for the steam, get off there and wait with the bags for the real *Wolverine*. Couldn't leave those bags. Well, the *Wolverine* finally comes and these people are giving me a hard time because they think it's my fault. It was my fault for not checking and that woman just looked at me and shook her head. She wasn't going to pay me and I didn't expect nothing, but I guess she was happy to get her bags back after all that.

I think that evening shift was the best shift to work. "Money shift." They'd put the younger men on days because they could run. During the summer they called days the "schoolboy tour." That was when all the schoolboys would come and work to get money for college. We produced a lot of prominent people from the redcaps: Adam Clayton Powell; Judge Livingston Wingate; Sam Battles, who got to be corrections commissioner. They all worked in Grand Central at one time.

It started to go down the drain in the late fifties when you saw those great liners disappearing one after another. They had some of the prettiest Pullman cars you'd ever want to see on those trains. The Cascade cars, the Imperial cars. They had drawing rooms, compartments, double bedrooms, real class. They never did run any cheap day coaches on the *Century* until the end. When you saw them putting coaches on those fine all-Pullman trains you knew it was going downhill. The *Yankee Clipper,* to Boston, the same thing. When it began to carry coaches it was finished. We had as many as fifty big trains a day at one time and I don't have to tell you what's out there now.

Towards the end it wasn't fun anymore. Sitting around waiting for people wasn't for me. I mentioned the skycaps before, that they belonged to our union. Some of the men went out to the airport to work. Started going out there in 1939, 1940, when they opened up La Guardia Airport. The money was better out there. People traveling by airplane had more money, I guess. You didn't have to work as hard, either. Just take the bags from the curb to the counter in the airport. I thought about going out there once when I was furloughed for about a month in 1963. But then I changed my mind. I'd been at Grand Central Terminal for twenty-seven years and I was definitely a railroad man.

G.C.T. 314

When he retired, Clinton Graham didn't find a porch with a rocking chair. Head of the water service and assistant chief of the fire department in his community, he is also an accomplished cabinetmaker. And he plays the piccolo, too.

CLINTON M. GRAHAM
Sandia Park, New Mexico

Like everything in the West, railroading was big. The largest engines that ever ran in the world, the longest tunnels and the highest mountains to cross. These same mountains created some of the most beautiful scenery that could be seen from a train window. Most men who ran these engines sometimes found a celebrity or two in the cab with them to share "the best seat in the house." Clinton Graham was no exception. He was joined by Jimmy Durante, Fibber McGee and Molly, Jack Benny and Edgar Bergen, to name a few, when he ran the Super Chief *through Glorieta Pass and the 13,000-foot Sangre de Cristo Mountains near Santa Fe. Pop Graham lives with his wife, Rubye, in a house he built himself in Sandia Park, New Mexico. Glorieta and the Sangre de Cristos are still there, but the* Super Chief *has declined to Amtrak's plebeian* Southwest Limited, *on which no celebrity rides.*

I had always been interested in mechanical matters. My mother said I was of a mechanical turn of mind. Our neighbors, not so charitable, said that I had wheels in my head. We lived on a farm in Virginia, eighteen miles from Washington, D.C. We had a few cows, a general store and the post office. My brother-in-law wrote that the Rio Grande Railroad was hiring apprentice machinists and said he'd get me on. I had to argue with my mother, since she wanted me to be a doctor, professor, some profession like that. Finally she saw it wasn't any use and I sold a calf I was raising and bought a ticket to Salida, Colorado. I got to Salida in August of 1917 and got indentured as a machinist's apprentice on the Denver Rio Grande.

You want to know wages they paid in those days? Ten cents an hour for the first year. Fifteen cents the second year, twenty the third, and twenty-five the fourth and final year. They took one half cent per hour out of your pay and when you were finished, they gave that to you in a lump sum. Then you had to go out and work for another railroad for at least six months before you could get a job at your home shop.

When I'd been there about seven months, the machinists called a strike. According to the Articles of Apprenticeship, we weren't called out, but we quit anyway. The master mechanic in Salida was E. G. Hastings. We called him "Beak" because of his huge schnozzola, but never to his face. Beak was of the old school and believed that the master mechanic was the lord of all he surveyed, and was ready to prove it. He was widely respected for his ability as a supervisor and a pugilist. I played the flute and piccolo in the local band and was the only person in town that could play those instruments. Beak was a great lover of music, and when I said I was going to go someplace else to work, he asked me, if he got me another job, would I stay and play in the band? I liked it there, and so I said yes. I went on as a painter's helper and extra call boy. (A call boy tells crew members when to report for duty.) At that time all of the standard-gauge trains were double-headed and most narrow-gauge trains were three-engine trains, so calling was quite a job. It paid $50 a month for a twelve-hour shift. We had to go in the whorehouses and saloons to get the men and I really got a view of the rough side of life.

Callers weren't supposed to go into such places to get men, but we always did. It was sure to bring us a tip, and besides, if we hadn't done it, the men would have gotten us fired. Of the six callers I worked with, only two of us didn't use cocaine or drink. Joe and I often worked two or three jobs to protect the other callers who had passed out.

There was other outside money, too. This one engineer, Windy, had a pretty sporty wife and she had a sweetie. Whenever Windy was coming in, I'd call her up and she'd have a hot meal ready and get rid of her friend. Windy had a sweetie, too, and two or three times a month he'd go to the roundhouse and lay off for a trip without telling his wife. Then he'd arrange with us callers to give him a fake call about eight in the evening and he'd spend the night with his sweetie. That was a double shuffle. I'd be walking down the street on payday and meet Windy and his wife and she'd say, "There's that nice call boy. He always lets me know when you're coming in so I can have a nice hot meal. Give him a dollar." He'd give me a dollar, but he'd already given me another dollar for making that fake call. I was making about $100 a month from everything that was going on in that town.

Salida was a wide-open town. There were thirteen saloons and about twenty houses of prostitution. One February night there was a bad storm. It was 25 degrees below and snowing and blowing. I had pulled the top button off my storm coat and hated the thought of facing that storm with my coat open. The only place I thought I could find a woman with a needle and thread at two in the morning was in one of the bawdy houses. I went to the first one I came to and knocked. I knew the girl, Elsie, and she asked me who I was looking for. I told her what I wanted and she invited me in, looked up a needle and thread and went to work on the button. As she was sewing I noticed tears were running down her cheeks. I supposed she had pricked her finger, but she dropped the coat and came and put her arms around me. She said that if she had remained true to her husband she might have had a boy of her own to be sewing for. I asked her why she didn't leave that life and get into something decent. She said, "Maybe I will." I took my coat and went about my business and thought no more about it. The next night her place was dark and no one knew what became of her. She was never seen around Salida again.

Those were the days of the boomer—the drifter who moved from railroad to railroad to "see the world." Boomers had to be good, especially the firemen. If a fellow drew more than two pay checks in the same place, he was a "Home Guard." When you were calling, you had to learn a new set of faces and names about every payday. There was one boomer, Tanner, he had service letters from sixteen different roads. When Beak asked him why he left his last job, Tanner told him, "Me and the engineer had an argument. He got a fourteen-inch monkey wrench and I got a four-foot start. We run a race and I beat him." There was a park across the river from the roundhouse and in good

That's not Clinton Graham running this "dinky" engine. He's riding the running board. They were building the Storrie Dam near Las Vegas, New Mexico, in 1916 and he's sightseeing.

"Side Car" Graham at Camp Funston, Kansas. After landing in a ditch several times, he decided that it would be safer to fight the war from a locomotive cab.

weather the boomers would gather there and swap yarns. If we ran out of firemen, I'd go over and ask if any of them wanted a job. They'd pull out some change or a meal ticket and say, "No, Jack. I can eat for a couple of days yet. I'll come over and let you know when I want to go to work."

September 22, 1909: President Taft was going to Gunnison, Colorado, to open an irrigation tunnel. They were going to run three specials. The first was the pilot train. It was going ahead of the main train to see that everything was all right. It carried Secret Service men and company officials. Then the main train with the President, and that was followed by a relief train—doctor, nurse, machinist, in case anything happened to the main train. Well, there was a masked ball up at the skating rink that night. The engineers and firemen for the pilot and special were the oldest men on the seniority roster and they answered the call, but the relief crew was to come from the regular freight roster. I found the engineer, but when I went up to the skating rink, everybody was masked and dressed up as Napoleon or the Devil or such. You couldn't tell one from the other. Of course, nobody would admit who he was because they didn't want to leave the party. I went back to the roundhouse foreman and told him I couldn't find anybody. I told him I thought I could fire that engine. He didn't want to send me out, but there was nobody else to go, so finally he told me to get ready to go.

I borrowed some overalls from a boilermaker's helper and everybody turned out to get the engine ready. We left Salida only five minutes late. I'd often ridden engines and I'd taken my turn with a scoop, so I wasn't exactly a beginner. I managed to "keep her hot" all the way up the Tennessee Pass and we arrived on time at Minturn. To be safe I wired the master mechanic for a pass to return to Salida. He wired for me to get back the way I got over, so I fired the same outfit back. That's the way I called myself for my first firing job.

I'd made four or five trips when the superintendent called me into his office. He asked me how old I was and I thought I could bluff it out. I told him I was a little over twenty-one. He laughed and said, "Don't you remember when you hired out here? You had to get your mother to sign your release because you were under twenty-one." Of course he had me, but he was pretty nice about it. He told me I could go back to my job calling and when I was twenty-one he'd see about a job firing. But I had firing in my blood by then, and after another week calling, I quit the Rio Grande and headed west.

I got a pass as far as Salt Lake City, hoping to land a job on the Western Pacific. They didn't have anything, so I drifted up to Huntington, Oregon, to work for the old Oregon, Washington Railroad & Navigation Company. After about six months of that I went to Pasco, Washington, because I heard that the Northern Pacific was hiring firemen. Come 1915 there was a kind of depression, and nobody could find a job. I was laid off and got a pass to St. Paul.

That was the end of the NP, and was as far as I could go. When I got down there I went to an employment agency one afternoon. About four-thirty it looked like nothing was doing and everybody started to leave. I had a hunch to go back, and sure enough, the man in charge was putting up a job on the bulletin board. A farmer needed a hand to

milk thirty cows. I knew farmwork, paid the employment agency man $3.50 out of my last $5, walked two miles out to the farm and started milking at four the next morning. Did it again at four in the evening and did chores in between. After I'd been there six weeks, a fellow came along and said he'd work for just his board the rest of the winter. I told the farmer I was entitled to a little money so he gave me $15 and I went back into St. Paul.

I got a job there in a restaurant washing dishes for my dinner and supper, no pay. There was a fellow who put up some beaverboard partitions in an old store and you could rent a room for twenty-five cents a night. Slop jar in there, no indoor plumbing. I tied up there and I'd smuggle out enough food for breakfast. Sometimes I'd steal a quart of milk off the milk wagon if I had a chance.

Then I decided I wanted to get up to my mother's for Christmas. She'd moved to Portland, Oregon. I still had my return pass the Northern Pacific had given me and I started for home. I got off at Jamestown, North Dakota, to eat breakfast and left my coat hanging in the coach. When I came back, my wallet was gone with my last $2.50 and my pass. Now, the Brotherhood had an agreement that a "fireman seeking employment" could get a pass to the next division point, so I got back to Pasco. There I got a Spokane, Portland & Seattle train and made it as far as Fall River before I got put off as a hobo. They were rough on hobos. Stayed all night with a couple of hobos in a shack and figured out how I was going to get on a train. The engineer and fireman were looking back and the hind-end

This is what happens when you don't have enough water in the boiler. The remains of engine No. 1604 that Clinton would have been firing if he hadn't gotten a flat tire.

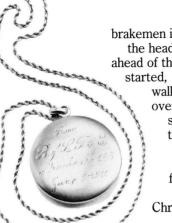

brakemen in the rear were watching the head end, so I got a little way ahead of the train and after they got started, I got up on the pilot and walked over the boiler, back over the cab and tender and stayed there until we got to Vancouver, which was the end of the line. That was just over the river from Portland and that's how I got home for Christmas. I got a job riding a motorcycle delivering telegrams. Eventually I got called back to Pasco and worked there for a while until May of 1916, when I took a notion to visit my sister in Trinidad, Colorado. She had a couple of kids and I sported around spending my money like a drunken sailor, and the first thing you know, I was broke. Well, a good fireman could get a job and place in those days and I went down to the Santa Fe roundhouse and hired out as a fireman on the New Mexico Division. That was June 1916. New Mexico was said to be the hardest division the Santa Fe had; it was nothing for a fireman to put fifty tons of coal into one of those 1600s.

One afternoon I had checked in, but they said it didn't look like I was going out before midnight. So I took my girl friend out for a ride on my motorcycle. On the way back from the ride I hit a washout and doubled up my front wheel. In those days every motorcycle rider was his own mechanic and carried a bunch of tools. I managed to get the wheel straightened and got back to town. I found out that the dispatcher had sent out a coal train, and since I wasn't there, they had called an extra man. I was called to take the next train out. Up at a place called Blanchard we went into a siding to let a regular passenger train pass. We waited an hour, but no train. Then a signal maintainer came up on a motorcar and said Train 1604 had a blow-up. That was the coal train on which I should have been. We were to proceed there and pick up a survivor. We cut the engine off and went to the rear of the train where we took the caboose and headed for the wreck site.

Now, when the boiler exploded it killed the fireman and head brakeman and blew the engineer, Lou Welch, clear over the right-of-way fence into a field. He was stripped naked except for a pair of sixteen-inch boots. He was badly scalded except for his right side, which was out the cab window, but he was still alive. When they tried to pick him up, chunks of flesh dropped off, so they went back to the caboose and got a blanket. A sack of flour was spilled into it and they carried him to the caboose in that. The other men who had been on that train let the caboose roll down a long hill for twelve miles with only the hand brakes to control it. That was pretty daring in itself because of the steep grade, but they made it. The operator on duty at the next telegraph station was Mrs. True Barnes. She got some of her bed linen and olive oil and doctored him up as best she could and rode the caboose with him to Las Vegas. The Santa Fe had a hospital there and he lived for three days.

The Brotherhood sent out a team to observe the investigation and I was on that team. The crown sheet of the fatal locomotive was burned as blue as a gun barrel and had torn loose from the crown bolts and side sheets. The gauge cocks which show the water level in the boiler were plugged with scale and this had led the crew to believe the water was higher in the boiler than it really was. Welch was known to be a careful, efficient engineer and we knew it must have been something like low water. The Brotherhood gave Mrs. Barnes a gold locket as a token of our appreciation for her services. The lodge has disbanded and my wife now has the locket.

About that time, World War I started and I, along with about half the firemen and brakemen, went to war. I found myself at Camp Funston in Kansas as a motorcycle instructor for a bunch of Kansas and Missouri farmers. I was to teach them to ride a motorcycle with a machine gun in the side car. These fellows were used to riding solo, and instead of turning the handlebars when we got to a curve, they'd lean and we'd end up in a ditch. After nearly getting my neck broken several times a day, I requested a transfer to a railroad outfit. They said I could not be transferred because I was a noncommissioned officer. I soon took care of that. I took a motorcycle and went AWOL to Kansas City for a few days. When I got back they busted me and I went to France with the 30th Company of the Railroad Transportation Corps.

We had French locomotives when I first got there, but we started getting American-made engines later on. The French didn't have automatic couplers, and the brakeman would have to go between the cars and pick up a chain and drop it over a hook. They had buffers on each car, and after you had them coupled you'd have to wind a turnbuckle to take up the slack. Pretty slow deal. Locomotives were different than ours. Throttles that were vertical, all kinds of things like that. Instead of a reverse lever, they had a screw—a wheel about twelve inches in diameter that you turned to reverse the engine. You'd have to guess for your cut-off. They used pressed coal brick for fuel and the Frenchmen didn't use a shovel. They'd pick up three or four of those bricks and throw them in the firebox.

We were in what they called a General Intermediate Depot. They had ninety days of supplies for everything in there in case the submarines got active and cut off the ships with materials. The depot covered at least a hundred acres and looked like a young city. The French were pretty accommodating with their waybills. They'd paste them right on the boxcar door. Tell you what was in the car. Any of us fellows wanted something to eat, all we had to do was break into a car. They must have known what was going on, but nobody said anything about it. Grub was pretty scarce there for a while. They'd give you a canteen of coffee and a rice and bacon sandwich to last you until you got to the next division point. Sometimes you'd be twenty-four hours on the road. Maybe a bomb would bust up the track and you'd have to wait for repairs. We didn't see too many airplanes because we weren't near the front, but the Germans would fire shells back where we were to tear up the railroad. Have you ever seen those little engines that ran in the trenches? Used them for ammunition. Covered everything with a tarp, cab and all, at night. When the fireman opened the firedoor, you wouldn't see the glow, but you'd just sweat to death in there. I had friends in them.

After I was overseas for nineteen months I was mustered out at El Paso, Texas, married the girl I am still living with after sixty-two years, and was restored to service as a fireman. You retained your seniority while you were away to war. I was promoted to engineer in 1920 and worked in New Mexico from Las Vegas to Albuquerque until 1947. Then I took a job with the civil service as special agent for the Interstate Commerce Commission until the old rocking chair got me, in January 1959.

I enjoyed my railroading and I think we "tallow pots" were a hardy lot in those days of the hand-fired coal-burning engines. After a twelve- to sixteen-hour trip, putting thirty tons of coal into one of those 1600s, we'd still walk that mile and a half to the Harvey House, eat our fill and then walk half the distance back to the roundhouse to Old Joe Shoup's Rooming House where, for twenty-five cents, one could rent a box stall, complete with single bed, chair, washstand with a bowl and pitcher, and a slop jar. We'd go to sleep, and when we were called again, walk back to the Harvey House, eat all we could and then walk to the roundhouse for another round with a Number 3 scoop, clinker hook and about thirty tons of Morely coal. Some of us called it rocks painted black. One of the questions asked firemen up for promotion was, "What is coal?" One man answered, "Don't know. Never saw any on this road."

These worthies are all Americans who were in engine service before coming to France during WW I. Clinton took their picture at Gievres in front of one of the famous "Pershing" engines built in this country and sent to Europe for the war effort. They were, of course, named after General "Black Jack" Pershing.

61

Take out the push-button phones and the Richford, Vermont, station doesn't look much different than it did when Cecil Jones was the station agent. However, one thing is missing. The *Red Wing* and the *Alouette* stop here no more.

CECIL O. JONES
Richford, Vermont

The job of dispatching on the railroad is like a giant game of chess. Instead of knights and bishops you have locomotives and boxcars. The board is a hundred and fifty miles of complicated track, switches, sidings, and branches. With today's centralized traffic control and radio communication, the dispatcher is in constant contact with the trains. When Cecil Jones was dispatching at Farham, Quebec, in the 1940s, he depended on train orders sent to the operators out on the line. The dispatcher had to know the terrain, the tonnage of the trains, the motive power and what crews could do with it. He was constantly arranging meets with opposing trains on single tracks according to train classification. A breakdown or storm could change everything and the dispatcher would have to start from scratch to get his railroad moving. It was not a job for the easily flustered.

I had in mind as a kid that I wanted to be a doctor. When I was fifteen or sixteen years old, I found that I should have taken Latin. My people couldn't afford to let me take another year to pick up Latin, so that was that. The procedure in those days when you lived on a farm was for the kids to do quite a lot of the farm work. I had my share. So, not being able to continue my schooling, I applied at one of the local banks in Waterloo, Quebec, for work. I also applied on the railroad, the Canadian Pacific. The railroad called me first in March of 1916. Don't know what would have happened if the bank had called me first.

I wasn't quite seventeen years old and they wanted me to come to work right away. So I went and put in twelve to thirteen hours a day, and the first few months my salary was $25 a month. It took me about one and a half hours to get to where the station was. I was expected to arrive there and get the place cleaned up by seven o'clock. I had to sweep out the old-fashioned waiting rooms, take care of the fires in the stoves and get things lined up for the crews that were coming in. Then I'd help load baggage and mail and milk on the passenger train. When that was taken care of, my responsibility would be freight handling. By the time my hours were up, and I finally got home at night, I was really dog tired.

Watching these crews while I was working there, I decided that if I wanted to get ahead I'd better learn Morse code so I could become an operator. I got one of these practice sets; you connected it to a battery and could practice as long as you wanted. It wasn't much fun doing that by yourself, so I got in touch with a girl who was also learning code down near Drummondville, Quebec. We used to practice in the evening after I got through my day's work and before I went home. I don't know if she wanted to learn telegraphy because her daddy was station agent or because she just wanted to fight boredom. Maybe it was the challenge of playing a game with a couple of boys her own age. My friend in the next town and I took turns practicing with Alice. He later was appointed station agent in his town, and since our road did not hire lady operators, Alice accepted a position as railroad clerk at Drummondville. After the war she became an agent, and then I lost track.

After I'd practiced for a while, I decided that I really did want to get on as an operator. I got a rule book telling what I should do and what I needed to learn to make myself capable of passing the test. The T. Eaton Company sold these little railroad rule books in those days, and I got one and studied it. So there I was, studying Morse code, practicing with that little girl, studying the book, and then when

When the railroads moved just about everything, freight and people, the station agent of a small town was a very important part of the community. East Ryegate, Vermont, 1932.

ROBERT JONES COLLECTION

I got home, practicing again and taking my share of the chores at the same time. I was still living at home because at $25 a month, you couldn't live anywhere else. Anyhow, that went on for about three and a half years. Then, in 1919, they decided they needed some new operators. I had a friend who was assistant superintendent and he put in a word to the chief train dispatcher. Said he thought I'd make a good candidate. I was called in to take the test and I passed it on my first try.

That fall they called me to work in the small station at Mount Orford, Quebec. Delaire, they called it back in those days. The trains used to break and rebuild there. One train would bring up a load and drop it there and return. Then the next train would come along and fill up to tonnage for the trip east. Anyway, I worked there that winter. There were three of us operators. I worked four to midnight. Another fellow worked midnight to eight in the morning, and still another the day job. When the St. Lawrence River was opened in the spring, and when the ice was gone, they discontinued that little station until the next winter. They'd start using the boats instead of the train.

Then I was called to do relief work. Relieve different agents and operators. My first job that summer was at Knowlton, Quebec. To relieve the agent for three weeks. Now, I was green to many of the procedures—accounting, paperwork, general work. I wasn't too proficient yet as a telegraph operator either, but I got by. At those little stations then, you took telegraph messages and train orders on the wire. As I said, I got by and apparently I was noticed by the chief dispatcher because he gave me the job at Sherbrooke to relieve the operators there for their vacations. That was a busy job, more than they should have expected any man to do, but I made out all right. Then I was sent home for a while, until they opened another winter job up near Megantic, near the Maine border. They had had some accidents up there, so they put us up on top of the hill just before the trains went into Megantic. We worked there that winter, three operators, and when the winter season was past and things were more normal on the railroad, they sent us home again.

I was sent back to Sherbrooke, I guess because I had handled that job all right. That was a hell of a job because back in those days there were no highways from Montreal to Sherbrooke. Those commuter trains then were just filled with passengers. On Fridays and Saturdays, the mills usually let their help out for the weekend. These trains would be loaded and the passengers would be stretched out for half a mile waiting for tickets. In addition to our work as operators, we had to sell tickets. I'd be passing out those tickets as fast as I could. Between the age of five and twelve it was half fare and if someone came to the wicket and you couldn't see them, you knew it was half. If by chance someone came up and I couldn't quite see them, I'd say, "How old are you?" Then one day this particular voice said, *"Vingt-sept ans"*—twenty-seven. She was a midget lady and she just stared at the child's ticket I'd given her. She and her friends giggled all the way from the ticket wicket to the train.

That winter I was sent to Gould Station. We had water tanks in those days for the steam locomotives to take water, and the operators at some of those stations were required to run little steam engines to pump water to fill the tanks. If you got that little engine on dead center, you had to take a crowbar to pry it off center or it wouldn't turn over. That was an all-right job and we had a good boarding house. From there I worked at Sherbrooke, again, until 1926, when there was a job vacant at North Troy, Vermont. An operator's job up for bid. I worked there as an operator for four years, from four to midnight.

In the meantime I had gotten married and we set up housekeeping at East Ryegate where I was sent next as station agent. After I got the station cleaned up and the job under my belt, I was a little bored with the work. There wasn't enough to keep me occupied, mind or body. So I got it in my mind that I would like to become a train dispatcher. Now, that is quite a job. I studied it and watched and listened on our wire to the dispatchers work. I then asked to be given a chance to see if I could qualify. The preliminary work was to go up and sit in with some of the regular dispatchers and watch them work. I used to drive up from East Ryegate to Farnham, a hundred and twenty-five miles, on weekends. Work with this fellow all day and then drive back. I'd take care of my agent's work during the week, go back the next weekend, study a little bit more and get in a little more practice.

Eventually they decided that I was ready and I qualified to take on a regular dispatching job. That was in 1942, pretty much at the height of the war. The Germans had made the way into the Gulf of St. Lawrence very dangerous, and Canada was sending her grain and freight by rail to St. John, New Brunswick. Freight was also coming from the Middle West of the United States and it was altogether a pretty busy piece of railroad. Single track from Montreal to the Maine border, that was our division. I worked from four to midnight that first winter, and that was one hell of a job. We had more trains than we had passing tracks to clear them. If you've got more trains than tracks, you've got to put them some place; double up. As an operator, I had previously walked most of the trackage, since I had worked relieving at some thirty-five different stations, so I could appreciate the ups and downs that trains were up against. I could arrange my meets because I knew the terrain. The dispatcher who came on at midnight to relieve me said, "How come you put out these meet orders on trains and I don't have to change them?" Somebody else piped up, "Well, he's walked that track so much he knows where they are."

You didn't want to stop a train on a grade. Maybe they couldn't get going again without stalling. Of course, the direction counted, too. The superior trains had to be considered in meets with inferior trains. Classifications, they counted too. Some trains were superior on the timetable. We had the timetable in front of us. We handled these trains by train orders. We knew a regular train was due at a certain place, or we thought we did. Always check. It was done with train sheets. Trains going this way on one side, trains coming this way on the other. You worked to match the meets according to train classification. All paper, no diagrams. We never made these meets by memory. Always work from the timetable. Check the timetable, it's so easy to remember wrong. It's something that's stayed with me all my life.

Anyhow, it was interesting. You had a lot of responsibility. Troop trains were going east along with freight trains. Trains with the wounded were coming back. Banana trains, full up, a solid train. They expected fast service on traffic like that. We were on pins and needles. However, when I left my day's work I shook off train dispatching. I was able to forget it. It's the only way you can survive a job like that. Do it while you're doing it and then forget it when your day's work is done. One thing I did do, when I sat down to take over my job, I had just a silent little prayer. Now, that sounds funny to fellows who don't believe in things like that, but a little prayer to ask for help always seemed to do the trick.

A train dispatcher knew his crews. Knew who he could depend on. In making his meets, he knew that such and such a crew and such and such an engineer could be depended on to make time. We had one engineer, I knew him, a fine fellow. We'd pick up the Boston trains at Woodsville, New Hampshire, heading to Montreal. If the Boston train was given to us, say half an hour late, and we had an engineer we could depend on, we egged him on a little bit. You could do that. This fellow, he would follow my lead and he picked up so much time he was exceeding the speed limit. You always liked to get the trains into Montreal on time. I preferred the fellow that had a piece of machinery that he was proud of and knew how to run. He didn't like to be held back. Well, that engineer finally got a reprimand and I couldn't get anything out of him after that.

One experience I used to dread was when the chief dispatcher would come in as I sat down at four in the afternoon. We had a lot of storms. It seemed that those years I was up there were very stormy winters. One winter we ran snowplows, it seemed, every day, The chief dispatcher would come in as I'd take over my shift and decide to run a snowplow ahead of No. 40. Now, this was a passenger train due at Farnham about four-forty. That meant you had to catch all your trains along the line and arrange for the snowplow to wiggle its way ahead of that passenger train. We had areas where you couldn't get in touch with some of your trains straight off to get them into the clear. Eventually they'd get clear, but it would be some time and the chief dispatcher sitting there watching. I don't know

64

The Canadian Pacific depot at Richford, Vermont, 1944. Left to right: Al Purdy, U.S. Customs Officer; Cecil Jones, operator; "Dutch" Shattuck and Hayden James, freight clerks. The arrival-and-departure board on the station wall is just a memory today.

how I did it sometimes. Many times like that, you couldn't even get up to go to the toilet, couldn't even eat your lunch. You'd have breakfast in the morning, sit down, and there wouldn't be any getting up until your shift was over.

There were accidents to be sure. To be frank, there was always the possibility of human error. One accident on another division stays in my mind; there was a mistake, and two trains came together over at Foster, Quebec. There were no passengers killed but one poor devil of an engineer, quite dead, hung by his foot from the locomotive. Things like that happened and will always happen.

While I was working as a dispatcher one of our fast freights went off the rails. There had been a flash flood, and water came down a hill and undermined the track. Without warning this train plowed into it and a couple of fellows lost their lives. We had no way of foreseeing that sort of thing. As I look back, I believe the operator out on the line had a burden of responsibility under the train order system as great or greater than the train dispatcher's. True, the dispatcher, with his knowledge of terrain, tonnage, motive power and the like, arranged the meets with opposing trains, but he depended on the operator to see that his orders were carried out. When accidents happened and the dispatcher was at fault, the punishment was in the form of demerits. Sixty-five demerits automatically meant dismissal. Dispatchers found responsible in the case of serious accidents were released from employment for various periods and taken back only after due consideration. This type of punishment applied to all employees.

We were given a lot of leeway to use our own judgment when I was working. There were dispatchers who'd ask the chief dispatcher for something or other every time they turned around. I used to take quite a lot of that responsibility myself. There was one time that I get a kick out of, even today. I was working from four to midnight. It

was No. 40 again, and I knew the number of cars on that train, knew her weight, her tonnage. I knew the hauling capacity of that steam locomotive, and knew her crew. So, knowing all that, I let that train out of Sherbrooke with one locomotive. It was the fall of the year and maple leaves in that area were falling—and, sad to say, falling on the rails, as slippery as grease. Now, that locomotive couldn't pull that train. He'd stall out trying to get started. He was late, hours late. The train finally got in, but I should have put a helper on at Sherbrooke. Oh, I was criticized, but they couldn't say too much because the locomotive under normal conditions should have been able to handle the train. Took a while to learn all the conditions and things that could arise on the railroad. You kept learning from the day you hired out until the day you quit.

I would have had to move to Montreal to continue dispatching and it was almost impossible to find accommodations. My two boys were in high school, and I wanted them to go to college, and with the economy as it was in Canada, I wasn't doing too well financially. So I decided to come home and take over the work as an operator at Richford. I retired as railroad agent on April 30, 1964.

There, now, in a nutshell, that's the life of a dispatcher and no dull moments. They had a little testimonial and they complimented me on my record when I left. A clear record, and I'm proud of that. I was telling my wife the other day, I wasn't a person who made a lot of intimate friends. I think I had to stand on my own two feet my whole life. The powers that be always seemed to give me work that was just a little beyond what I could reasonably be expected to do. My first job relieving the agent, for example, I didn't know the book work because I hadn't been taught. I was expected to keep it up, just like that. You didn't have a chance to learn things, you had to get right in and do it and you were expected to do it right.

In his backyard museum, Lewis Freeman is surrounded by some of the rail-roadiana he's collected since his retirement from the T&P. The watch was his father's; W.J. Freeman was an engineer on the same railroad for fifty-six years.

ELMER L. FREEMAN
Shreveport, Louisiana

Not very many people have a museum in their backyard, especially one that would make some small cities envious. Lewis Freeman says that he didn't think that much about the equipment he worked with on the railroad until he retired. Then he became interested in collecting and bought everything he could lay his hands on. Lanterns, watches, switch-stand lamps, even a locomotive bell. Photographs of Texas & Pacific engines line the walls, many with Lewis and his father in the cab. He ended up with so much railroadiana that he had to put up a building to keep it in. Lewis loves to show people through and explain where the various pieces came from. His favorite items are the conductors' uniforms hanging on the wall, complete with caps, buttons and badges. These he prizes most because they were entrusted to him by the men he worked with.

Everybody loves the old railroads. I don't know whether you found that out or not, but they just love them. People are fascinated by railroads, especially back in the old times. I've got a friend here in Shreveport, "Kit" Robinson, that took these photos you see of me and my father. He started taking them when he was about fifteen years old. He don't have to work, he's a millionaire. He has stocks and all. His biggest job is waiting on the postman to make his deposit, see, but he thinks I'm something because I'm a damn old railroad engineer. He comes visiting me all the time, and gave me some of these pictures he took when he was a boy. When he was a little boy, his old great-aunt took him down to the depot to meet somebody that was coming in. Little bitty boy standing by the track and that big old engine come a-roaring and a-rumbling and a-shaking the ground. He said he never seen such a sight in his life and it just struck him and went into his heart. It just growed and growed. I think that was what it was like for a lot of people with the old steam engine. I been on a trip with him where we went to see some land or cattle or something. I'd say, "That's some of the most beautiful cattle I ever looked at across there." He'd say, "Yeah, it sure is, Lewis. Do you remember that old No. 702?" Bring the conversation right back to railroads every time.

I run this business selling railroad antiques. I started this little home museum I've got here. Took a booth at the flea market. People love to stop by and look at the lanterns, cannonball markers, all that sort of thing. Some old fellow's wife comes down the aisle and stops at my place and says, "Well, by God, this is the first place that's even worth looking at." She had been through about forty to fifty of them others, see. It never got fascinating to me, collecting this stuff, until I retired. That's something, isn't it? I worked all through that and never gave it a second thought. But after I retired and got to looking around, this or that old piece looked pretty good to me. I wasn't a railroad man anymore. At least not working anymore, so this keeps me feeling like I'm in touch. Friends gave me things. Still do. Switch keys to put up. Must be a hundred of them up there now in those cases. A lot of different people give me things. Some of the conductors that I worked with, they even gave me their caps. Now, isn't that something when you think of what those men feel about those caps?

There's my favorite conductor's hat, right up there over my granddaughter's picture there in the center. Joe Lasiter's. We worked together all our lives. First thing we'd do each day was belly up to one another and jerk out that

railroad watch. You look at yours and he looks at his and see if they're right together and all that. We worked together for forty-five years. One period of time we worked on a passenger train with each other steady for five years. Never had a cross word. Not one cross word.

Old brakeman we had was Frank Brown. There's his cap up there on the other side. All three of us was old heads. We'd have a different fireman once in a while. Fireman, he'd get old enough to go running the midnight switcher, or get bumped, or something. Firemen come and go, but us three always stayed. Get up at one o'clock in the morning and get on that passenger train. Anybody feels bad at that time of the morning. A body could get upset or cross at one another, but we never did. I don't care how fast I went, that feller Joe never did give me a signal to slow down. I'd look out the window and I'd see him back there . . . go, Lewis, go! Always thought he had confidence in me, which I had the same in him. If he said, "We better do so and so," I'd say, "Okay, Joe." He run his business back there and I run mine up in the front. We got along so good together. He's still living. I've got to call old Joe. He comes out once in a while and we talk over those days. I want to get old Joe's hat down and show it to you. There, always looked neat as a pin. He was wonderful.

I've got the names under their hats now. This one's gone . . . He's gone . . . This one's still living. That's old Frank Brown. Man, Frank must be ninety years old now. There's no such things on the railroads as them hats any more, or the men who went with them. Some of them railroad fans, they'd give you their right arm for these. That's what those railroad men thought of me to give me those things. These are the buttons Joe had. Right off his coat, his best, really dressed up. He was fine-looking in those days. I mean, he was neat. He looked like the passengers. He was just the image of what a conductor should look like.

Ed Robinson took this photograph of a very proud engineer in 1941. When someone asked Lewis about railroading as a career, he replied, "I wouldn't trade jobs with Roosevelt."

It was a different railroad then, let me tell you. I've got this lantern here, belonged to a switchman, yardmaster later on. He was working when I was a little boy and I used to go down in the yard and watch him work. I'd go down with a couple of cronies and we'd look at those old steam engines kicking them cars around. He would say, "Boy, did you know this lantern can talk? Now, you watch it talk, boy." Sure enough, he's giving that engineer a signal all the time, you know. *Boom, boom, boom,* here comes that boxcar. We thought we were seeing something else, I'll tell you. That man is ninety-seven years old and still living.

I was born in Greenville, Texas, July 17, 1913. My daddy was a railroad man, and we moved to Marshall when I was about five or six years old. Then we came to Shreve-

This doesn't really need a caption. It shows exactly what made the job of running a steam engine so exciting for these men. Almost fifty years

old, this lady is doing seventy-five miles an hour in the 1940s with Lewis in the cab.

Just about his whole family is there to wish W. J. Freeman the best on his last trip in 1963. The train was the *Louisiana Limited*, and the station, Shreveport.

port and he got me a job when I was sixteen. He had fifty-six years of railroading in him. I went to work in 1929 and retired in 1973. We had a hundred years of railroading between us. I actually fired for my daddy, and that was some experience. That was the roughest trip a man ever had, firing for his daddy. Boy, he was tough. He was some man, that dad of mine. He shoveled enough coal to cover up this town. I never did have to shovel coal, thank God. The Texas & Pacific was one of the first to use oil.

Back in those days it was kind of a father-to-son hand-down. Of course, we didn't all go into engine service. Some man would be a switchman and his son would be a clerk. There was two or three of us that went in with their daddies and I was one of them. There was Frank Moxley, Senior and Junior. And Joe Green; he was an old-time engineer and his son went into clerking. You know, I've actually run a train and met my father on another train out on the road. That's some experience. I know I had a great feeling about it and I'm sure he did too. His little boy, he called me. Called me "boy" until I was sixty-five years old . . . right up until he died. He was something else. He lived and breathed that railroad. I've got a front-page picture of him when he stepped off that last run. Of course we all have that. They gave him front page, ending his career and all that. I thought they were going to have to send down five men to drag him out of that cab when he turned seventy. Didn't want to quit, no sir. I just lost him last year and you really don't know what a man was until he's gone. You get to thinking about all this, you see.

I started as a caller in 1929. That's where most everybody started and you clerked and then you went on up. I've done a little bit of it all. I've switched, done everything on the railroad except being a conductor. Took me all the way to '41 to go firing engine. Twelve years before that of doing other things. You know, during the Depression they didn't hire any firemen. As soon as they hired one I got the

job and from then on I worked in engine service. Saw the Depression face to face and that was something. I was in a different department than my daddy, of course. He got cut off first in 1930 and I didn't get laid off until 1932. We worked on a farm and if I hadn't been strong and young, I couldn't have gone through that. I don't see how some of the old people ever survived it. My daddy would be out in that field and he'd say, "Hear that train blow, boy, hear that train blow." I knew what he was thinking about. His heart was breaking for that railroad. I hadn't been in it for as long as he had. It hadn't got as deep into me.

I went ten months without a dime in my pocket. It's hard to believe, isn't it? That's a fact, ten months, but it taught me something, a real good lesson. If you got started again, you'd be sure you had something to lean on. When I got back on that railroad I almost kissed every rail, I was so glad just to get back to work.

I fired about five years before I was promoted to running. I was an engineer since '46. I told you that the T&P had gone to oil. You had to watch an oil fire just like coal. Keep the water just right and the oil just right, and you had all kinds of gauges to look at and valves to turn. You had to keep the fire just right and every time the engineer would change his throttle, you had to change with him. You didn't go to school a week or two and learn that. You had to learn that by experience on the road. Oil didn't mean you just sat back and took a ride for your pay. I ran between Shreveport and Alexandria, south. Shreveport to Mineola, west, and then up through Marshall, Texas, to Texarkana. I went three different ways.

I was on the first diesel that ever came here. They put it in the roundhouse and got it all ready and everybody who was drawing $1 a day was there to see it. I was on duty and got to climb on it and back it onto the turntable and take it up to the yard. It was fascinating for a short while and then you didn't like them, or at least I didn't. Those old heads, oh man! It was like putting them on a bomb or something. They knew every inch of those steam engines and didn't know anything about the diesels. Later on, though, they got to be masters of those diesels, some of them. It kind of separated the men from the boys, steam engines did. These little college graduates, they would get up there on a diesel and take a couple weeks on them buttons and run one of them things. But when older men started on the steam engines, firing, and when we asked to be allowed to run them trains maybe just part of the way, those old-timers would look at us like we done lost our minds. I remember one old boy, I asked him if I could come over there and run and he just looked at me and said, "It took me forty years to get over here." That was that.

It was something to wrastle one of them big steam engines for sixteen hours and I done it thousands of times. The engines we had were fine—the 600s for freight, the 900s for passenger. They were so huge and powerful that as much as I've been around them, it still fascinates me to look at a locomotive today. But they scrapped everything on the lot except for three engines. I never dreamed that would happen, but before anybody could think, they were just cutting up those engines for the weight of the iron. Just for the weight of the iron, which wasn't much back in those times! Now, could you imagine what a 600 would be worth today? How about that 600 that the Southern Railroad still has, what's she worth?

Back in my days, when the caller would call you the first thing you wanted to know was "What crew?" and the second was "What engine do I get?" They'd say the 703 or something, and you'd say, "Boy, that's a good steamer and we're going to make some time tonight." Each one had its own personality, you might say, and you got to know them. The yard engine which built up the train—"the switcher" we called her—was No. 492. She was a powerful and wonderful engine. The men who worked with it called it "The Silkworm." Quick and powerful and smooth.

The 666 I always remember. Are you too young to know what three 6s are? It was a medicine they advertised way back then on every barn and fence that you took for fevers, chills, that kind of stuff. It was just the bitterest stuff that you ever swallowed in your life, but it drove the fevers and chills out real good. Three 6s on the side of that engine, so we called her "The Bitter Dose." All those 600s were good. All the 900s were good too, and 901—she was one of my favorites. They had such huge drivers. They'd ask you, "What are you going out on today?" And you'd say, "I'm going out on a high-wheeler." That meant a passenger train. I guess those wheels were as big as this room is high. When those drivers turned, you moved fast.

We handled some great passenger trains on the T&P, beautiful trains. We were up front, engine rumbling, popping and all that noise, heat, dirt, but those people in the back, they were living some fine life. They had the best, just the best. *Sunshine Special* and the *Texan* that went to Marshall. Came down out of St. Louis going west to El Paso. They were the two main ones out of here along with the *Louisiana Limited.* We left Marshall and took that train down to Alexandria, Louisiana. People really rode on those big trains. If you wanted to, you could just get up and stroll around the train. It seemed like a mile walking down one of those trains, seeing different people eating, some sleeping, some talking, some playing cards. Just really enjoying life and all that scenery outside swishing by you. I noticed every bit of it. I also noticed every bit of it when they started to cut off service. When this other railroad took over, the Missouri Pacific by name, that's when they started chopping things off. I guess the stockholders wanted to get the passenger trains out of the way and make room for the big-revenue freights. We had some fine people right here in this town of Shreveport, and I seen them with my own eyes being shoved and pushed trying to get on those trains. Cut the trains back, so they were always crowded. Cut the sleepers off, so that took care of the long-haul people. Then they cut the diners off. If people had to get somewhere, they had to take a lunch. If someone had to go a hundred miles, that took care of them. Then they gave the mail away, that took another car out. Next they cut the club cars off, until it was nothing but just plain seats and a baggage car, and they finally got it down to one of each. That wasn't even a train anymore. Oh, one of the first things they did which I forgot to mention was to close down the fine depot we had right in the middle of town and put up this dinky little depot, if you'd want to call it that, back of the airport here. It was about as big as my workshop here. They did everything in the

world to run the passengers off. I'm fully convinced that if they would have just halfway took care of the public, those trains would still be running and running full.

The railroads today are not at all like they were in the past. The Texas & Pacific was—and a lot of them thought like I did—one big happy family. If you did something wrong and got in a little trouble, you'd go tell the man and he'd say, "Look, just be more careful and don't do that anymore." But the Missouri Pacific, they just looked for things to fire a man for. I don't know why they were so

W. J. Freeman (left) in this family portrait from the late 1800s. Also in the picture are his mother, Annie, brother Elmer and sister Olga.

nasty unless they were trying to cut back on the manpower. They would hide in the grass at one in the morning trying to catch you doing some little thing to bring you on the carpet and have an investigation. Try to fire you. I know, because I've had it happen to me. All them Texas & Pacific officials, they would stay in their offices and tend the railroad, but those Missouri Pacific fellows would get out and sneak like rats out in the weeds beside the track, sometimes one hundred miles out in the country. I just don't understand that kind of thinking. How could a man have his heart in his job with that kind of thing going on? When I was working with the T&P I could hardly wait to get to work and try to do a marvelous job for them, the best I could. I put everything into it and gave them a good job. How can the new managers expect people to have that kind of feeling when they run things the way they do today?

Built in 1901, and now serving the town of Kingfield as a truck garage, this building was once a three-stall engine house. It's been almost fifty years since an engine spent the night in Kingfield.

HERSCHEL P. BOYNTON
Kingfield, Maine

Some of the people who appear in this book are institutions in their communities. Talk to just about anybody in Kingfield, Maine, and you will be told about Herschel Boynton and the railroad he worked for. This is rather extraordinary, since the Sandy River & Rangeley Lakes Railroad ceased operations in 1936 and totaled only 110 miles of narrow-gauge track. It was truly a railroad from another era and Herschel is the last man alive who worked on the Sandy River. After his railroad career was over, he labored for years at other types of jobs, but people think of him only as a railroad man. They want to hear him tell about the engines, the great snows of 1919–29, the old-fashioned coaches with their potbellied stoves. Soon we will only have the fading photographs to help us remember the golden age of railroading.

I was born May 28, 1888, in East New Portland, Maine, and started with the railroad in 1906. East New Portland is a town that joins Kingfield. I lived there until I was eleven years. Then my family moved to Kingfield in 1901, and it's been my town ever since. The Stanley twins, who invented the Stanley Steamer Automobile, they were born and brought up in this town. Their sister, Chansonetta Stanley Emmons, was a well-known photographer. Yes sir, she was a smart woman.

I had several jobs as a boy. Worked odd jobs around the mills, but railroading was the best there was around here as far as I was concerned. The people that worked in these mills did ten hours a day, six days a week indoors. I didn't want any of that. I liked the outdoors. The railroad was built into Phillips in 1879. They celebrated the 100th anniversary of a train coming into Phillips in 1979. Old Home week, that's what they call it. Too bad there's no train to ride into Phillips or anyplace else around here today. The railroad from Strong into Kingfield came here in 1884; from Phillips to Rangeley in '90 and '91—twenty-nine miles of railroad. The railroads were real busy in those days. There was a lot of lumbering going on in Redington. They had a branch line, the Eustis branch, that came from Greene's Farm. A lot of lumber was hauled out of that valley by rail. I didn't work over on that side much, mostly over here on the Kingfield branch.

I was seventeen years old when I went on the railroad. Made my first run as a fireman for Charlie French. I was promoted to running in 1915, and I had an engineer's job until the road quit in June of 1935. I fired a long time. Promotion was slow on such a small road and you had to wait for someone to retire. I put in almost thirty-five years. Yes sir, it was a busy road there for a while. They had a very good machine shop at Phillips and they made all of the railbuses there. Those boys could do just about anything in those shops. I run the first railbus they had. Built it from a Model T Ford in the 1920s. I didn't like them at all. You were more like a bus driver than an engineer. They had an engineer and conductor on when they started, but after a year they took the conductor off and left the engineer alone in the thing. He had to do everything, collect tickets, run it. I remember the first year we ran it, I came into Salem in a snowstorm. We didn't run them in the winter, but it was an early fall storm and the wind was blowing something fierce. We had about a dozen passengers, and I decided that we weren't going any place in that motorcar. I telephoned the station in Kingfield and had them send out some teams to get the passengers, and we left that ma-

Fireman Bernard Doyle (left), engineer Herschel Boynton (center) and brakeman Philip Porter take time out for lunch sometime around 1916 near Carrabassett, Maine.

chine right there in front of the station. That morning we went back and the wind had blown hard enough across Salem Flat to knock down seventeen lengths of telephone line. I pictured what would have happened and was very thankful that we didn't try to get home that night.

We had a lot of bad snowstorms here and it caused a lot of trouble; we had to fight snow all winter. I spent nearly a week steady on the job one winter because of it. We had a bad snowstorm on a Saturday and left Kingfield with a plow. It snowed, blowed, rained and froze. We got to Strong all right, but the train up from Farmington was snowed in, so we couldn't meet her. We spent the afternoon plowing the tracks at Strong so we could just turn around and head home. Then we were told to lay over for the night at Strong. We spent Sunday plowing the yards and then headed to Phillips to clear that other line. The snow was so deep we had to come back to Strong and stay another night.

Everything was snowbound by this time, and we spent the next two days trying to clear the tracks to Farmington. Then we tried to get to Kingfield. One of the brakemen who was riding on the top of the plow where he shouldn't have been was thrown off when we hit a drift near Harlow Cut. He separated his shoulder, and now we had both the snow and an injured man to contend with. He didn't get too much sympathy from the rest of us. When we finally arrived in Kingfield the flues on our engine were leaking in good shape. However, they sent us immediately to Bigelow. We'd back up about a quarter mile to get a run on a big drift, open her up, and when she struck that snow she was really sailing. By this time the snow had turned to rain and had really frozen up. We had that plow off the iron seventeen times going sixteen miles. The plow just kept riding up and fishtailing. She wasn't heavy enough to cut the frozen snow. Had to sit there with one hand on the throttle and the other on the brake. We didn't put the engine off; she hung on. Each time, we'd set the rerailers and haul the plow back on. We returned to Kingfield from Bigelow and they told us to take No. 18 to Phillips for repairs. We got back into Kingfield about midnight. We slept in a real bed for the first time in a while and went out the next morning to Bigelow on what would have been our regular run.

When that storm was over we had been on the job almost constantly for pretty close to a week. That was before the sixteen-hour law went into effect. Speaking about plowing, we had a trick we'd use on bad spots where the snow drifted bad. We'd nose the plow into the drifts and shovel a hole just above the rails for a bit. When we hit the drift going fast, this would help the plow get a bite so she wouldn't ride up off the rails. When we did have trains go

The Kingfield baseball team of 1910. Herschel Boynton is in the front row (far left). Flave Vose, in the back row (third from the left), was also an SR&RL man. Baseball was a popular game in small towns during that era, and the railroad had its own team for many years.

off because of the snow, we'd jack them back on or haul them on with block and tackle.

Like I said, snow could cause you all kinds of problems. I was firing for Charles Hodgman one winter and we hit a drift with No. 18 and she stopped cold. The drivers and valve gear got centered and nothing would move her one way or the other. We decided to call Phillips for help, but they said they couldn't get to us until the next day. We all discussed the predicament and finally took the screw jack off the engine and set it under the valve-gear coupling. A few turns moved the eccentric off center and in minutes we were on our way home. Never saw anything like that before or after. Another time I got caught a half-mile out of town in the snow with one of those bobtailed engines, and after a while we were running out of water. I had to shovel snow into the tank. Had to put some steam back in that snow and melt it so we'd have water. The conductor and I stayed with that engine all night. The engineers always used to have a saying, "Trust in the Lord, but keep two gauges of water for your own self."

We had some good engines, starting with quite small ones, but they kept getting bigger as time went by. We had the Forneys and the Moguls. Which I liked best depended on what I was using them for. I liked that No. 24 engine. That's the best engine they had, according to me. She was built in 1919 and was the last engine they bought. Good steamer, had a nice braking system. Latest and best system for its time—the Westinghouse ET style. Had a nice bright headlight. An awful nice-riding engine. I never knew one to ride nicer. Always ready to go, that one. No. 19, that was quite a nice engine, too.

We used to have quite a few tricks up our sleeves and we often had to use some of them to get our trains over the road. I remember one time I had No. 18. Her flues were leaking like the devil. When this happened we used to put three or four pounds of bone meal into the tank and that would usually plug up the leaks—at least until we could get in with the engine. Well, this time I couldn't find any bone meal so I took a bucket and scooped up some horse manure and dropped that into the tank. I was ready to try anything. The manure went up into the boiler and did a good job of sealing up the leaks, and I made it in without any trouble.

The railroad was under the control of the Maine Central at one time. Had its own name but was owned by the MC. All of the Moguls were sent to the MC shops at Waterville at one time or another. They put on new boilers, headlights, trailers, steam generators and air brakes. They'd put an engine on a standard-gauge flatcar and take it right over there to be fixed up. The trailers were put on to improve the ride. They really helped. The locomotives wouldn't jump at a low joint and were easier on the track. Some of them were easy to fire, some of them not so easy. You had to know how. We used those bobtailed shovels. Didn't have a lot of room to swing a big shovel around in those small cabs.

Nos. 20, 21 and 22 were built to run on the Eustis branch. They were the bobtailed engines. Good and strong and all that, but they were bad on the track. They'd slide back and forth because the wheel base was so short. No. 8 was a Mogul. She was very top-heavy. Had an inside frame instead of outside. She was just like No. 9, with that difference. Why they made it that way, nobody knows. She was an awful light-riding engine, but she'd go into a curve and lay over and wouldn't come back. Frank Hodgman was killed in No. 8. I was in Strong waiting for the train to come and she never did come. We went up there to get the passengers and mail. She'd gone down the bank three miles north of Farmington. Broke a steam pipe and scalded Frank. He spent ten weeks in Lewiston in the hospital before he died. Had some close ones myself, but none like that.

On May 29, 1922, we were on the Kingfield branch. I was firing for Charles Hodgman, Frank's brother, and we were crossing the trestle over the South branch of the Carrabassett River when the bridge broke in two. I was sitting on the seat ringing the bell for the next crossing. Suddenly it felt like we were being pulled backwards. I looked back and didn't see much except thin air. The tender, boxcar and baggage car formed a V-shape at the bottom of the river. Good thing we had the boxcar in back of the tender or we'd have gone in, too. The bridge was built a number of years before, and traffic was getting heavier all the time. They didn't change the bridge and she simply just wore out. The baggagemaster and a few passengers were shook up, but no bones broken.

Another time we were coming through what we called Brackley's Pasture near Summit with an Eastern Star Special. We found four or five cows on the trestle with their legs between the ties. The crew and several of the passengers lifted them out and then slid them on their sides along the rails to the end of the trestle. Didn't lose a one!

I had the record for pulling the longest train out of Strong. We went up to Perham Junction to get thirteen loads of long logs and a flatcar loaded with a steam boiler. We could only pull a few cars out of Strong if we had to stop there. Well, when we got down to Phillips I told the brakeman to tell the conductor to telephone down to Strong and have the iron and signals set for Kingfield and we'd go over with the whole train. That gave us a running start at it. She went up there, I'll say. Like the fellow said,

the "old lady" had her high-heeled slippers on and she went downtown in a hurry!

Our day was from the time you left home until you got back. Didn't make any difference how many hours, you did a day's work. Sometimes we'd work seven days a week, sometimes six depending on when the trains ran! $1.50 a day, $9 a week, $39 a month. You wouldn't call that much money nowadays, but it was in those days. You could get good room and board for $3–$3.50 a week. Any time the rest of the boarders didn't eat something, "Put it into Herschel's dinner pail," they'd say, and you'd never see it again. I used to have a sugar bucket to take my meal in. They accused me of taking two meals and one night's lodging for my money.

Yes sir, she was a busy road for a while. Hauled a lot of lumber out of those mills. We gave good passenger and freight service until there were so many trucks and passenger autos that we couldn't compete with them. The railroad finally had to quit. Of course, when the railroad quit, why, I quit, that's all. Trucks and autos took the place of the railroad. They sold the whole thing to the junkman in 1936 and shipped it over to Japan. I presume we got some of it back during the war in one way or another.

After the railroad quit, there was a year or two during those bad times when you were glad to work for $1 a day. Then I was in jail for seventeen years, in the Farmington County jail. I was the turnkey. Served six years as county commissioner. Like I said, railroading was the best I ever had. Hated to see it go.

A fellow by the name of Pratt bought the bell from No. 18 at auction and took it to Prince Edward Island. A few years ago I decided I wanted to see the bell again. I'd rung it quite a few times, you know, when she was on top of No. 18's boiler. I'd heard that Mr. Pratt had given the bell to a church in the town, so I paid a visit to the man living across the street from the church and told him why I was there. He gave me the key to the church and told me to go right in and ring it all I wanted. I really enjoyed that day, I'll tell you.

There wasn't much time left for the SR&RL when Herschel Boynton (left) and Charles Hodgman stood in the snow next to engine No. 18 in Kingfield. The date was January 12, 1934, and the railroad would be out of business a year and a half later.

When the New Haven closed its Maybrook yard, they wanted Mary Carmody to move to New Haven. With a backyard like this, who could blame her for not leaving Walden. Tina wasn't too impressed by the camera.

MARY V. CARMODY
Walden, New York

"I usually knew where to find them." Mary Carmody's job was exactly that, to find the men. Unless you had thirty-five or forty years' seniority and could hold a regular job on a train crew, you worked off the extra board. When your name got to the top of the list, you were called for the next job. If you missed that call, you went to the bottom and lost at least a day's pay. Before telephones, the callers went out and told you when you had to report. Phones made it easier, but there were still times when a caller would have to go out in a blizzard or thunderstorm to find you. Crew members would make it their business to let the office know where they would be. When Mary calls the railroad a "second family," she sums up this relationship between the caller and the crews. It made living your life next to the telephone a little bit easier.

I grew up in New York City. I was raised in orphanages for eighteen years. Dominica was on East Sixty-third Street, and the Charity nuns were in Brooklyn. I don't know if either of them are still there. My parents died when I was a baby, my mother at only twenty-one, and I didn't know anything about myself until my cousin came up from New York to see me. He hadn't seen me in years and somebody told him I was in Walden and then one of my neighbors told him I worked on the railroad. I was born in New York City in 1909, but I didn't even have a birth certificate. Both of my parents came from Ireland. My father drove a double-decker bus on Fifth Avenue.

All the kids were treated the same in the orphanage. We were all one number and that was that. The nuns were good to us and they made us very independent. They made you do your share of the work, and if you had a handicap (I was born with just one hand), you still had to do what the other kids did. There were three of us that were handicapped and we had our work assignments, just like the rest. I can still remember the nun sitting in the middle with all our chairs around her. She'd tie a rope to each chair and tug it if we fussed. They did what they could for us because there wasn't really enough of them to go around for all the kids.

Then when I was thirteen, my aunt took me out of the home. She lived down on Lewis Street, off Houston Street in Manhattan. When I saw the pushcarts and everybody out on the fire escapes and caught the stinking smells, I knew, back in my mind, this wasn't for me. She had six kids, and the boys used to tie my braids to the bed when I was asleep. Always playing tricks on me. Those boys were hellers! They were on the street all the time. My aunt would make up their lunch and they'd throw it away and steal from the pushcarts all the way up the street. I said, "Enough of that!" and I ran away. Well, the cops found me and then I was sent to the Brooklyn orphanage and stayed there until I was eighteen.

You had to be out of the orphanage by that age. Be with your family, if you had any, or get a job. Start being self-sufficient. I had an uncle who lived in Walden, New York, and he said he'd take me in. I came up with a nun on a boat and saw this big fat Irishman. Big mustache, army coat. He came right up to me. He said, "My gosh, you look just like your mother." He recognized me right away.

I started working in a factory, cutting thread. They made pajamas, that sort of thing. Everybody worked there: only place in town. It's long gone now. It wasn't all work, though. I started going to dances with my girl

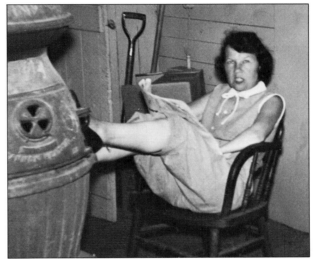

That potbellied stove must have come in handy on cold nights when Mary was working at Maybrook. A railroad yard in the winter time could be one of the coldest places in the world.

friends. Oh, I loved to dance. I remember the first pay I got, I went in the shoe store and bought myself the highest pair of heels I could find. I walked home in them so my uncle couldn't make me take them back. Gray tortoise shell. I can still remember them. Gorgeous.

I met my husband at one of those dances. My friends told me not to get married, but you know how kids are. We had Leo, my son, and then ended up getting separated. Then I went up to Bridgeport, Connecticut, to work. I would come home to Walden on weekends, but I was staying up in Bridgeport with friends. I was working for Bridgeport Brass. They were making bullets for the war.

Then my husband died and I came back to Walden to live. I didn't know what I was going to do, or how I was going to make out. I didn't have a car, I had nothing. But there's a way God works things out for you. My boy had a toothache and all I had was one dollar in the house. I told him I'd go up to the drugstore and see what I could get. When I came out of the store, there was this man in a car out in front. He got out and told me he was George McBride. His daughter used to do my hair. He asked me what I planned to do and I said I didn't know. He told me not to go back to Bridgeport. Everybody here would help me out. I told him I wanted a job, that's all. So he asked me if I'd like to go on the railroad.

"What would I do on the railroad?" I asked him.

He told me to come down in the morning and they would give me a job carrying bills back and forth from the office to the platform and that sort of thing. I went over on the work bus in the morning and got a job. First thing you know, I'm in my overalls like everybody else.

Oh, I enjoyed the railroad. I got so healthy, my legs were as hard as a bullet from walking. I was the only one who stuck it out, stuck out the walking. When I first started I'd be so tired when I came home from all that walking that I'd lie down and when I woke up I didn't know if it was six o'clock in the morning or six at night. A lot of people couldn't, or wouldn't, do it. Me, I knew I had me and my kid to take care of, no matter what the conditions were.

Today's people, I don't know if they'd do what I did. They'd be right there for the welfare. Not me. The only thing I say is, thank the Lord, he made me Irish. He gave me a hell of a lot of guts. I used to say, "I'm never going to be licked." I did all my own canning, kept my own house, raised my boy. Did it all myself. "Be independent," that's what I said, and the railroad was perfect for me. It was really a second home. Going to work was the happiest part of my day. Working with all those people. They were a wonderful bunch.

In those World War II days, there were other women

working for the railroad. There were a lot working as clerks. Some of the women were washing engines. I was the only girl caller. I started at $19 a week. Seven days a week. That's how I learned to stretch and stretch a dollar. I told George McBride, "I can't pay my bills with this money." He told me to be patient, it would get better, and he was right. The rates started getting better after a while, and then the union came in. At one point everybody had to join the union and it got a lot better. When I retired in 1969, we were doing okay.

When I started I was carrying the bills, but they put in this underground machine that helped with the walking. It took you so long to get through the snow and ice that after a while they put that tube in to save time. It had those containers like they have in department stores. Same kind of thing but with air pressure. You'd put the bills in the container, put them in the tube and there was another one down at the other end where they clanked out. They spent a lot of money because that was a long runway through the yard, past the icehouse, and then another long run to the main office. Saved a lot of walking, let me tell you. When we used to have to walk that all the time, everybody used to get sore feet. I just happened to be the lucky one and I could take the walking. All kinds of sleet, snow and ice. I loved the outdoors and never minded the weather.

That snow would get so high, the men would reach down from the engine and pick me right up by my shoulders. It was a funny sight. Many a time I'd climb up and ride between the cars so I wouldn't have to walk all the way to the office. I got on a train one day, and there was another train going up as I was going down. This conductor was on the roof giving signals. He happened to look over and saw me. Oh my God, he jumped right off the top of that train, got up on the ladder, and hooked me on his arm. Swung me right off that train. I was so scared. That train was heading for New Haven. Now, can you imagine me riding to New Haven between two boxcars? I'd have froze to death. He said, "If I ever catch you on there like that again, I'll kick you right in the pants." They were always looking out for me.

I don't think there was another girl that could have fit into that job like I did. There were some devils out there, and you know how boys will be boys. Sometimes they thought they were real funny. One day I had a nice blue snowsuit. Turquoise-blue. We had these pigeonholes where they threw the bills and I'd give myself a boost to get up on the ledge so I could get at them easier. Somebody slid a carbon sheet from a pad under me and I had to work all day with that ink on me. I was so mad. Another time they had a box at the platform and they told me to take it down to the office. I figured it had supplies, that sort of thing. The next day they'd have some other things going to the platform and they'd tell me to take that box back. I did that for a while and then one day I got smart and looked in that box. There were just a couple of two-by-fours in there. I saw those guys laughing and I stopped carrying that box. They'd start over from the pit with a steam engine and they'd pull that thing to work up the steam when they got near me. That spray would come right over to the hump. When I first started, I thought it was just cool dew. I found out. My clothes, my hair, I

couldn't get it out. I had long hair then and from the way it looked you would think I worked in a coal mine.

During the war there were these Army guys out there. They went over to the YMCA and took showers and put on their nice tan gabardine uniforms. One even had a white uniform. They were standing down in front of the engine house and somebody let the steam go. You should have heard that one! There were two steps on the platform and I'd sit there in the sun waiting for the bills to be made up. First thing you'd know, they'd put a little hose behind me and I'm getting wet. I had to go through the yard all wet.

When I look back now, that was a great time to work on the railroad. It was the best time. We worked hard and got the job done, but we had a good time doing it. I'll never forget another time, when we had the steam engines. I got

Three smart-looking young ladies in 1929. Mary and her two chums show off the latest styles.

a mess of those bubble-girl decals. You know, those sexy bubble girls you put on the wall and things. I pasted them all over the engine. The engineer said to me one day, "My God, Mary, an inspector was out here the other day and he asked us who put those girls on the engine. We didn't dare to tell him because he'd throw you in the firebox." You learned real quick with the railroad men. One day one of them tried to give me what he said was chicken. The other guys kept winking at me and I knew he was pulling a fast one on me. Kept saying what good chicken it was. Turned out it was woodchuck. He ate it, not me.

I'd been carrying the bills for a while and then the war ended and the fellow came back who had my job before I left. He bumped me under the union rules and I ended up in the engine house as a crew caller. I'd have to call the men for their jobs. Engine crews, conductors, brakemen, all of them. Some of them wouldn't take calls by phone, so we'd have to go get them. At one time it was set up so they had to sit home all the time because if you couldn't find them right away, they lost out on the job. They changed that to where you had to give them a two-hour call. If the job was going out at two in the morning, you had to call them at midnight. They'd usually tell you where you could find them if they weren't going to be home. Sometimes they'd be at the barber's, someplace like that, but you could usually catch them someplace. There was a YMCA in town where the railroad men stayed who didn't live there. You'd slip the note under the door so they knew what job they were going out on. I was pretty good at finding the men. Nobody liked to miss a call.

When I first went on the railroad, those engineers looked so nice. They had nice white railroad caps, the red checkered scarfs around their necks and the pinstripe overalls. Boy, they looked good! They were real efficient men and went by the rules. You'd see them get their watches out and check them when the noon whistle would blow. Then, when the younger people started to come in, there were no railroad hats, no scarfs, just T-shirts. They didn't look like railroad men anymore. They're a different breed. Today's young people, they don't seem to be as enthused as we were. It's just another job to them. They hired a young guy one time, a fireman. They stopped the train and he got off. Went swimming someplace. He thought you only had to work eight hours, then you go home. They had to tell him that you work until the job goes back into the yard.

We were so busy during the war, you can't believe it. I knew a girl who couldn't believe her husband was doubling. I told her he was working two shifts. Told her to get in the car and I'd show her. I brought her over and there the men were, all working. I told her not to ever doubt him, he was a hard-working guy. They were all hard-working in those days. Those older men, they took care of those engines like anything. Those steam engines, especially. Oh, they'd fuss over them like babies. When they tied up for lunch, they really went over every inch of the engine. Walked around it and got the dirt off. Put a bit of oil where it was needed. Ralph Burr, he was one of those older men. Such an easy-speaking, wonderful man. He always looked so nice, like a real engineer. He used to ask me, so slow and low, "Mary, are you going uptown? Will you get me a cigar?" Such a good man.

I felt business dropping off in the 1960s. All the big shots used to come out and every time we saw them come through the yard, we knew what they were there for. They were there to cut jobs. First thing you knew, this was shut and that was shut and it wasn't long before we were all booted. They were sending in all these college men who were going to save the railroad. They didn't know the first thing about railroads. Two of them went through the yard and had the men take up some tracks. But later they ended up having some more laid down. Until you see the real yard and work in it, nothing matters.

Before the railroad closed up, the agent was dismissed, the general yardmaster was dismissed. I don't think they did fair by those men. When I saw that they were getting it like that after so many years of service, I felt in my blood that we weren't going to last much longer. At the end they didn't even have parts for the diesels! Closed up the shop and didn't even have a nut or bolt for an engine. They were taking from one engine to put something on another to keep at least one of them going. There was nothing to work with. One locomotive didn't have a seat one night

Mary and her son, Leo, in 1953.

and went out with the engineer sitting on a wooden box. When you can't even get a seat for the engineer, things are pretty bad.

Well, I turned out to be right, and they closed down everything in early 1970. I got mine in 1969. There's nothing over there in Maybrook yard anymore, just a parking place for trucks. Makes you sick to see it. I could have gone to New Haven to work. What do I know about New Haven? Had my house in Walden and everything. Had my friends. Didn't want to move. I got my severance pay and it was okay. Then I went to unemployment and they sent me up to the Hot Shoppe on the Thruway. They couldn't believe that I could operate the cash register with only one hand. I did all right. Ever see a Hot Shoppe? All the people, all in such a hurry. Each one wants to be first. Some of those girls that worked there, they'd rave about the truck drivers, and what fine fellows they were. I used to tell those truck drivers, "You're nothing like the railroad men." They didn't like me saying the railroad guys were better. It was family on the railroad. I used to come home at night and bake pies and cakes for those men. Just let anybody get sick, you didn't have to say anything. Right away, somebody would put up a notice. Everybody would help out with what they could.

Like I said, such a good bunch of fellows. I will always be grateful for that job I had on the railroad. There's a track just up from my house and I used to lie in bed and be able to tell you every train that was coming through here and who was on it. Oh, I miss that. Missed it for a long time. I've even dreamed railroading. Many a time I woke up thinking I was right in the yard. Railroading gets right in your system and we couldn't believe it when the jobs were gone. Even now, I go shopping and a railroad man will spot me and come over to talk to me and give me a little kiss. We often talk about what a nice family it was. We were that close. When we see each other, you know what we talk about the most? Railroad! I'm telling you, railroad!

It's hard to believe that this neglected building was once a symbol of American industry. The tracks and turntable are long gone and instead of Pacifics and Mallets, they store fertilizer in what's left of the Oneonta roundhouse.

PERCY S. SMALLIN
Oneonta, New York

It took a lot of phone calls to find Percy Smallin. There were several cousins, second cousins and a niece or two before his daughter, Mary, was located. She explained that Percy was living in an adult home in Otego, New York. His health wasn't that good, but she thought he'd be interested in talking about his railroad career. Railroad engineers' daughters are their fathers' biggest fans and proud of what they did. They can also be very protective. She thought trying to take photographs of him at the Oneonta roundhouse would be out of the question because he would have to use a walker or canes. Percy, indeed, said he'd love to talk about his days on the Delaware & Hudson. When the problem of the photograph was explained to him, along with his daughter's reservations, he hesitated a moment and then asked whose photograph we were taking, his or his daughter's? The message came through loud and clear and you can see for yourself where Percy Smallin wanted his picture taken.

When you go to bed at night you're reaching for water in your sleep. Looking for water, that was always on your mind. Without water you were in for a real ride, you know what I mean? If the fireman doesn't change the supply of water going into the boiler it blows up and puts everything including you on the ground. I remember a fireman who forgot what he was doing; his water pump was putting the water on the ground instead of in the boiler until he got to a place called Hungry Hollow, where she blew up. No. 1510 blew up July 15, 1941. I came by right after: the engineer lay up there on the bank like a bag of bones. The brakeman, the fireman, lay down in the cut, two more bags of bones. I always called her "the ghost," that engine. They revived her and put her back in service within that year. Couldn't rebuild those men.

You could say that 1510 was my favorite engine because she didn't cause you any trouble. That is, she didn't cause *me* any trouble. Caused those fellows a lot of trouble. Our 1500s were marvelous. They were articulated, which means they were hinged between the two parts. They were the biggest engines in the United States when they came out. Well, those engines most always had a little bit more in them. If you were stuck somewhere, you could put them down on their knees and still keep going. We had the 300s that came out during the war. They were high-speed. They were used on troop trains, in passenger service. There were a lot of different types, the 700s, 900s, 1400s, I loved them all. But those 1500s, they'd get you out of a hole. It's like the farmer with a plow horse, he'll go slow and easy. What about a race horse? A race horse is high and mighty and full of zip. Sometimes you'd get an engine that was full of that zip and then some days you'd get an old plug that was off the farm. I liked the old plug because she wouldn't fall down. You could keep that engine going and get in somehow.

I had an engine go over on us—December 30, 1946. It was the 905. Loggers had been skidding logs over a crossing and it was still full of ice when we came along. Right down the bank we went. The fireman, he came over and shook me after we'd stopped sliding. He said, "Come on, Percy, let's get out of here." There wasn't any light in the cab, there was just a peephole. We were down in the dirt. We had big shakers on those engines. We'd shake the grates with those to get a cleaner fire. We had an extension pipe we used to get more leverage that was probably five feet long. When the engine tipped, that shaker lever went right up in the air and stayed hung up on two valves, right up over our heads. If it had ever come down, it would

Before there were motor homes, this is how you went camping: a Model T and a tent. Percy, his wife, Edna, and daughter, Ruth, at Gilbert Lake, New York, in 1916.

have killed us. It was the hand of the Lord.

Another night I came through Central Bridge, west of Albany, and I saw smoke. I thought it was just hot wheels but when we came around the other curve, I see it was a hot box. I nursed it until we got up into the woods and then I saw the fire had gone out. When the fire goes out, that's when the bearings start cutting, the grease is gone and it gets dry in there and you start chewing things up in the wheel. I told the brakeman we had to stop and he said if we stopped we'd have to take the car up to the switch, anyway, to set it off, so we might as well keep on going. So I kept going, and within five hundred feet of the switch, the wheel dropped and I went eight car lengths and tore up a lot of track and that's all there was to it. Doesn't sound like too much trouble, but that's when the work starts with something like that. It doesn't have to be a bad wreck to cause a lot of trouble. We had to take the head end up and set it off on the siding. Then go back and pull the rest of the train back and then come back around the stop and pick up the head end and go down to Mohawk and set the train off. I made it in an hour and ten minutes. I had that engine going about sixty miles an hour when I went back into Mechanicville. The trainmaster called me up and wanted to know what happened and I told him just like I told you. He said, "Perc, you really made the per diem tonight."

We didn't make any bluffs. You thought you could make it, you did it. You went too far out to get back and sometimes you didn't quite make it. You've got your own thinking to do in that engine. You're out in the woods at two o'clock in the morning and you've got a green fireman and brakeman, and one of them says, "That switch is all right, that signal is all right." I say, "No, it isn't." And he says, "Yes, it's all right, got the top green." I stop the train and tell him to go up in the tower and tell them who we are. If the operator says anything and I'm wrong, tell him I saw fire flying back there and that's why I stopped. The signal was wrong. The operator thought we were the Albany freight going to Albany. We were going home to Schenectady. I was right.

I could go on and on. I could tell you the good ups and the bad downs. You learn from other people's downfalls, and you learn to keep your train together. Some of those places, if you broke it in two, it would take you all night and the next day to get out of the way of somebody. The D&H was a hilly road and you had to know those hills. As you passed by the hay barn or went under the overhead bridge, you didn't have to look out to see where you were day or night. You knew the road and you knew your job and that wasn't something to be learned out of the old Sears, Roebuck catalogue.

Take braking. You learned something every day. I had No. 1500 and I would go down into Mechanicville, and right around the curve there was a block signal that you might have to stop for. You wouldn't have a lot of time to see the signal. You had to be down to five miles an hour until you got that signal. I would go down in there with the brakes on a bit and with a little throttle open so as to hold the train tight together. I'd keep it *chug, chug,* until I got the signal and then release the brakes and everything is just fine. No chance of slack breaking the train. Going over a hill you went over with ninety pounds of air, that's what you wanted. When we were going up we'd pump them up to maybe eighty-five pounds of air pressure and leave a little bit of slack back there. The first thing, going over the top of the hill, you might get a red flag. You hadn't expected it, but there might be a rail out or some such thing. It'd take eighteen or twenty of those pounds to get stopped. When you got down a little bit farther, you might get a yellow flag. Some more work going on. You'd have to get down to ten miles an hour or slower. Now you'd lost some

more and how much of that were you going to get back? Maybe four or five pounds. You get way down to the foot of the hill and you get another flag and you've got to stop and your air is down to forty-four pounds, how do you feel? Is that forty-four going to stop you down there?

An engineer I knew went down there and he hit a hind end, and when they dug him out of the coal, they found his watch in his stomach. I have seen trains in the cold weather that I would put the air on to make a test at the top of the hill and the pin would just keep going right down. Do you trust that gauge? Is it reading wrong? Froze up? How are we going to go over the hill? Are we safe? I took chances on it because I couldn't tell something I didn't know to the office. Yet I went down those hills with just as nice a braking train as I ever had. I wish I could tell you what the matter was, but I can't. You know, those are the things that bug you, and after you get to bed at night you wonder if you should have done it.

I grew up in Maryland, New York, up near Twelve Miles. Lived on a farm for twenty-two years. I was the only child. I drove my grandfather's horses, mowed and cradled, used the reaper and ripped oats. I tried it all, but didn't really want to be a farmer. If you've got a lot of money and a good herd of cattle, you're okay. But farming today is like the story of the old man who lived on the farm: he had a good team and he made lots of money. So when the old man got to the time that he couldn't work it, he gave it to his son and he bought tractors and hay loaders and cutters and got in debt, and there went the farm. I went to school in Schenevus, not far from Cooperstown, and there I carried mail and taught school.

I didn't like any of that, so I decided to go to Detroit to make my fortune, but I didn't go with the right bunch. I didn't end up with a job, so I came back and worked in the forests cutting wood. I decided I'd try the Delaware & Hudson railroad. I weighed 125 pounds and they wanted me to go braking, but I didn't want to do that because I felt that I wouldn't last very long. In those days, going down the hills, the brakemen had to go up on top of the cars. I started firing February 5, 1916, and I had to fire a long time. I was promoted on Decoration Day, 1942. There were seventeen men below me laid off during the Depression. What men were left working, they could make up to forty hours a month. If they got in their forty hours before the end of the month, maybe those laid-off men would get a handout, work those last few days of the month.

You know about President Loree of the D&H? He was always buying new engines, building new engines. Bigger, bigger, bigger, so they pulled more cars instead of pulling any promotions. He was quite a boy on new ideas. He spent time in Europe and he changed from the slide valve to the Walschaerts valve gear. That was just a wonderful valve gear. They were always taking an engine out of service and rebuilding it. Putting this or that experimental thing on it. We had water pumps from Austria. You name it, we had it. I ran a test one time for him. The man they sent sat on the seat box. He checked every scoop of coal I put in the firedoor, every time I took the hook down, every time I looked out the gangway, took a drink of water. Every time I did any single thing he checked it on a list he had. After a while he went to sleep, so I don't know what

Percy and Edna in front of her parents' home in Cooperstown Junction, New York, in their courting days.

became of it. One thing he did have was a thermometer with him and he said to me, "It isn't even hot up here in this cab." I said, "Put it down on the coal doors where I am." He did, and it said 120 degrees. Then he said, "I can't leave it there, I borrowed it, and it's going to break." He made me mad because I was between the coal doors and the fire. You leave the door open for more than three or four scoops of coal and you commence to dance and sing. You learned to give two or three scoops and get the door shut. Get in all you can before your overalls commence to smoke.

The only thing that L. E. Loree didn't want to put on the engines was stokers. I remember he said that he wouldn't put an automatic stoker on an engine as long as he could buy a scoop shovel for forty-seven cents. He thought you should earn your wages with that shovel. You take sanitation. You wouldn't drink out of my glass here, would you? From 1916 up until we got into the diesels, three men on the head end tipped a two-gallon water bucket. When the conductor and middle man came over from the hind end, there were five of us drinking out of the same spigot for all those years, but I didn't hear of anyone catching anything.

My God, I don't know how I put in eight hours' work some days. You know how fellows kept awake? You put a monkey wrench on your leg and when it fell off, it woke you up. Sometimes you'd give anything for five minutes of shuteye. And sometimes you worked with men who didn't make the job any easier. I remember Peg Leg Kane. He had a game leg and he'd put the reverse lever so he could rest his knee against it. Never changed that lever uphill or down. Made it very, very hard work for you. Going up the hill he'd take the fire right out from under you. When you came down you could catch up with him, but he was not a good engineer. The engine ran him. Now, I ran those engines and they didn't run me. I worked enough years with enough different men on the road to learn what a good man was. We had wonderful men and we had a lot of poor ones. Some of them that were reported as being awful tough were the best men to work for. I had "the Sydney drop"— that was a job where we had to get all the cars that the other trains had dropped and bring them in. Back and forth, you worked all day, twelve, maybe more hours. Your engine was old and so were you by the time you were finished. Then I got a man on that job name of Old Slashbar. I thought, My God, I've got Old Slashbar. I'd heard of him and thought anyone with a name like that was going to be bad. Well, he was a jewel to work with. After working with him you could go home and play, while some other fellow, he would have you down on your hands and knees.

Another man, Henry Clark, he was beautiful. When I don't go to sleep early, I watch my digital clock and when I see 10:18 I think of a trip we had one day going to Carbondale. We had that engine, No. 1018, and I remember looking at the roof of that engine and there wasn't hardly a pipe that wasn't leaking or squirting. They had men out looking at her and Henry said he'd take her. Now, this is way back in '21, '22, and I went to Carbondale with Henry and never saw an engine steam so good. I never had such a beautiful trip, and that engine was in bad shape.

Oh, I had so many good eggs I worked with, so many good eggs. I'm not bragging, but I didn't have any trouble

We can only wonder at the significance of the draped chair, but Percy looks happy. With him in this photograph from the late 1800s is a neighbor's daughter.

running, myself. I've been up to see the trainmaster, Mr. Clemens, and he said, "Percy, your judgment is good enough for me." He told me that right in his office. Your judgment has to get you over the road; sometimes it did and sometimes it didn't. A little luck helped too. It was 1916 or 1917, and I wasn't married at the time. I sat in the house all day waiting to be called. I got mad about five o'clock and decided to go see my girl friend. It turned out that they had me on the board, but the caller didn't get to me. Around eleven o'clock the phone rang and the operator asked for me and was surprised to find me. There had been a wreck at Howe's Cave and it was reported that either Harding or Smallin was on the engine. Now, you put that together and you see the picture. Harding got the job I was supposed to go out on and the office didn't know who was on that engine. I reported on and went out on a fast freight pusher, and when we got to Central Bridge to take water the fireman on the lead engine came back and says to me, "Let's go down to the morgue; they just dug that fellow out of that wreck." We went down and saw that both of his legs and arms were burned off like fenceposts and his throat was cut from ear to ear. That was what was left of Harding. Was the Lord on my side of the fence that day? Oh, there was one thing more. Jimmy Fisher, the engineer on that engine. He wasn't hurt, but he took right off and he never showed up again. That's the story. That was the end of Harding and the end of Jimmy Fisher.

The classic wooden bench that George Rudolph is sitting on is located in the Harrisburg station that once belonged to the Pennsylvania Railroad. It is a reminder of the elegance that at one time was taken for granted in everyday life.

GEORGE E. RUDOLPH
Camp Hill, Pennsylvania

The conductor on today's railroad has a thankless job. He's usually explaining why the train is late, too hot, too cold, or not moving at all. More than one conductor has been assaulted by angry passengers. That's a far cry from the relationship that George Rudolph had with his passengers. To begin with, George didn't have to apologize very often for the service on the Pennsylvania Railroad. The "Standard Railroad of the World," as the PRR was known, knew how to treat people and also knew how to be on time. In those days the conductor was called "captain." The engineer ran the engine, but the conductor was the final authority on the train. In the very early days of railroading this authority wasn't always taken for granted. More than one train was late while these two worthies decided who was in charge with a fistfight. Things had settled down by the time George Rudolph was working as a conductor, but he still knew who the boss was.

There's nothing harder to handle than the traveling public. I used to work a job out of Philadelphia that left at eight-fifteen in the evening. Local train to Paoli. A fellow would get on every Saturday night and he'd always hand me a $10 bill for a thirty-five-cent ticket. I'd say very nicely, "Do you have anything smaller than that?" He'd always say, "That's good United States money." I'd get his change for him, somehow—the sixty-five cents and the rest in bills. Sometimes I'd have to go through the whole train before I could get enough change.

I went out one Saturday morning and got $10 worth of nickels, dimes and quarters. That night he handed up his $10 bill as usual. I asked him if he had anything smaller. "That's good United States money." I told him to sit tight and I'd get his change. So I went to the rear end and got all that silver. I told him to hold out his hand and started counting it all out.

"What am I going to do with this change?" he said. "I'm going to a dance."

I said, "I don't know, mister, what you're going to do with it, but it's good United States money." I never had a $10 bill from him after that.

On the local trains we got to a point where we would never punch a ten-trip or monthly ticket until we bent and flexed it. You'd be surprised how many punch cuts would pop out of a ticket. They'd pick them up from the floor and iron them back into the ticket at home. I picked up one woman's ticket, ten-trip, and it had twenty punch cuts on it. Well-dressed men on the through trains did it too. Just trying to get a free ride.

You'd be surprised how quick some people could go to sleep. Sit down with a newspaper, read it a little bit, and when the conductor came through they'd have their head down, pretending to be asleep. It was amazing how you could pick out people after you'd done it for so long. They hadn't been on there before, but it was just something that seemed unnatural about them. Most of them always had a ticket, but if they could save that ride, they thought they were getting away with something.

Most of the people who rode were pretty decent. I had another job out of Philadelphia at eight-fifteen in the morning. We had two cars on the rear for kids going to the Main Line schools. One for boys and one for the girls. I never had any trouble with any of them except one little fellow. He was just mischievous, full of life. I sat him down one day and explained how he could get hurt running around the train. "Jolt or something and you could take a bad fall." He looked at me and after that I never had any trouble with him. That was during the Depression in the thirties and I

was being taken off that job because an older man with more seniority had bumped me. Not thinking anything about it, I told one of the boys that such-and-such a day was my last trip on the train. He asked me why and I told him about the older man getting the job. He said, "They can't do that." I said, "They're going to do it."

A couple of days later I saw this boy with a paper and he was going to every boy in the car. Then he gave it to a girl in their car and she took it around in there. I had no idea what was going on. I walked into the crew dispatcher's office, where we got our instructions and orders, a few days after that. The crew dispatcher looked at me and said, "Rudolph, you run on the eight-fifteen?"

I told him yes, that was my train.

"Well," he said, "You must be well liked on there."

I said, "I don't know, I do my job, take care of the kids. Don't know anything else about it."

"Well, they just sent a petition to the general manager to keep you on that train."

Of course, I couldn't keep the job, but that was the greatest thing that ever happened to me.

My father, at one time, was a farmer. I don't know how he ever got on the railroad. Just one of those things you don't think to ask at the time. He was the freight clerk at Frazer, Pennsylvania, when I was growing up. We lived right over the station and that was where I was born. They said it was snowing and blowing that night. My father held me up to the window in the morning and they said the first thing I ever saw was a train going by. I started with the railroad on August 25, 1909. Never had made any real preparation for a job. I was at the station at Malvern one day and found out that this fellow had quit a job there to go to a steel mill. I went home that night and asked my parents if I could quit school and take a job. They never hesitated and that morning I was on the first train to Malvern.

My first job was telegraph messenger and mail carrier. At that time the company furnished a man to go from the station to the post office to get the mail. You'd bring it down to the train, put it on and take the bag that came in on the same train back to the post office. Some of the trains stopped and others you'd have to hang it up on a special arm and they'd pick it up on the fly. If you missed getting a mail bag they fined you $1. At $22.50 for a month's pay, you didn't want to miss too many of them. I was there for a year and two months. Then I just happened to walk into the freight office one day, and the agent was talking to someone on the phone. He hung up, turned around and said, "Tomorrow you go to work on the baggage stand."

Malvern was a hard station to work because it had such heavy baggage and freight. I'll tell you, that was a tough

Baggage trucks like these weighed over two thousand pounds when they were loaded. George Rudolph at the Paoli station in 1912 trying to get the gate closed and push the cart at the same time.

The Paoli station (above) where George worked on the baggage stand. Behind the small door on the right is the men's outhouse. The Frazer station (right) is where George was born.

job! You would unload the cans out of what we called the milk train. It started out of Lancaster and they would make stops to pick up those twenty-gallon milk cans that the farmers would bring down to the station. They'd have blocks of ice in the cars to keep them cold in summer. Regular milk cars. You'd unload anywhere from one hundred to two hundred cans off that train for the condensed-milk factory. You'd be surprised how few would get spilled. From the time they hit the platform until they went in the wagons, they were on the roll. Just put your hand on the lid and roll them right along. Then we'd load the milk boxes from the local dairy onto the train going to Philadelphia. Pile them in pyramids. We checked trunks. I've checked them all over the United States. We had plenty of trunks, let me tell you. Summertime, some people would come with a big truck full of them. If they lived in the neighborhood, they'd have the man from the livery stable come to the station and drop them off or pick them up.

The railroad was just about the only way to ship anything in those days and it was busy. At that time the railroad company had made arrangements with the stores to ship their products by train. If you bought a pair of gloves, they'd send them out in the baggage car for a nickel. We did a big package business. Sundays, coming out of Philadelphia, we'd have a car that was three-quarters filled with ice cream tubs, shipping out along the Main Line. All packed in ice in a regular baggage car. They very seldom laid around very long because the people were after them right away. It wasn't like today where you can just go to the store and buy some ice cream. Then it was a real treat. We had one fellow, quite often he'd be away and his chauffeur wouldn't come after his ice cream. We'd wait until the last train had gone, in case he'd come at the last minute. Then we'd call up and tell the ice cream company that ordered it for him that it was there. They'd tell us to send it back and we'd tell them that there wasn't another train until the next morning. "Well," they'd say, "you better eat it." We wouldn't let it go to waste.

I worked at the Malvern baggage stand for about a year and a half. Then I was on what we called "the west end relief" job. You had five different stations to work in, all west of Philadelphia. One day a week at each station so

George in front of his wife's home in 1913. No matter how hot it got, you were expected to wear the full uniform at all times, including the vest and hat.

that man could have a day off. Go to work at seven in the morning and get through at seven-thirty or so at night. No eight-hour day in those days. Did that until 1917. Just when that was starting to get boring, I was called into passenger service as an extra passenger brakeman. I always liked the extra list. Even when I became a conductor in 1941, I liked the extra list a little better than a regular job. You'd get all kinds of tickets. Never knew what you'd get. All the different trains. Tickets clear to California.

We had to punch the tickets in different places, depending on what kind of ticket it was and where the passengers were going on the through trains. You'd get the tickets from the Pullman conductors and punch them in a certain place. It was interesting work. I've kicked myself ever since I retired for not trying to keep my punch. There was another fellow by the name of Rudolph who worked from Philadelphia to Washington, and when he retired and I came up, they gave me his punch. It was an old one, I'll tell you that. Mine looked a little bit like a doll with a body and a little bit of a head. We'd get women a lot of times who asked me to punch this card or that letter for a little girl. Each punch had its own cut.

When you worked extra you'd go out on any train that needed a man. Every day was new. At one time the Philadelphia Division was rated as having the finest brakemen and conductors on the Pennsylvania Railroad. When I first went braking, the front brakeman would have to ride in the mail-storage car. They had one car for the clerks, the sorting car, and the other was for the mail bags. They'd come up and get a bag or two and take them back to sort. I'd be in that car and on every curve, as front brakeman, I'd have to pass on the signal from the flagman at the rear end of the train up to the engineer. No fire flying from the wheels. Hot journal boxes, stuff like that. Just open the door long enough to get my head out and look back at the train.

For a while I was working a Pittsburgh baggage car. I really liked that job. You were in there all by yourself and you were your own boss. You were supposed to stay in the car until it was unloaded in Pittsburgh. Well, if the baggagemen were busy, you'd maybe have to wait a half-hour, even an hour. An old fellow who had a regular job saw me waiting. He said, "I'll tell you what to do. You go up to the cigar store when you're in Philadelphia, and get a quarter's worth of those Philadelphia handmade cigars, six for a quarter. All these guys can get are those Pittsburgh stogies. You give the foreman a couple and one to each of the men." I never waited for a baggage car to be unloaded after that. "Get out of the car, get out of the car," they'd say. "We'll take care of that." They wanted those cigars. You learned in a hurry. I had to unload and load that fifty-foot car three times between Philadelphia and Pittsburgh.

They say that the *Broadway* was the best train the Pennsylvania had, but I say it was the worst train to work. People trying to get away with using only half a ticket. You'd have to wait outside the compartments in the morning when they were getting up to see that their tickets were in order. Take a lot of cussing because you made them get their tickets out. They expected you to treat everybody with respect. That's what I always tried to do. On the other hand, I never took any guff from anybody, either. On a train like the *Broadway*, there'd be one conductor, and two, maybe three brakemen. All depended on how many cars they had on the train. You wore your uniform buttoned right up to the neck. In the summertime it didn't make any difference how hot it was, you had to wear your coat and keep it buttoned. Wear your vest and keep that buttoned, too. Keep your hat on. We bought our own uniforms at Abrams in Philadelphia. I got several uniforms, they wouldn't fit, no how. I went in one day and told the salesman, "Just between you and me, I think you people are just good tent makers." He almost threw me out of his

office. At one time, you know, conductors wore long-tailed coats. When I was working the conductor had gold buttons and a gold badge on his hat. Brakemen had nickel buttons and badges on theirs.

When you were in passenger service, you saw it all. Coming into New York one day, a man came up to me just as we were leaving Newark. He told me there was a woman lying in the women's washroom on the settee with her wrists cut. Well, I got hold of the other brakeman and we went in and used our handkerchiefs as tourniquets. All we could get out of her was how she'd always been told she had blood on her hands and now she had her own blood on her hands. No name, nothing. We got an ambulance in New York to take her to the hospital and that was the last we heard of her. An unfinished story. Many a time you'd see a man and woman come down to Penn Station and she'd be getting on the train alone. She's crying and carrying on. Kissing and hugging him. It wouldn't be until Newark and she'd be riding up in the club car drinking with some other guy.

One day on the *Trailblazer* there was a woman who asked a porter what time we'd be getting into Chicago. He gave her all the information. A little later the conductor was coming through the car and she asked him the same question. She didn't see the porter behind him. After the conductor had answered her, the porter looked around him and said, "Lady, now you've got it in black and white."

When I first went on, they didn't have air conditioning. They had screens in the sleepers, but in the coaches the windows were just wide open. Cinders coming in all the time. You may not believe this, but remember the old wooden matches? I used to always carry one or two of them. They used to put horsehair in men's coats. In the lapels. I'd double up one horsehair and wrap a rubber band around that and the match. Many a woman I'd take out on the platform and get a cinder out of her eye with that. You wouldn't do that in the car because, if she was next to the window, you might have to lean over another woman to do it. That wouldn't do.

That was one good thing about the electrics, you didn't have the cinders like the steam engines. I never worked behind the diesels. Just steam and electric. They ran behind steam from Harrisburg to Paoli and the steam engines would lay over there and take the trains back the other way. Later they electrified the whole railroad from Harrisburg to Philadelphia. Those GG-1 electric locomotives were powerful and they could start a train real nice. Some engineers could really handle a train. You usually knew who was up there in the cab by the ride you were getting. Even with the steam, they could take ten or twelve cars out and you'd hardly know you were moving. Those men would fuss over those steam engines. We'd see them coming early and wiping their engines down. Shine the bell, the whistle. One of our jobs as train crew was to crawl under the train and take down the brake rigging if it came apart. We had one engineer, he was a prince of a guy. He'd tell you, "Get away from there, I've got my overalls on." He'd get under there and do it and we'd keep our uniforms clean. Kastrivic, that's who it was. Most of them were good but I never had one better than him.

We had good engineers and bad ones, same as anything in life. The conductor was the boss of the train, even in the steam-engine days. He gave the engineer orders, and as a rule conductors and engineers got along pretty well. I did have trouble with one fellow one morning. We came out under the East River towards New York City, heading for Philadelphia and Harrisburg with a mail and express train. We had a lot of freight cars. It was during the war and they needed all the cars that they could get their hands on to haul mail, express, and things like that. I was riding in a caboose. Of course you've got a speed limit coming through the East River tunnel and that engineer didn't observe the speed limit, not a bit. Freight cars are wide and he grazed the platforms in Penn Station as we raced through. All you could see was sparks and smoke flying. Cars were just swinging and dragging against the platform. I had no whistle to stop him because we had the freight cars and he tore through there something awful.

He just kept it up. We ran from what we called Holmesburg Junction to North Philadelphia in seven minutes. That was normally a twelve-minute run. I had a big raw-boned Irish brakeman on there with me and he was sitting there holding on to the cushion for dear life. He was scared to death. When we came into North Philadelphia there's a switch where we changed from one track to another and when we hit that switch, I mean to tell you, I thought we were gone. I thought that cabin [the caboose] was going to turn over. When we reached 52nd Street, there was a steep grade and we slowed down pretty good. I gave the flagman a fusee, lit it, and I lit one for the other side, and we swung them out the sides of the caboose. I can still see the fellows in the freight yard running. They dropped their brooms and shovels and ran for the office. They thought we'd had an accident and wanted the train stopped. You should have seen all those men running.

We got between 52nd Street and Overlook Station and they took the power away from us. When the train stopped, I started for the engine and met the fireman coming back. First thing I said to him was, "Is your speedometer working?" He said it was. That's all I needed to hear. I walked up and crawled up into that engine and asked that engineer what my instructions had been. "Didn't I give you orders that we shouldn't go over fifty miles an hour because of those freight cars? You've violated every rule so far. You came through New York going too fast."

"Yeah," he said, "I knew I was too fast there."

I said, "You almost upset us back at that switch."

"Well," he said, "we were in a hurry." Turned out, as I found out later, that there was another crew ahead of us and he was trying to get in before them.

"If I have to wreck this train," I told him, "I will throw the air on you if you violate that fifty-mile order again."

He just looked at me. We went to Harrisburg without any more trouble.

That isn't an O&W bridge in back of Oscar Bennett. There are a few O&W bridges standing, but they don't look like this Conrail bridge in Hancock, New York. Trains are few and far between, but Oscar never misses watching them.

OSCAR O. BENNETT
Hancock, New York

According to some railroad historians, the Ontario & Western Railroad should never have been built in the first place. Torn up in 1957, it was nicknamed "the Old Woman" and "the Old and Weary." The employees even worked for reduced wages the last few years to try and keep the railroad going. Oscar Bennett never badmouthed the railroad, especially the men he worked for and with. He did have some choice things to say about lawyers and politicians, but never his fellow railroaders. They had a true brotherhood and the men believed in each other and the job they did. Railroading was their way of life and they gave it 100 percent, sometimes more. The last day he ran, Oscar took a full train out of Mayfield yards and was hoping business would get better and the railroad would be saved. When he came back to the bunkhouse and saw them taking the lockers out, he knew the O&W was finished. He said it was the saddest day of his life.

On January 1, 1900, my father gave me a ride on his locomotive and he said, "This is a new year and a new century, and I don't want you to forget it." From then on, everywhere I went I had to get into an engine. When I went away to college, I couldn't get it out of my mind. I wanted to run a locomotive. That was my biggest ambition. It probably ruined me, but I fulfilled it.

I was born and raised around Hancock, New York. My father was an engineer on the O&W. I also had two brothers who worked on the railroad. A real railroad family. Guy was an engineer and ended up as the road foreman of engines. Roy started out on the O&W and finished up on the Delaware & Hudson as a trainman. My father quit the railroad. He had a couple of close calls and didn't want to get himself killed on the railroad. In those days the railroads were a lot more dangerous. No signals, no air brakes, there were some real bad wrecks and a lot of men killed and injured. Well, he said that when he found a farm he was going to quit running engines and he did just that.

When I was in high school, they double-tracked the Scranton Division. They used mules and two-wheeled gigs for the job. Just below our house there were two shanties for the laborers—one for the Mexicans, and one for the Italians. They were always drinking and fighting on Sunday. They'd be using knives and razors and get cut up real bad. I went into one of those shanties one morning and the man in charge of the explosives was thawing eight sticks of dynamite on the stove. I wasn't long getting out of there.

One of the Italians came to our house on some pretense and tried to attack my mother. He chased her upstairs and she grabbed her Smith & Wesson .38 and took a shot at him. Our house was off limits after that.

My father didn't want me on the railroad. He wanted me to get an education. I went to college in East Stroudsburg, Pennsylvania, East Stroudsburg State Teachers. It was a four-year course, but I took it in two because I had a high school education. You didn't get any time off in those days, and we couldn't even leave the campus. I came out a schoolteacher of Latin and English.

I began my teaching career at Poyntelle, New York, which is near Hancock, in a one-room school with fifty-six students. That was 1915. In October of that year the station agent told me that the first O&W Bull Moose locomotive would be coming through town that afternoon. I held recess so the children, and I, could see it. No. 357, huge and shiny. I didn't know that afternoon that years later I would be an engineer on those monsters. I worked up and

became the vice principal here in Bainbridge, New York. I taught Latin and history. I was getting $90 a month . . . I started out at $40 a month teaching, but the first two weeks I worked on the railroad I drew $156.

I went railroading on February 12, 1920, because I never could get it out of my system. I ran some fast ones—big ones, good ones and even some bad ones. Railroading was tough in those days. It was just a strong back and weak mind for a lot of it. You didn't have generators, stokers, air-operated firedoors, you did it all by hand. You couldn't have a dream that was as bad as railroading was in the twenties. You came in at two o'clock in the morning, and you had a hand-fired engine, and you had to go 122 miles. You fired up the hill, and then you got to roll down the hill and you could take a rest, but the brakeman went out and he rode on top of the cars. He'd go back and meet the middleman, and they'd come together and they'd sit out

Conductor Marcus Hart, engineer Oscar Bennett, and brakeman Whistler Wells, at the Mayfield yards in Pennsylvania. It was March 29, 1957, and one day later the last train would run on the O&W.

there on those cars . . . twenty-five below zero sometimes, sometimes colder.

We had bad tunnels on the O&W too. That Northfield was a killer—1,152 feet long. No ventilators, no nothing. You had to go full power through it going south because you were on a grade. Sometimes two pushers on the hind end, and no place for all that exhaust to go. I had a fireman jump off in there because he felt so suffocated. Took the lesser of the two evils, I guess, but he lived. You'd take a big piece of waste as large as the bell, soak it with water, hole your head right in it. Your neck would be blistering. I even had two firemen go unconscious in there, and we had two engineers died from all that smoke and heat.

But things did gradually get a little better. We had steam locomotives that were forty-six years old. You couldn't wear them out, so of course they took their time getting new ones. In those days every engineer had his own engine assigned to him. Then somebody got the bright idea that they would put the engines into pool service. The engines deteriorated after that. When a man had his own engine it was like his watch. He took care of it. Later, when you got off, you didn't know who the heck was going to get it. It was too bad. Later on they bought the Mountain type, the Y-2. They all came equipped with stokers and they were a pleasure to run—the ultimate in locomotives on our railroad and maybe just about all railroads. They had 225 pounds of steam and a big wheel. I've had one up to ninety-six miles an hour on our tracks. The Y-2, you couldn't beat it. It was all locomotive! It was easy to run and had a wonderful throttle. Then they got rid of all the steam engines for the diesels.

We were the first road to go 100 percent diesel, in 1948. I would take a diesel train out of Scranton, Pennsyl-

91

vania, and go to Norwich, New York. I would get off, the next man would take that train and go to Oswego, New York. Then he would come back and I would get on again and take it back south, and she was fueled over here in Pennsylvania, that's all the service she had. No water, coal, all the stuff that kept a steam locomotive going. In the steam days, though, in the big Mayfield freight yards, for example, they had fourteen pusher engines in the pool. That meant fourteen engineers and fourteen firemen who were guaranteed at least thirty-eight days of work a month. There were engineers at Cadosia, extra firemen, brakemen, and there were pushers going constantly. There was a pusher at Livingston Manor on twenty-four-hour service. A pusher at Summitville, twenty-four-hour service. When the diesels came, these men were unnecessary because you didn't need pushers. You didn't need machinists, boilermakers, you didn't need anything.

There wasn't any transition to the diesels. Nope . . . just jump off the engine and go to church! Didn't even have to wear your overalls. A chair as nice as any you've got at home, a comfortable height, air conditioning. You could do everything just using your little finger. The hardest thing to do was to blow the horn. The responsibility was gone, because you didn't have to watch the water, you didn't have to worry about this or that or anything else. Anything went wrong with the diesel, you didn't know what the hell to do. With a steam locomotive, you knew instantly what to look for, but with a diesel with all those high-flown gadgets, you didn't stick your finger in them. No sir! You didn't really run a diesel. The steam locomotive, you ran them. You ran them! I wanted to be the best man that ever

ran one and I was as good as any because I made a study of it. See, we had the Baker valve gear here. You could play with them and really make a locomotive behave.

When business was good here, I'd go to work, I wouldn't know which locomotive I was going to get. Whether it would be a New Jersey Central, a New Haven, or whatever was up. We were doing such enormous business. There was no end of railroading in sight in those days. I used to get that 875, she was built by Baldwin. She was New Jersey Central, and she had a chime whistle on her and coming down through this valley, you could hear her, it was music . . . not like these damn diesel horns, those whistles were music. I never liked the Pennsylvania whistles, though; they screeched.

I'll never forget, after the diesels came, I had four units one winter night. We were leaving Cadosia, New York, with a heavy train and there was about six inches of new snow on the ground. When we started to make the descent down Rock Rift Mountain I applied the brakes, and when we came out of the cut I saw a railroad motorcar going down the track ahead of me. I stopped as soon as possible and the motor- car continued for about a hundred feet and stalled in the snow. We looked around for anybody who might have been on the car but couldn't find a soul. Couldn't even find a footprint in the new snow. When we got to Walton we reported the accident, but the mystery remained.

A few days later they solved it when somebody opened their mouth. Walton was a "dry" town in those days and the nearest place to get a drink was at the Dew Drop Inn at Cadosia. There was a section boss at Walton who, unbeknownst to the railroad, took his friends every Sunday on his motorcar to Cadosia to the tavern. He had always got by somehow without meeting a train. On this night, they were in their cups. They put the motorcar on the track to come home and gave it a shove to start the motor. The motor caught and it ran away from them. They gave up chasing it and went back to the Dew Drop Inn to finish up the night. The motorcar stalled behind the Presbyterian church in Cadosia and I unknowingly picked it up on a left-hand curve where I couldn't see it. I pushed it ahead of my engine to Rock Rift, which was about eight miles, and when I made my first application of air on the grade, it went out in front of me. That was the first I knew of it.

The section boss was discharged over that one, but was later reinstated to service. I don't think, however, that he used his motorcar for any more trips to the Dew Drop Inn.

We got the old Bull Mooses in 1915. They were going to be the wonder wagon of the world. I was firing for Eddie Clark, who never swore, a real gentleman. He didn't use tobacco, lose his temper or anything. We had one Bull Moose that was riding so rough that I got back in the tank. I couldn't stand to ride in the cab of that locomotive. When we got back and put her on the receiving track, Eddie walked up and kicked one of the drivers as hard as he could and called her a few names. Oh, they were wicked. They were the dirtiest, meanest, rottenest locomotives ever built. I ran diesel 801 the first trip after she was delivered to Maybrook and went to Mayfield yards, where I was to catch her back. They told me I had to take a Bull Moose instead. I had no gloves or overalls, and a white shirt on. You should have seen me after I got back to Maybrook.

There was a wrecking shop in Middletown, New York, one of the best-equipped places for any wreck or mechanical problem. You could go in there and see steam engines being repaired. They'd seem just like corpses, but you get 'em out, and the pumps running, and the live steam, it was a different thing. Like a human being. People used to be out waving at you. After the diesels came, you didn't see any waving. It was a change of atmosphere, there was something wrong. I think it was that the sound was gone. The steam locomotive was railroading to me.

When the O&W went out of business, whole communities vanished. You can't find a piece of them today. There's Franklin up here. You go up to Franklin, that was a booming little village. They had a big coal pocket, a feed mill, they had a store; now there's nothing, not even a house. The railroad built the towns like Lakewood. There is nothing now at Poyntelle. The O&W station was open twenty-four hours a day. There was a blacksmith shop, a creamery, two feed mills, the school, all those things. All gone. They weren't there before the railroad, and now that the railroad's gone there's nothing again. Terrible thing.

The railroad didn't go bad, the people did. It was the big boys playing ball again. Right up to the end I was coming out of Norwich with a four-unit diesel every day with never less than ninety-eight to a hundred cars. Sometimes as much as a hundred and twenty. But where did the money go? There wasn't a station or anything to maintain. Here was a railroad one hundred and thirty years old, being stolen right there. There was $10 million worth of business from Cadosia alone, for 1957, even before Route 17 was going to be built. All the cement and stone—we could have hauled it. On July 31, 1957, the last through freight came through here.

I could tell you stories about the end of the O&W until midnight. Now, you take this big mill down here at Parksville, the Purina people. They put up this factory, getting eighteen cars of feed out of there a day. They wouldn't have built that factory if they

knew if would only last six months after they finished it. DeCamps put one up, and that didn't last six or eight months. Everybody thought the railroad was solvent or going to be soon. The New York State Highway Department and the New York City Water Supply wanted the right of way and they got it. I don't have to tell you where most of Route 17 runs, now, do I? Right on the O&W roadbed.

I'd come out of Norwich with thirty-forty cars of rock alone, that was all pure profit. We had all that Armstrong work, all Nestlé's products. We had all that Rome airport work, we had everything, everything but the money. They paid a lawyer $1 million every year for the last ten years. Then you wonder why the money ran out. The railroad couldn't pay us our full salary. We worked for less than union wage to help the railroad the last few years. The railroad worked out an agreement with the union to try and keep the railroad going. They owed me $28,000 when they folded. Management told us it was going to fold, but everybody thought that the New York Central would want it.

I just never believed it would go under, not even in the end. Did you ever see one of these piggybacks go through here on the Erie Railroad? It doesn't use as much fuel as a big truck. That one engine. You have more than two hundred trucks on that train, and one man doing it all. But then, that gang is in there, that power gang. All the billionaires. They put the trolleys out of business. Ripped them all up and burned them. Now they're doing the same thing with the railroads. They're building these highways for trucks, not for you and me! The highway goes right through where the railroad yard was in Sayerville. There were sixty trains coming into that town every day of the week. A lot of people used those trains. Shipping things and riding places. Now there's not a one. I've seen some awful changes and I think we're going to see more.

With his distinctive baseball hat, Oscar checks his train at Delhi, New York. To Rogers Whitaker, who wrote under the pen name of E. M. Frimbo, the O&W was one of his favorite railroads because "The O&W were pioneers in reverse. They were keeping the old nineteenth-century style of railroading going in the twentieth century."

Before the diesel engine, a set of overalls like this was as necessary as a good watch. Taking time out between runs at Steamtown, Andy enjoys another important piece of equipment, his cigar.

ANDREW A. BARBERA
Bellows Falls, Vermont

There are busman's holidays and sometimes even busman's retirement. Retired as a Lackawanna engineer in 1967, Andy Barbera now lives in a refurbished coach at Steamtown, a railroad museum in Bellows Falls, Vermont, and runs its steam trips. A few years ago he was at the throttle of the great Berkshire, ex-Nickel Plate No. 759, on a fan-trip to Boston when the fireman got in trouble and the steam pressure started to drop. Andy had been trying to answer everybody's questions when he noticed the gauge. Getting off his seat, he grabbed a rake and told everybody to stand back. Five minutes later, back on his seat, with the pressure rising, he mentioned that the fireman wasn't used to such a large engine and that it was up to the engineer to pay attention to such things. Andy must be a good teacher; he had all the steam he needed for the rest of the trip to Boston.

I was born and raised in Hoboken, alongside of the railroad. It was an interesting place to be in those days. My mother and dad would always take us children down on Sunday to look at all those beautiful clean engines. The Lackawanna Railroad kept them so spotless. There was something you could really enjoy about them. The sound, the bell ringing, the whistles, and the exhaust going *choo-choo-choo*—it gets out of sight and then you don't hear the sound anymore. One of the most important pieces of machinery, I guess, that was ever invented. Built America! If they hadn't had the railroads back then, we'd never be where we are today. You couldn't have ever done it with mules and canals.

When I got old enough to get a job, I quit school and went firing on the Jersey Central in June 1915. I had to lie, I told them I was eighteen. In those days they didn't bother you too much. I worked there for two years and four months. The war came on and I quit the Central. I wanted to get into the First World War and tried to join a railroad battalion so I could get to be a second lieutenant or something. But I couldn't make it. I think I still got my card here. I did want to get in that war so bad. Maybe it was for the best, though. Some of them went over there as firemen and, gee, they wound up just laying ties and rails.

I was about four months or so out of work when I heard the Lackawanna was hiring firemen. I went over there and got a job. I was always kind of a rail fan and wanted to run those Lackawanna engines. I had five brothers, they all had what I guess people would call good jobs, well educated. One was a priest, one a lawyer—I was the only one ended up on the railroad. It was something that just stuck, the railroad was the one dream I had. I fired until 1927. Promoted in 1927 to engineer and was running in 1928, on and off. When there was no work for an engineer and you were the youngest, you went back to firing. That's how it worked. Didn't bother me a bit. When I went back to firing I was on a crack train. When I was an extra engineer, I'd be here and there and all over, I qualified only for freight. I had to wait for two or three years before I could qualify for passenger.

It was a tough life then, long hours away from home. I never knew what holidays was, worked every day in them days. In later years you got two days off a month on a regular job. I started at fifty-five dollars a month back before the first war. The unions were a good thing for us. They helped us out a lot. The railroads treated men like servants. Any work that had to be done. Like a servant had to take out the children for a walk, or to get their hair cut.

In one of the Pocono engines that he liked so much, Andy and his fireman are ready to leave Hoboken with a passenger train sometime in the 1940s.

You had to come back when they wanted you to do this or that. Then the unions got a bit stronger and organized and made it better for the men. That was no more than right. I remember when I was a fireman; you'd get your fire down right, get everything ready to go—and you'd be all sweated up. Then you had to go over and get the ice for the cold water. They used to have a big chunk and you had to go over to the ice car and put it on your shoulder. They didn't even have tongs in there and one day I wouldn't do it. I wanted the hostler to put the ice aboard with the rest of the tools. They said I wasn't going out until I got the ice, so they called up the boss. The boss said, "All right, send him in the office and put somebody else on there." I was out two days. Later on they got the firemen's organization and they had them put on the ice with the oil, lamps, and everything else. In the beginning you belonged to the railroad just like the engine. The unions made them stop a lot of that and hire laborers for the stuff that wasn't really your job.

I worked until October 30, 1967, and ended up in regular passenger. I finished the *Phoebe Snow*. Thought she would finish me out, but I finished her. She went into service in 1949, as the *Lackawanna Limited*, but then they streamlined their engines and coaches and painted them with their gray and maroon color and named it the *Phoebe Snow*. You wouldn't want a prettier train. I wanted that train and I want to tell you how lucky I was to get it. There were two men older than I was—but one of them turned out to have a murmur of the heart and the other had high blood pressure. So I got the job. Couldn't miss, you see, 'cause I was next in line. One wouldn't talk to me anymore, I had been promoted with that guy. He used to go by me without a word. Didn't even say hello. But he had the high blood pressure and I didn't have anything to do with that.

When I started out, railroads was something that worked. Something that was fantastic. The country let it go down the drain. Instead they should have helped the railroads. They can move in almost any weather conditions. This highway business with trucks can scare the hell out of you. It isn't safe for people going out with their touring cars. It's too bad the government didn't subsidize the railroads. If they ain't got the business, they can't operate. They rip up tracks, rip up the stations, and I'm wondering if they're ever going to get back to anything. I won't see it, but in ten or fifteen years, there are going to be very few railroads around. You ain't going to see any short lines . . . just coast to coast. Sell the property . . . sell the land . . . sell the buildings. First they sold that hotel across from Penn Station. Then they sold brand-new beautiful engines. Five cents a pound for scrap.

The Lackawanna had passenger engines built in 1937. They ended up in 1945–47 using them on freight trains because they had done away with so much passenger work. They were Pocono types, the 1600s. A nice engine, one of the nicest, finest engines that was. The ones I liked best in steam were the Hudsons. The 1500s and the 1100s. I liked them the best. They were a more "designed" locomotive or something. It wasn't so rugged-looking or heavy-looking. They were real nice, like a lady, if you know what I mean. They were made of real heavy iron just like the rest, but they didn't look that heavy. Everything was better in the later engines. We had a lot of double cab engines [cambelbacks] when I started. Cab on both sides of the boiler, and the fireman all the way in the back by himself. They were kinda hard riding. You rode over the main drivers. I tell you the truth, I always used to be in fear in those engines. If the main rod ever let go, the thing would come up through the cab. When you climbed up the ladder you couldn't see nothing outside nowhere. It was like being in the bottom of a ship. It's not like a regular engine, where you can look out the windows.

The first I was firing was in the wintertime on the one of those camelbacks and the goddamn airpipe froze up on the steam gauge. They had them curled pipes that came up underneath the gauge. Well, it froze and the damn gauge run up to 400 pounds. I was scared stiff, being back there by myself and seeing that needle run up like that. Like I said, I was pretty new and I thought that engine was going to blow sky-high. The next stop, I run up and tell the engineer that the goddamn gauge back there is at 400 pounds. He says, "No." I says, "Yeah!" He says, "Get your torch and hold it on that pipe under the gauge." You see, he had a gauge up with him and his was showing the real pressure, so he knew we weren't about to blow up. We didn't have generators in them days, so no electricity for electric lights in the cab. We had a torch and oil lamps in the cab for the steam and air and water gauges. We used signal oil so they wouldn't make a lot of smoke. It was what they used in submarines. I took the torch down and held it there and pretty soon I had 175, 190, whatever the hell it was. I never had an experience like that again. To think about it afterwards, it was very funny, but not then.

During the thirties the builders were making something more like what I call a normal American locomotive. They started to look beautiful. I used to just like to look at those ladies. They streamlined some of them in the thirties too. I ran them, the 1151, 1155, all of them. They sent the 1151

to the New York World's Fair. Renumbered her 1939. They had stainless steel on the sides. They were designing them better. Just like the automobile, they grew up. What did we have in 1909? Henry Ford's Model T. We had a Maxwell in our family. When they started up again after the war the companies put out better-looking cars, better mechanics, better style. After the war everybody got ideas, everybody got smart, pitched in—and how they invented things!

In steam, all the motion was thrilling. But in a diesel engine, you don't see nothing. It's all hidden away. It's nothing more than a glorified Mack truck. I didn't much care for electric engines, either. We had lots of them and I called them trolley cars. What do they look like with that umbrella up there, what they call the pantograph? Nothing more than a bunch of trolley cars put together. Electrics and diesels I had no love for. The diesels we had, the gas fumes used to come up into the cab. We used to get the heat and fumes and the walls would turn yellow. When we got the cabs washed, you ought to see the difference. You'd think it was enamel, yellow enamel. That didn't do no harm to your insides? Steam engines had fumes and heat too, but not that foul stuff.

A steam engine was a good teacher. A cabbage cutter can't teach you anything. When the teacher doesn't take an interest in you, you ain't going to learn nothing. Today

Standing on the steps of a "cabbage cutter" in a Paterson yard. Andy was working local passenger between Hoboken and Paterson when this photograph was taken in 1955.

everybody wants to get dressed up, and nobody wants to look dirty. With these here diesels and electric trains, you don't know whether they're employees or passengers. Engineer used to come along with an oil can, waste in his pocket, and looked like a workingman. Today nobody looks like a workingman, no matter what his job is. I wore those pin-striped coveralls since 1915. I was proud of those coveralls and I was proud of working for the Lackawanna. That railroad was a gold mine! It was one of the neatest, cleanest railroads there was. You had to be on the ball! The stations were clean, the roadbeds were good.

The railroad used to have roses along the sides of their stations and all along the fences. They had men cutting the lawns and everything. It was one of the nicest little railroads in the East. They had their own coal mines, and for a 410-mile railroad, it was a very good one.

Then they merged us with the Erie and outright ruined the Lackawanna. I think some of the officials on that Erie line were a bunch of crooks. Lackawanna men were stricter. The Erie was sloppy and they just didn't care too much for our ways, the way we worked our railroad. After ten years all this was forgotten, but when the merger first came we were the better road.

I don't think any of those mergers done any good. They all merged for a reason—to eliminate tracks and maintenance, and to cut payrolls. In a couple of years, they all went into bankruptcy. How do you figure that? If I got a store and you got a store, and you turn around and say, let's merge our stores, we eliminate costs. How did they go bankrupt all at once? That's what happened to the Lackawanna, what happened to the Pennsy road and the New York Central. It was all in one pocket. So what happened? It wasn't business taken away from them. Business was taken away from them years back, by trucking. The railroads were like a good neighborhood you live in for twenty years. People start to move out, and things start to deteriorate. They deteriorated, the railroads, every one of them. They cut down maintenance, let things run down until they were gone—to where they had to cut the speed down in order to keep 'em on the tracks at all. Our railroad was still in pretty good shape when I left it. Now, a conductor I worked with over there, he told me, "Andy, the track where you ran eighty miles an hour has been cut down to fifty." I said, "You're kidding!" There were so many speed restrictions it was hard to believe. You have to have speed instructions on a panel board so you know where you are. He gave me one to look at and I couldn't even read it. I threw it away.

Fifty years I was running on the Lackawanna and I didn't want to see that to remind me of what had happened to my railroad. Fifty years I never had any accidents. Never killed nobody, hurt anybody. I went right through. If you liked your job, you certainly didn't want to abuse it. You ought to have seen that machine shop, they had machines in there was big as a railroad car. All the excursions going to Asbury Park, Cranberry Lake with those white "extra" flags flying. Beautiful bunk room, showers, wash-up areas and everything else. I can't understand how it disappeared. Just like it was a thousand years ago for all that's left of what was.

They talk about bombing Europe—Jesus, we got bombed one way or another in this country by ourselves. It even hurts me today. At least I can say I grew up when the world around me was like a rose coming up and blooming. Now the world is getting old and I'm getting old with it. I don't regret the time away from home. It had to be just that way with the type of work. I didn't know what the heck holidays was, Easter, Christmas—I never had a birthday in my house. I never had a birthday cake or party until I had retired and come up here to Steamtown to work. I don't regret it, though; it was real interesting work.

The last run of the *Phoebe Snow*. The train was named after an imaginary Miss Phoebe, who kept her white gown clean because the Lackawanna burned smokeless anthracite coal. Andy shakes hands with his conductor, Ray Holleran, on the sad day, November 27, 1966.

In the kitchen of the dining car of the *Lakeshore Limited*, the last train with full dining service still running out of Grand Central Terminal. With Johnnie Heyliger (right) are Emmet Dixon (left) and Nathan White, two chefs of today.

JAMES J. HEYLIGER
Jamaica, New York

Twentieth Century Limited. *The most famous train in the world. The last run was in 1967, but the legend lives on. Most legends tend to get bigger than life as time goes by and the railroads are no exception. In the telling engines go faster, snows get deeper, and the service one could find on trains like the* Century, Super Chief *and* Broadway *gets better every year. However, if Johnnie Heyliger is typical of the men who worked on the* Century, *that train must have been exactly as people describe it. Johnnie knows only one way to do things—the right way. Even when he serves a visitor a drink in his home, the ice is in a silver bucket and he uses silver ice tongs. He never refers to the people who rode the trains as passengers or customers. They were always guests.* Century *service was a fact and the dining cars of that train were where a great part of that service took place.*

NEW YORK CENTRAL SYSTEM

A lot of places I go, people are afraid to give me something to eat when they find out I was a chef on the railroad, on the *Century.* I tell them, "Don't worry about me, just give me something I can eat." Other times they say, "Here comes Johnnie, let him cut the meat." I tell them that I didn't come to cut the meat. I have to admit, I did have a pretty good hand for cutting meat. That was before they had all this electric-knife stuff.

I really liked working the *Century.* On that train the guests knew they could get anything they wanted. People are easy to take care of when you got the right supplies. You didn't mind serving that class of people. They were friendly, not trying to monopolize all your time without giving you something for it, like you got sometimes on other trains. Gloria Swanson, Tim McCoy, John Boles, Chrysler people, Ford people, I've handled them all. We had all those folks. Not stuck up at all. Very friendly. In fact, sometimes you didn't want to take anything from some of those people because you were just doing the job you were supposed to do. You appreciated the way they accepted you. The way they appreciated you on your job. That's all the *Century* was, movie stars and big businessmen. Wanted to be in New York or Chicago the next morning. There were times when I wished I'd ridden on all the trains. I'd hear all these stories of how much fun these other guys would have when they went places on these football specials. New Orleans, Cincinnati, all those places. They wouldn't let me go on those specials. I had already bid on the *Century* and that was that. I'd ask about those specials and they'd say, "When the *Twentieth Century* pulls out of here, you're on your football special."

We'd be on the train no later than one o'clock, even though it left from Grand Central at six. You did all your preparing at the Mott Haven yard. Get all your supplies on board there. We had brass floors in the kitchen, and with Bon Ami we'd get down and scrub those floors. Make them shine. Then we'd put newspaper on it and when we got down to the station, we'd pick up the paper and sweep the floor. Inspector would come in and look at that floor. See if there was dust, dirt in the corners. Check out the whole car. Garbage cans had to have clean aprons on them. Inspector came on and if they were dirty, he wanted to know what was happening. Everyone was very particular about things on those trains, especially the *Century,* that's for sure. They were right, too. You had the door to the kitchen open, you wouldn't want the guests seeing a dirty apron on the garbage can.

We were strong on keeping the door open. It'd get hot at times because there was no air conditioning in the kitchen. They had screens in the windows. Small screens because they couldn't put large ones in there. Let too much dust in. The faster the train ran, the lower we had to do the windows. When we were burning coal you had a lot of grit coming in. I'd tell those men, "We want to keep the door open, it has to be clean." You had to be smiling all the time, too. Kitchen was on one end of the car. There was a hallway that ran next to it and the people would have to pass that door. Look right in the kitchen. Not like a restaurant. We were right out there for people to look at. I could tell when they were at all interested and I'd ask them if they wanted to come in. In they'd come. The first thing they'd always say, "How do you work in here? Where do you put everything? Where do you cook everything?" If I had a few minutes, I'd tell them, show them around.

Preparing dinner on the *Century* in the 1950s. The kitchen of a dining car was a masterpiece of functional design with a minimum of wasted space. It was truly the original high-tech kitchen.

ROCHESTER DEMOCRAT & CHRONICLE

They'd bring the train down to the station at five or so. Back it in. The conductor would come by and see that everything was right and in working condition before we left. Make sure you had a full crew. If he thought it wasn't right, he'd just cut your car out. Put another car in there. They always had an extra car ready in case that happened. If a car went bad out on the road, first station they got into, they'd wire ahead and the yardmaster would have another car ready to put on the train. Set the bad one right off, especially if there was something wrong with the air conditioning. They'd put the people back in the observation car until they could get into a station and put the new car on. On a less important train, the passengers had to get to where they were going with the bad car. Not the *Twentieth Century,* or the *Commodore.* Not on those fancy trains.

As soon as the train backed in, you were ready for business. Some people wouldn't even take their luggage to their compartment. Just give it to the porter to put away and come right into the dining car for dinner. First thing you might serve them was a shrimp cocktail. We had all that kind of stuff. Clam bouillon, hot consommé or cold. We had it all. The guests had a real meal on that train, let me tell you. Soup to nuts.

I ran on the *Century, Detroiter, Commodore Vanderbilt, Lakeshore Limited.* All classy trains. They all had the same quality of food, but they had more of the fancier cuts on the better trains. Steaks, roast beef, Chicken Tetrazzini, those were some of the favorite dishes on the good trains. We had a recipe book and when they came out with a new menu, there'd be a recipe for you to go by. However, most of the time, you'd been cooking so long you didn't need the recipe. You knew what goes into something.

Sometimes when we had a special on the menu, I would make Chicken à la King. Then you could use the chicken for Chicken Tetrazzini. Just strain the peppers and the pimentos out. You had to be thinking a lot while you were cooking. You had to employ things in different ways. If you had a roast beef and you cooked too much, you'd make a roast beef hash for breakfast. Very seldom did we get a well-done cut of roast beef on the *Century*.

I was born in Bermuda, and my family came here in 1919. I started with the railroad in 1921. I had a brother and an aunt who were here already. We lived up on West 138th Street in New York. My brother had a grocery store. I had nothing else to do but go on the railroad. Things were slow in my brother's business. Men who worked on the railroad would come by the store and I'd ask them if they could get me a job. One of them asked me if I wanted a job washing dishes, so I went over to the New York Central and got a job. I was twenty years old then. Wages weren't even worth telling about when I started. We used to have to work two hundred and forty hours in a month. I got $57 every two weeks. That isn't much money, is it? But times were different. You could do better in those days with a little bit of change than you can in these times with the hundreds of dollars we get.

You started as fourth cook. That was the dishwasher. That's about all you did, wash dishes. Clean the kitchen and keep things in their place. You went from fourth to third, third to second, and then to chef. I stayed fourth cook for about six years. You learned from watching the other men work. They also had a school you could go to at certain times during the week. It was in the yard in an old coach. The chef or steward would tell you about the new menus when they came in and what you had to know to prepare the food. After a while they put more of a regular school in Grand Central. Every Thursday afternoon we'd go down there.

The number three cook was the fry cook. Anything fried, he'd take care of that. Oysters, breaded pork chops, that sort of thing. Second cook was the broiler man. All meat broiling was his job. For me, three to two cook was only a matter of two or three years. I got promoted real fast, I think, because I was interested in the job. Some men were indifferent. I believed that if you were going to do a job, you should do it right or don't bother doing it at all. I've always followed that method and so far I've done pretty good with it. Any time that the second cook didn't show up, the chef that I was working with would put me in his place. You learn fast doing that. Same way I got promoted to chef. I took an interest.

When we first went on the *Century*, they didn't have colored chefs. Used to have white chefs and colored help from second cook on down. Sometimes those white chefs could be mean. Stewards were always white, too. Then the company started getting good recommendations on the colored cooks, and let us be promoted to chef. In some places they'd say the passengers would rather have a colored crew on there instead of a white one. They started using black stewards in the late forties, early fifties. They were waiters who were good enough to become stewards. In the beginning they were on different trains, not on the *Century* or anything like that. Finally we had two black

stewards on the *Century*. They were men with light complexions. They were both A-1 stewards. With the class of people that we traveled with, it never occurred to me that they felt any different about my color.

Every man had his job, every man had his station. In the kitchen, chef was "in the hole." That's what we called the serving window between the kitchen and the pantry. Four cook was next to the chef washing dishes. Three cook was in the middle, and second cook was down by the door. We had enough room if everybody worked right. There was no confusion. You didn't pass nobody. When I was chef, I always kept an eye open in the back of my head in case someone needed help, but there was no food being cooked in the hole. Everything was coming down from the other men. The people didn't get anything to eat until the guys in the back gave it to me. I didn't have any misunderstandings during the meals because I didn't allow it. My rule was like this: if you know what you have to do, do it. If you don't know, ask me, I'll tell you. If you ask me and you still don't do it, you're no good to me. Change you when I get back to New York. I think some chefs had to be mean because the help was indifferent. I was just lucky enough not to have that situation with the men I worked with.

They had it pretty convenient in the kitchen for us. You had a hot oven and broiler ran down the length of the kitchen. First the stove, then the broiler and then you had the steam table. Heat for the steam table came from the stove, just like a furnace. We burned coal in the stove. Regular coal. Only other thing we used for heat was the sterno under the coffee urns. There was a warming area under the stove. We had a big walk-in refrigerator in the kitchen. All the meats would be there. The roast of beef, usually we'd have three of them. Shelves for everything we needed. We'd have the nice sliced ham in this drawer, down below the bacon, next door would be sausages, all very nice. Best meats you could buy. We used ice for everything. Didn't have any kind of mechanical refrigerators on those cars. They'd bring ice on the train practically every four hours. Stop in Albany and we'd ice up. Didn't have to call the iceman, he was right there when we came in. That's the way things worked. Things were there when you wanted them. "How much ice do you want?" They had these huge pails of chipped ice. Kept things like the juice cold. Ice for drinks. Water was in tanks up above. We'd fill them up, too, every time we stopped.

The pantry was right next to the kitchen. That's where the steward was. The serving window connected the kitchen with the pantry. That's where the steward mixed the drinks. The steward didn't do nothing except steward. Mixed the drinks and operated the car. Make sure everything was going smooth. There were six waiters on the car with us. They were rated just like the cooks. First waiter, he was in charge of the pantry. Another one of the waiters was in charge of the silver—polished it up before each meal. Fourth waiter was the linen man. He'd see that we got the right amount of linen, uniforms, tablecloths. Every time you came in, you'd change your uniform. You'd go to the commissary for pants, hats, got as many as you wanted. Coats came on with the provisions. They didn't want any dirty coats on the cooks and waiters. No dirty aprons. We made out a linen slip just like we made out a slip for

In Harlem, Johnnie Heyliger (left) and Henry Sleming, a waiter with Johnnie on the *Century*, look like a pair of wandering troubadours. The year was 1932.

meat and other things. What we put in the linen bag, we'd get back clean.

Everybody had his job and everybody did his job. We could walk through the train before or after the meal was over, but not in our uniform. Walk back to the observation car and have a drink. Let's put it this way: you wouldn't want to walk through with your uniform. Not on a train like that with those people.

Coffee urns were in the pantry. First thing you'd do when you got up in the morning was put fresh coffee on. Table supplies were in the pantry too. Linen closets were in there. Everything was in the place. Very convenient. When we were moving on the road things were set up nice for us. The pots sat in something like a shallow basin. They couldn't slide around. Everything had heavy covers so things couldn't spill around. They had chains on the broiler. If the train went around a curve, whatever was on the broiler could only go so far. On the range they had a rail so the pots couldn't slide off. All the dishes were in closets behind doors so they couldn't come down on us. You have to remember, the roadbeds were perfect in those days, so the train wasn't bouncing around. Our cars were heavy and with those roadbeds we had a beautiful ride. Even so, we had to have those shoes with steel tips on them, just in case anything did fall on you.

We all had our own knives. I carried mine in a bag. Still got it downstairs. French knife, paring knife, Parisian cutters, different knives for different things. They had a place in the yard where you could sharpen your knives. You could come in once a month and bring them to the shop.

Polishers and everything. Sharpen them on an emery wheel. Wouldn't let another man use your knife. Some men would take a knife and do something with it that it wasn't for. Use it to chop anything. Puts a nick in it. Once you got a nick in there you've got it forever. I had a slicer about twenty-five inches long. Nobody got to use that. Used it to cut roast beef.

I forgot to mention that on the *Century* we really had seven waiters—one extra because we had what we called "upstairs service." Sometimes the guests would be down in their rooms and didn't feel like going to the dining car. The porter would give their check to the steward. He'd send the food right to their compartment. That's where the extra waiter came in. You would be surprised what those guys could carry. Train moving, opening and closing doors between cars. You had to learn how to stand, how to brace yourself. I never saw one lose a tray.

Some of the passengers would stay up all night. Not interested in sleeping, just eating and drinking. If they wanted to eat until two o'clock in the morning, you fed them. They'd have parties in the dining car. Somebody like the Dodge Brothers would take two tables. As long as they wanted to party, we stayed. However, after twelve o'clock, if you didn't need everybody, you would send two of the cooks to bed. If there were a lot of people and you needed the whole crew, you kept them and they'd get paid extra. The chef and the steward always had to be there. Oh, they had some parties on those cars! They'd tell the waiter, "Ask chef if he can make us a cake."

I made many a cake on the *Century* and the *Commodore*. No mixes! We didn't have any mix on those trains. We made biscuits, muffins, waffles, that sort of thing on the train. The Pennsylvania Railroad even made all the cakes and pies on the train. They had a stock car on their trains. Had a lot more room for things than we did. On the New York Central we got the baked things from the commissary when we were getting ready in the yard. We'd order what we needed and pick up things along the way when we stopped. We'd get the rolls in Albany that we'd serve for breakfast the next morning. I would make my muffin mix at night so it wouldn't be rough in the morning. You learned little things like that. A little flour, baking powder, stir it up and you'd have it. Same thing with a cake. After you've done it so many times, you don't even have to look. It was quite an experience when you think about it. Being out on the road like that. It teaches you. Prepares you for just about anything that's going to happen and that's been a real help for me in other things.

The last run on the *Century*, we got into Chicago and people were waiting at the gate. Asking us if we had any souvenirs. I told them no, just some menus. One guy asked me if I could get him some menus. I went down and got some. He paid $10 for four of them. That great train ended up in Chicago and we came back on another one. The last trip wasn't sad at all. People seemed to be happy, but I don't know if they were happy because of the trip or because of what they were drinking. It was a beautiful trip. The guests were just giving money away, like it was water. Came by the kitchen and asked me how many men I had in there. I'd tell them four and they'd hand in $40, $50. A beautiful trip. I guess everything has its day.

Although there's only three feet between the rails, the locomotives of the East Broad Top are far from dainty. Engine No 14, built in 1912, steams behind "Buz" Pheasant between trips in the railroad's Orbisonia yard.

JAMES A. PHEASANT
Rock Hill Furnace, Pennsylvania

The East Broad Top Railroad, in south central Pennsylvania, still looks, smells and sounds a lot like 1940. Abandoned in 1956, it reopened in 1960 as a tourist railroad and was spared the unfortunate Bicentennial red, white and blue paint jobs or false gingerbread touches that have ruined some other operations. "Buz" Pheasant is the only man still alive who ran the engines on the EBT when it was a revenue line. He doesn't go down to the railroad very often because he doesn't want them to think they have to let him run the engines. That's a shame because when he does, the engine sounds different. The exhaust is sharper, more accurate, more businesslike. Even the whistle has more authority. The people who run the EBT today are doing an excellent job but you have to give the edge to the man who ran the engine when they were actually hauling coal.

I started out on the East Broad Top Railroad as an engine helper in 1923. Taking care of the engines at night and getting them fired up for the morning run. Made sure they had a tank full of water and a load of coal. Took care of the sand, too. Then later I got on to the job of firing when they had an opening. The railroad seemed to be the only thing you could get a job on around here at the time. I always had to get out and make my own living because my father died when I was about a year old. I worked for the railroad until it went out of business in April of 1956.

It was real busy here when I started. There was eleven hundred men back at that time digging coal in the mines in the mountains around here. We had a miner train. It would leave Rock Hill Furnace at five-thirty in the morning and they ran that one on schedule south to Robertsdale. It was one of the few trains that really ran on schedule. We'd pick up them miners all along the way. Then, that train would stay up there until four in the afternoon and we'd fetch the miners back home. During the stay up there, we'd make up the trains, distribute hoppers and stuff like that to the mines. You'd also pick up the coal and weigh it and get other trains ready. That's about all they had here, the coal and ganister rock. They'd haul that ganister into the brickyards and make firebricks out of it. They had what we called the mail train, too. Combination passenger, mail and freight. They tried to run that on schedule too. Other trains left when they were full. You'd take all the empties into Robertsdale and then you'd fetch the coal into Mount Union. You generally figured either one trip a day from Robertsdale near the south end to Mount Union at the north end and then return, or from Rock Hill Furnace which was in the middle of the line, to Mount Union, then to Robertsdale and back here again.

Mount Union was where our narrow-gauge railroad tied in with the standard-gauge Pennsylvania Railroad. They had a big crane there at Mount Union. Cables ran down from the crane to a sort of a yoke. They'd hook it under the coupler and just lift the car up. The men would have to do some unhooking of rods and things like that, then they'd run the standard-gauge trucks out and put the narrow-gauge trucks under the car. The crane is still there in Mount Union. They could take gondolas, or standard two-door hoppers, through our tunnels but anything bigger wouldn't go through. They could take a standard-gauge boxcar up as far as Saltillo, nineteen miles, but not through the tunnels beyond. The boxcars were just too high to get through. We had two standard-gauge engines that belonged to our railroad to switch the cars around. They had

Narrow-gauge lines were usually built because it was cheaper and they could go places their bigger brothers couldn't. Except for a few instances, they have disappeared. Drew Collier (left) and Jim Pheasant in 1956.

two couplers on them, one standard-gauge and one narrow. One was higher and the other was lower, so they would line up with the right coupler on the car. The yard rails at Mount Union ran inside each other so that both kinds of equipment could use the same track.

I have an idea that the reason they built narrow gauge in the first place was the curves. We had what we called the "Seventeen" Curve. You'd come down a grade and go right around the mountain. It was real sharp and you had to watch your speed on that curve. Standard gauge wouldn't have gone around there without some kind of extensive work. Everything would have had to be bigger and more expensive if it had been standard gauge. The country was awful rough around here and we had some real steep grades. We had to go through nine miles of tunnel through two mountains to get into Robertsdale. I think that was why we kept steam when others were using diesels. They always figured the smaller steam engines we had were proper for this railroad on account of those same tunnels. If they had gone to the diesels, they would have had to make the tunnels bigger. Any diesel engines that could have gone through those tunnels wouldn't have had the power to pull the trains we had. We also had no trouble getting coal for the locomotives, with the mines being right here and all. Had the fuel right in our own backyard.

The biggest problem we used to run into on those mountains was when it was wet or when there were leaves coming down in the fall. You take wet leaves on the tracks in those mountains, that's worse than anything I can think of. You'd get up there and the leaves were falling and it'd get to raining a little bit, not enough to wash them off, and you'd do a lot of slipping. They'd get just like grease. You'd have to be real careful to keep from slipping too much or you'd send your fire flying right out the stack.

They had all the locomotives here before I started to work. Never needed any more. Everything is pretty much the same here as it ever was as far as equipment goes. They did sell No. 6 engine, but everything else here, with part of the railroad restored and running as a tourist road, is just like it was. They only use a few miles of it because the tunnels are in such bad shape, but I think they want to fix up some more of it. No. 6 was one of the standard-gauge engines at Mount Union. They kept all the narrow-gauge engines. Shops are still here, everything like it was.

Our engines were easy firing. They didn't have any arch brick in the firebox, only the big engine, No. 3, had any. The boilermakers had to adjust the front ends to take care of that so it wouldn't cut your fire too hard in front. The engine would be working your fire too hard and put holes in it, just tear it up. We had a regular boilermaker here in the shops, Orlando Halibaugh. You'd tell him what was happening and he'd adjust that front end—we called it "the petticoat"—so that wouldn't happen. Do that about every six months. We had a whole shop then, so everything was taken care of right here. Must have been sixty men working here when things were busy. Had a foundry, blacksmith shop, car shop, paint shop, everything's still here, but the men are gone. Still got some working in there to keep the engines and cars up, of course, but not like it was back then. Anything you wanted done on an engine, you had a book right there in the shop, and every evening you'd mark up what was wrong. If the engine had to go out early in the morning, they'd call men out to repair it at night. They kept their equipment in good shape. You told them something was wrong and it was fixed in a hurry. There wasn't much difference in engines either, only that No. 16, she seemed like she could haul better. She was quicker getting away, had a quicker exhaust. The engines were all made the same, but she was just nicer to handle. As I said, they tried to keep the engines in good shape. They would take one locomotive a year, tear it down and rebuild it. Rebuild it from the ground up. At the end they'd have a new engine, boiler flues, bearing, everything. They were still doing that kind of work when most railroads didn't have a steam locomotive on the whole road.

Of course, the Pennsylvania had lots of diesels coming into Mount Union when they got rid of their steam engines. We'd see them and it did look a whole lot easier to me. No water to look after in the boiler, no coal to shovel. Some of those engineers were even wearing white shirts and straw hats in those engines. If the railroad had kept going, we might have got into them—who knows—but we never had a diesel on our railroad. We used to get kidded a bit by them standard-gauge men; they would call us "the dinkies." They would ask us how our toy trains were running. We didn't mind their kidding too much because we always figured it took a lot more coal shoveling in those big standard-gauge Pennsylvania steam locomotives than we had to do on our engines.

There was generally a three- to ten-cent hourly wage differential between us and the Pennsylvania men because we didn't have to stay away from home like they did. On a railroad the size of ours, it was pretty easy to get back to where you started from the same day. When I went to work as a helper I was making thirty-seven cents an hour, and that was for a ten-hour day. Things got a lot better as time went by, of course. The union helped with that. The union was all right. We didn't have too many problems, though. On a larger railroad there might have been more trouble with more men working on faster schedules, more places for conflicts to occur. In a little place like this we didn't have much conflict between the men and management. We got along pretty good. Everybody knew everybody else and most of us lived pretty close to each other.

We depended on the mines for most of our business and jobs, but I was never inside a coal mine. Never really wanted to go in one. You see, some of them up there in those mountains had props holding up the ceiling only 2 feet 8 inches, maybe 2 feet 10 inches high. I helped cut a lot of props for those rooms before I went on the railroad

and I know how high they were. I didn't want anything to do with that. Of course, the headings were bigger, because they had to run the motors and mules through them. They got loaders later on, but when I started out, they used to have around two hundred mules in those mines. When there was a strike, you'd see all those mules out in the fields. My brother-in-law used to drive mules in one of the mines. The men would work that coal out of those tight little rooms, and then they'd haul it to the surface with the mules. Sometimes those miners would hit streams of water down there and they'd come out soaking wet. One that I think of, Meyers, before there was very many automobiles, he'd have to walk four or five miles to catch the miner train. Both morning and evening. I don't know how them men kept going, getting their clothes all wet and dirty and then walking home in the freezing cold.

When the miners didn't work because of a strike or such, things really slowed up around here, though the railroad would always find the train crews work around the shops or something. They were good about that. That's how they kept men. The railroad used to operate a bus line up here at one time, freight delivery, door to door. Well, come 1927, that's when the big miners' strike was on up here, work on the railroad was slack even in the shops, and I wound up running the buses and the freight truck. I done that, for six years. There wasn't much doing on the railroad and you had to eat.

At the end, they just run out of coal, that's all. You see, one company would be getting over in somebody else's mine. On the other side of the mountain would be another company, and they would be getting into their territory. The mines were just worked out and they'd have to go too deep to get it. Oh, today maybe you'll find a little house mine producing a little trucking coal, but that's about all. It just came on gradually— they'd keep shutting a mine down here and there. You had other things too. It used to be you had three brickyards in Mount Union, but they kept closing down too. It's things like that knocked a lot of men out of work. Not

"They just run out of coal, that's Steninger and Charlie Hooper.

only the railroad but in other types of jobs too. I would have stayed with the railroad if it hadn't stopped, but there wasn't anything anybody could do about it.

Towards the end, the railroad buffs knew we were closing down and they were after anything they could get their hands on. We'd get a written train order, we could hardly get up in the engine for someone asking for the order. You'd be out on the road and come around a curve and there'd be some guy pointing a camera at you. There was always somebody in the yards taking pictures of the engines and equipment. Some of the railroad men had little farms or something they could depend on, but I didn't have anything to fall back on, so I had to get out of Rock Hill Furnace and we moved to Elizabethtown, that's down in Lancaster County. I got a job at the Masonic Home firing the stationary boiler, making heat and hot water for the big home and the laundry and all that. Same way you made

steam on the railroad, but you weren't going anywhere. We burned a ton of coal an hour during the winter in that boiler. I believe they had between six hundred and seven hundred guests in that place at that time. Retired folks. They produce almost everything they need, or they did when we were there. Vegetables and everything. Now, I remember the first summer I went there. I started out with the engineering gang then, and along with everybody else, we'd go out and pick potatoes. I still remember the first day; we picked 3,900 bushels of potatoes. That was harder than any railroading I ever did!

I retired from there May 14, 1970, and came back here to Rock Hill Furnace. If the railroad had kept running, I'd never have left. I enjoyed riding along looking at the countryside, especially in the fall of the year. You had your ups and downs with the railroad, but after all, it was likable. But the coal just ran out, and that was that.

JOHN KRAUSE

all." The crew of the last freight train on the EBT, April 1956. From left to right: James Pheasant, Steve Painter, Drew Collier, Henry According to Jim, Charlie always wore a tie; it wasn't just for the last run.

The engine behind George Kelch is No. 611, one of the famous N&W stream-lined J engines. When this photograph was taken she was in the Roanoke Transportation Museum, but the newly merged Norfolk/Southern Railroad has recently restored her to running order.

GEORGE H. KELCH
Roanoke, Virginia

"They didn't realize what steam locomotives were. They had to be taken away from 'em to make 'em realize." When George Kelch said that he wasn't talking about himself. He hasn't forgotten steam locomotives, or railroading in general. Not many people, even ex-railroaders, have a locomotive headlight in the front yard and four steam boilers in the back-yard. The boilers work and have been used to usher in the New Year with the sound of a steam locomotive's whistle. When a fan trip is operating in the Roanoke area you can be sure that George and his wife, Gladys, are on it. In fact, George might even be running it. He's chairman of the board of the local chapter of the National Railway Historical Society and the Roanoke Transportation Museum. His enthusiasm and interest haven't gone unnoticed. The Roanoke museum has a passenger coach with big gold letters on the side: GEORGE H. KELCH.

My father worked for the railroad, and my brother, and my uncle, all that gang. It was all the same railroad family and I guess that's one reason why we got along like we did. There was ten of us in our family, and when we moved around to visit one another, that's all we ever talked about, railroads, because all of us worked on it. We never knew there was anywhere else to work.

I was born in a place called Brazier, Ohio. The railroad run through there, it was the Cincinnati, Georgetown & Portsmouth Railroad. There was a pond where you could cut ice and store it in the wintertime. The railroad had a big icehouse there, walls two foot thick, and a water tank for the engines. We lived on a big farm near there. I remember running around on that pond with the rest of the children. It's a wonder some of us didn't get run over, what with getting in the way of those trains and railroad men. They used to hoot and holler at us, "You damn Kelch kids, get out of the way!" Ring the bell and everything. I can just shut my eyes and see the stationmaster: "You young 'uns, out of the way."

I started in working as a kid in 1914. By then the CGP was an electrified interurban line and had only three steam locomotives left. My first job was in a substation at a place called Mount Washington—which is all Cincinnati now. I had two large rotary converters in there. These substations ran in unison in the daytime. At night you just cut one of those converters off when the traffic eased up. About one o'clock in the morning you shut down the other. It was my job at night. Thirteen hours I used to work. I'd close them down at night and then start them up again in the morning. I got $1 a night and thought I was doing a big job. I was rich. Most boys around there didn't have a job, but I was a big railroad man.

About that time electricity went into the town of Clare Junction, Ohio, where the Norfolk & Western Railroad had their roundhouse and coaling yards. I was supposed to be an electrician's helper, lugging wires around, and insulators—whatever they needed to get the place wired. I also got a job firing a little old steam locomotive boiler there. I don't remember what class engine it had come from, but it made the juice to light Clare Junction. It was the first electric lights they had there. It didn't take much seeing to. The boiler was about ten times bigger than the generator it powered. Get it full of water and once it was running you didn't have much to do for three hours. Well, that became my regular job and I think I got $2 a night for doing that. When that job was done, I floated around for a while and finally came up to N&W headquarters at Roanoke, Virgin-

ia, in the East End shops, firing stationary boilers.

That was the time that World War I was really opening up. Since the N&W is a coal hauler, business was booming; men were scarce, and they needed firemen—they needed anyone they could get. They knew what I was doing and asked me if I'd like to go firing on the road. That same day I signed up and went firing on the Radford Division. It was 1915. I was promoted to engineer in 1919. I had a time then, because the war was over and they were running us around anywhere they wanted to use us.

It was around that time that we put the engine in the ditch. Me and old man Clayton Lawrence, we had engine No. 348 when they were double-tracking the New River branch. We had two tenders and two little four-wheel cabooses. We were out there a month at a time. The engineers were digging out these granite rocks and dirt and dumping them over into the river to keep the water from cutting into the roadbed—building a dike of sorts. You were paid $3.10 for twelve hours' work at that time. I done the biggest part of running the engine because the old man had a bad leg and he couldn't get around good. The engineer and fireman was supposed to have one of the cabooses to stay in, and the brakeman and conductor had the other. Supposed to sleep in there, but they sure didn't do much sleeping. Just played poker in one of them all the time. They had three brakemen on that job but you never had more than one out working. And, of course, old man Lawrence, he was in there playing poker too, so half the time I'd have to run the damn engine and fire it too. We'd sit around and they'd be loading that rock with those steam shovels. I'd have a pretty good bank on the fire, so I didn't have to do much with it. Sometimes the brakeman would come over and fire a bit for me. We'd go eight or ten miles and then dump the rock. We'd stay out there until it was time to wash the boiler out on the engine, or until something broke down. Only time you'd get off was on Sunday. Lots of times Clayton wouldn't show up on Monday at all, and again, I'd run it all that day. Firing was some job in those days, but I loved getting my hands on that class of engine, getting to run it.

But about our going in the ditch—they had about ten or eleven dump cars out there and everybody was acting crazy; they were trying to get the job done in too much of a hurry. The cars were ramshackle and the rocks would fall off and roll down and get stuck in between the ties. There wasn't any need for ballast in there because so much stone was falling down. Well, one day we were pushing a group of them empty dump cars. I had just put in some coal and was standing on the edge of the tender when I felt the damn apron of the engine rise up. The bot-

A proud father with his two sons, James (left) and George Floyd in 1939. Both sons were on destroyers in World War II, and George had three ships blown out from under him.

tom guide yoke hit a rock and broke off. The yoke kept everything in line. When the rod came down, it had enough slack in it so it caught on another rock. Well, the rod acted just like a cantilever and you couldn't upset an engine better than that. The prettiest upset you ever saw. We were going about three or four miles an hour and I let out a war whoop. Them old-style engines had two top valves and the whistle stuck right on top of the steam dome. They broke off and all the steam got loose. Clouds of it! You couldn't see a damn thing. I knew Clayton was back in there because the engine had rolled over on his side. I thought, Oh my God, he's scalded to death. You couldn't tell anything because of that steam. I jumped back up in the cab and commenced to look and holler, but I couldn't hear a thing. Then I could just make out something, and pretty soon he comes crawling out of there cussing. He came right out of the coal pile, and that saved him from the steam. I gave him a hand but he never stopped cussing. He was a cussing man, old man Lawrence. The only time he stopped cussing was when he was eating.

In the meantime, I started studying. I took up this ICS [International Correspondence Schools] business and studied locomotive design, air brakes, drafting, all of it. I stayed with it, too. When we'd get to the YMCAs on a layover, instead of playing pool or something like that, I'd hunt up a *Railway Age* or whatever books I had with me and study. That's where I got a lot of my knowledge of engines. I wouldn't have minded staying an engineer; you know, they make good money now. I wouldn't have kicked about it too much, but that's not the way it worked out for me. One time when there wasn't nothing doing on the road, they loaned me out to the East End shops in Roanoke, to work as a shop inspector.

I was doing inspecting when the war business broke out again. World War II this time. They asked me if I would accept a job as a locomotive inspector for the War Department. I had already filed for a civil service examination for the ICC. I knew Congressman Clifton A. Woodrum; that helped, so I took the job. I didn't say anything to the railroad about it until the government asked them if they would release me. Of course, during wartime they couldn't do nothing but let me go. So I was working for the government from 1942 until 1950. The first job they gave me was inspecting and running engines on the test track for the Baldwin Locomotive Works over there at Eddystone Station near Philadelphia. There was about a mile and a half of test track there and we would work with the erecting shop while they were putting the locomotives together. When they got one ready to run, all finished, one of us inspectors would go out with it. They'd have a hostler fire for you and you'd run that engine up and down the test track to see how it handled. Then you'd have the hostler run the engine and you'd get out and ride on the running boards and watch the driving boxes working up and down in the frames, the equalizers, the running gear. You could usually tell right away if there was trouble or not. Look for binding, things like that.

There was a whole flock of us locomotive inspectors. They got roundhouse foremen, qualified engineers, master mechanics, anybody like that who knew locomotives. They had to get air-brake men too. Pulled men out of the railroad yards, everybody they could get their hands on. It had to be somebody who had the knickknack of what went on with a locomotive. You'd check out everything—the front heads, back heads, pistons. Look for leaks. All your brakes, piping joints. You'd have to go over all the air lines with a long skinny torch that you'd put through the driver spokes. Any leak would blow that flame so's you find it. You'd have to put three to four hours on a locomotive depending on the size. Usually you could do two engines a day. Maybe one of those Southern Pacific jobs with the cabs in front, in the morning, and an "iron doughboy," a Consolidation for Europe and the war, in the afternoon. Couldn't but one of you use the test track at a time. They kept that shop going day and night. Never stopped.

Then there was sabotage throwed in on top of everything else. By golly, what a time we had with that! They'd be putting a valve in. Of course the head would be off and someone would secretly throw a handful of one-inch nuts in there. When they got ready to set the striking points—that was the cylinder travel—it'd bump those nuts in there. You couldn't get the proper full distance to make the main rod line up. They'd have to take the whole thing apart and they'd find those nuts in there. Slow up the works. The tinners were fellows working on top of the boiler. They put the steel jackets on the boiler. Well, maybe one of them would drop a piece of steel sheeting or a ball of the cotton waste that we used for rags down the injector pipes when nobody was looking. They'd do anything to break things or slow down the assembly. Our security people told us not to say anything to anybody. Just to go on as nice as you please, never let on, you know. Everybody had a badge number and if you saw something, you'd go to the phone and call up the number that we were told to call. Tell them what you saw. When that fellow got off the job, there was somebody who would follow him and see where he went. They didn't want to arrest him on the job. They finally found out who the kingpin was. When they got him, then they arrested the whole damn bunch of them. I think there was sixteen or seventeen of them in all. We were real glad when they got those people.

We also went with a crew when they delivered the engines to the port of embarkation. One time we rolled into Hampton Roads with a bunch of locomotives—2-8-0 Consolidations—and we thought we would head right back to Baldwin. But they told us to take the whole bunch to the docks at Locust Point, Maryland. I heard later that the ship that was coming to get them at Hampton Roads had been sunk by a submarine. They tried to keep our movements secret if they could, so nobody knew exactly where we were going with the engines.

I stayed with that inspection business until the war ended and Baldwin started to slack off. My next job was working for the Reconstruction Finance Corporation. They were in charge of seeing what was going to happen to all of the surplus stuff that was left over from the war. We had 1,300 of these Russian "Bohunks," we called them. They were .2-10-0 Decapods built for the Soviets. Had a fence all the way around the running boards . . . couldn't fall off it if you wanted to. All of them had a big "US" on the tenders. They also had the instructions on how to run the locomotive printed on the tenders. They couldn't use them here because they were Russian 5′ gauge.

In front of his backyard steam boiler, George with son George Floyd, and his son's wife, Dorothy. The steam lines run into George's shop, where he operates several small steam engines. That's being in love with steam!

Another time, I helped put that *Jawn Henry* back together. That was the N&W steam turbine engine No. 2300. The blades came out of the turbine rotor and a mechanical engineer by the name of McFadden and me, we worked together putting that thing back together. We wouldn't let nobody else fool with it because nobody else knew anything about a turbine. I didn't know too much about one myself. But we put it together, put the vanes back in, and it worked. Granted that *Jawn Henry* had a lot of bugs, but what killed it was General Motors. Killed all the steam engines, no matter how good they were. No question about it. General Motors is the one that stacked up all the streetcars out in Los Angeles. Stacked up like cordwood. They talked the cities into taking out the streetcar lines and now there's talk about putting them back in!

I didn't like the diesel engines. You can smell the stinking oil when you start going on a trip behind one. Wasn't anything for the engineer to do, you could fall asleep in one of the damn things. That's why they had to have those dead-man throttles to keep the engineer awake. Very different running steam. Say you've got tonnage. Let's say you've got dry rail. You don't have much trouble. She'll run pretty good if you've got a fireman who can make good steam for you. But if you've got troubles, too much tonnage, wet rail, a bad steaming locomotive, then you've got

to know what you're doing. You start swapping water for steam. Cut the injectors off. Then your water commences to come down in your water glass a little. The steam gets hotter. But if you don't watch it, the water gets to where you don't have but about an inch in that water glass. Just as sure as God made little green apples, the damn injectors are going to start to sputter and start wasting water on you. All these things are going on and you might have to shut down, that's all there was to it. Get some water working and get some back in that glass!

On the N&W the Y-6s were more powerful than the As, but they were a little bit rough in the ride. Those As rode better than anything because the springs were curved more, I think. They'd just float along like you were on water. Like that old Cadillac I drive. The class J and J-2 engines were something. Streamlined. Shame of it is they ended up on freight when the diesels came. One of them was down on the Norfolk Division handling local freight. Was a shame to see that beautiful lady hauling an old freight train when she should have been on that fast passenger run. Just didn't seem right.

There's a place down there between Waverly and Wakefield, Ohio. It was just as straight as an arrow and they had good track at that time. Some of them fellows got to drinking up there before they took that train out and they got that thing really going. They were so drunk they forgot they had that lockbox on there. It was a box they weren't supposed to open, with a tape recorder in it. Recorded how fast you were going. At the end of the run they pried the box open because they knew they were already in trouble. Read that tape at 127 miles an hour! Deep trouble, but they had that engine running that night.

The fastest I ever run, it was on one of them K-2s. I don't know if it was No. 126 or 127. I was firing on train No. 3 one morning between Portsmouth, Ohio, and Williamson, West Virginia. The engineer, Mark Pleasants, had one bad eye, and he smoked a pipe that was upside down half the time. He was cantankerous and didn't feel like running that day. We were about an hour late when I told him, "Run the damn stoker and let me run the engine and we'll try to make up some of this time." I run down through Haverhill and Sheelersburg, and I'm telling you, that engine, it was right around eighty or ninety miles an hour for a while. I commenced to ease it off, you never shut one clear off, and I was still running sixty-five miles an hour when we came down through the yard.

You could run like that because we had the track in those days. Those articulated engines, they used them up in the hills, doing forty and fifty miles an hour, and the engines alone weighed 480 tons. We never had any problems with the road. Now they don't keep up the tracks like they used to. I had a test not so long ago. I took two thirty-nine-foot rails near here and counted fifty-five spikes that had worked up out of the track where you could put as much as one or two fingers under the head of the spike. Amtrak comes down that track at fifty miles an hour? No wonder they have the accidents they do. They thought the diesels didn't need the tracks the steam locomotives did, so they let it go to hell. It went too fast and it got so late they couldn't catch up. You wouldn't believe it, but they quit buying ties on the railroad for a while.

Outside the B&O museum, Clarence Knight stands in front of an old friend, No. 5300. When the railroad bought this class of engines they were called the Presidential Engines. The first of her class, 5300 was appropriately named the "President Washington."

CLARENCE R. KNIGHT
Hyattsville, Maryland

Although he lives in Hyattsville, Maryland, C. R. Knight had never been to the Baltimore & Ohio Railroad Museum, in Baltimore. Looking at engines he hadn't seen in twenty-five years was obviously quite a thrill. His daughter had brought a wheelchair, "in case Dad gets tired," and he gave it a look of disdain. After walking around the displays outside, Clarence gave in and was riding about indoors, "just to rest my legs." One of the displays inside the museum is an animated display which shows how a steam locomotive works. Push the button and the coal lights up red; blue water moves into the boiler; white steam goes into the cylinder. Finally the drivers start slowly to turn. King steam at work in slow motion. Clarence sat watching for a while and then said, to no one in particular, "That boy isn't in much of a hurry, is he?"

We didn't have the diesels long in my career, but I fell in love with them as soon as they came on the Baltimore & Ohio. I had run the gas-electric cars which operated very much like the diesels, so I didn't have any trouble with them. The diesel made a darn nice job. I was just about as much in love with them as I was with the steam engines. It was a pretty hard thing to quit, too, I'll tell you, but when I became seventy years of age, I had to quit that very day or I wouldn't be getting the check from the pension fund. If I'd worked one day over, I would have lost it. I retired when I came into Grafton, West Virginia, with Number 1 on the morning of November 23, 1957.

When they first got the diesels, they split them up so you had to run a steam engine one way and a diesel up the other way. We griped about that for a while. They just said, "Hold your horses just a little bit and we'll get diesels for all of you." The passenger trains had them at first. Those were very nice days on the railroad. I did like to be a bit more presentable. You didn't have to wear overalls like you did in the steam engine, just to keep clean. You didn't have to look like a tramp.

I had the first diesel in our division and I took an interest in learning something about how it worked. I didn't pretend to be a mechanic or anything, but just knowing something got me out of trouble out on the road sometimes. You know those brushes, the things that push down on an electric motor to make the spark and actually make the motor go? Well, them darn things would wear down to a little bit of nothing and then they wouldn't make enough juice. They'd get to wearing down and sometimes you could limp in, but sometimes you'd be out on the road with those long hills and you couldn't make it. You had to do something about it and get it going, or be out there all day and night waiting for help. One day I was hung up on a hill. Now, I'd watched the mechanics put in those spark brushes at different times. I'd seen them do it, but I didn't have the special tools to get into the things in the first place. They didn't want the crew fussing in there getting hurt. I got some cardboard and my fireman had a small hand and he pushed it in there to hold the brush down. I figured if we could push that thing down, there'd still be enough so maybe we could get over that hill and then we could get some help. Gosh, I got pretty near home before it went down on me again. That cardboard finally just burnt out. I told them what I'd done. The superintendent was out there because we were so late, two or three hours at least. He said, "Well, if the railroad had medals to hand out, I'd give you one because I don't think we have another

engineer on this division that would ever have known what to do."

A lot of the men made a big thing about the dead-man brake pedal. You had to keep your foot on it or the train would stop, and that was putting some people out. I said, "You're going to take your darn foot with you on the trip, aren't you?" It was right in front of you and you set your foot right there on it. That's all there was to it. Many engineers seemed to think they was suffering a hardship to do that, but I think they just didn't like the change from steam to diesel and would gripe about anything they could.

The diesel was, like I said before, a much nicer job in some way, but it still took a little something away from you. I was always used to hearing the pounding and the clicks of steam engines. Maybe they did something to my hearing, I don't know. I can still hear them engines in my mind, though. There was something about steam that you

About to leave Parkersburg, West Virginia, on the *National Limited* are Clarence Knight and his fireman, "Bo" Buffey. Clarence didn't dislike the diesels as much as some of the others.

always cherish. Something that was intriguing. I didn't think I wanted anything but steam until after the diesels came. I liked steam engines for a long time and I don't think I'd have been so taken by the diesels if I could have kept my regular engine. I suppose I was one of the last engineers on the railroad that had a regular engine. They made an exception for me. No. 5038, that was her. The master mechanic got her for me, and I shopped that engine three times. How long she'd stay in the shops depended on how heavy the work on her was. Usually a couple of weeks. Why, I even took my engine right into the shop myself. I'd make a trip down there and tell them things I wanted done . . . and I got 'em too! I'd have to put up with running something else for those weeks. I was awful glad when that 5038 came out. Didn't any of the other men seem to care.

Lots of changes on the railroad, I'll tell you. Look at those little fellows we started on, and then look at some of them nowadays. There's no end to it. The steam engine was a thing of the past when I quit, but sometimes I'd have liked to have a steam engine to help me out, even with the diesels. If a steam engine went bad, you could usually fix it up and get back in. Lot simpler than the diesels when you had to figure out what had gone wrong and try to fix it. I ran that Lady Baltimore locomotive. Have you ever seen pictures of her? Beautiful! Ran her on a train from Cincinnati to Baltimore. We had some nice power on the main. Never did have any engines I liked much on the branches. I didn't care for the Mallets either. They had two that we ran. We had twenty-three tunnels and fifty-two bridges on our 104-mile division, and those tunnels were too small for the big articulated Mallet engines. They've taken a lot of those tunnels out now, but then we could only run those

With a generous helping of officials and his wife, Virginia, Clarence has his photograph taken before his last run. The suit jacket that Clarence probably worn for his wife's benefit.

is wearing looks a little out of place with those overalls, but it was

engines part-way on the division because they wouldn't fit through those small tunnels. Once in a while someone would get sick and they'd ask me to go out to Martinsburg, West Virginia, on that run and I'd get one of those engines. I think I did that three times, but finally I said no, don't bother me anymore. I didn't really care for plodding along with those big engines.

I had the yearning for the railroads when I was real young. I guess the whole family did. My brothers Harold and Roy followed me onto the railroad and both of them became engineers on the B&O. Roy was killed in 1946 when an engine blew up. Ovid was a caller on the B&O for a while. The only one who didn't go on the railroad was John, and he went to college and was athletic director at Bethany College in West Virginia. I worked around the freight office, helped in the summertime. I used to mess around when the local freights would come in. Talked with the crews and got to know some of them. That was near where I was born, in Barbour County, near Grafton, West Virginia. Dad was in the sawmill and we moved a lot, following the lumbering. That was all Dad knowed. I drove a team for him and he gave me a man's wages, $1.50 a day, even when I couldn't put the harness on the team. I curried another fellow's team for him and he'd put my harness on for me. Then I got into the sawmill and stuck it out two years but decided I wanted to go railroading. I told my dad, but he said they wouldn't hire me because I wasn't old enough. I told him they'd hire me if he'd sign for me. He said, "If your mother says yes, I'll do it." That's how I started railroading.

Went to work in 1904 on the West Virginia Central, which later was the Western Maryland. It was a pretty primitive affair. When I went to work that was all virgin timberland. In spots the pines was so thick it was like going through a tunnel. They'd just cut enough so you could get a railroad in there. Now, you couldn't find a tree in a mile in some of those places. They gave me a job in the shops, but that wasn't what I wanted. I wanted to be on the road. Sometimes I was a hostler when they needed me. In them days, when a passenger train pulled into a station, the regular crew got off. The hostler had to take the train around a wye with the carmen and put it away. [A wye is a triangle of tracks, useful to turn a car or engine.] Then we'd move the engine to the fire track and change the fire. After we got done with her on the fire track we put her out on another track and dagos shoveled the coal out of a hopper car right into the tender. Later on they had a coal tipple at Elkins to drop it in by gravity, but that was after my time.

One day I told them I wanted to go firing on the road. The master mechanic said, "You're only seventeen years old." I said, "I know, but I was only sixteen when I said I was seventeen, so now I'm saying I'm eighteen when I'm only seventeen, will that work?"

One morning the roundhouse foreman called the master mechanic and told him he didn't have any firemen for a helper engine. "Put Clarence on," the master mechanic said. That was the beginning of my real railroading. I was never actually promoted on the Western Maryland, although I had run on it. You had to fire three years before you were eligible for promotion, but I'd hostled and done

113

all that kind of thing, and they were pretty anxious to see if they couldn't get me to run. The superintendent asked the Interstate Commission if they couldn't use me in an emergency as an engineer. They gave him permission. From then on I didn't do much else. He got his permission to let me work emergency and let the emergency last forever.

Then I quit the Western Maryland. My wife—well, we weren't married yet—was scared to death I was going to get hurt and said I'd have to quit the railroad or she wouldn't get married. I wanted to get married so I quit for about two years. Railroading really was very dangerous in those days. I can recall an awful lot of men who died railroading in my days. I had several wrecks myself, but I was never hurt in any of them. My best friend in the world, my roommate, he was on a train coming down the mountain into Hendricks and the train ran away. It went over Big Run Curve and he went over too. We got orders to go out to that wreck and the whole damn train was in the hollow. We got him out and took him to the hospital and darned if he didn't live. But he didn't railroad much after that, even after he got well.

I had an engine turn over on me one time and had to lie there for about five hours. I wasn't even pinched, but I couldn't get out until the wreck train lifted her. Wasn't speed or nothing like that entered into it, just bad washouts. She fell over on her side, lay against a rock. I wasn't even burned, but they thought they better put the fire out and started to throw water on it. I stopped that. I told them, "I'm not burned, so don't boil me to death."

I was off the railroad from 1907 to 1909, and did a little bit of everything. I worked for a natural-gas outfit on pipelines, and anything else I could get. I ended up in a tin mill. If you ever walked through a tin mill you'd know you never could be any hotter until you go down to that place below. It may not even be as hot there. I never was carried out, like some of the fellows, but when I went out of that mill that first evening I told the foreman to just give me an order for my money. He asked me what I was going to do, and I told him I didn't know but I wasn't coming back to that hellhole again. That was in Clarksburg, West Virginia. We lived with my wife's sister. I got on a train and went to Grafton and got a job firing on the Baltimore & Ohio. Some of the men there knew me from my days on the Western Maryland. I'd decided railroading was what I wanted and that's what I was going to do. That was in 1909, and in 1914 I was promoted to engineer. After I was promoted, I run pretty near a year before I went back to firing.

I'd be back firing for a while and then I'd be running a little. That's when I was in the holdup, I suppose you heard about that. I was firing then on Number One on the Parkersburg branch. The holdup man got on when we stopped for water. First thing I knew about it, we had pulled away from the water tank. I had put the rake in the fire and when I turned I was looking in the dirty end of a gun. He told us to stop where he said, and there was another one of these fellows waiting there. He made me go back and cut the mail car off. Told me to set my torch down, we used them in those days, and not to come between him and the torch. I assured him I wasn't about to do that. They knew more about what was on that train than we did. I didn't know we were hauling money on that train. After the robbers took off, I had to walk back about a mile to the first telegraph to tell the railroad we'd been held up. The police finally got them all and put them in the penitentiary. They had over a million dollars buried in some pipes under a gas station down in Texas. It was my very first night back firing, too.

It wasn't until after the hard times in the thirties that I got a turn I could call my own and be good for it. The last twelve or thirteen years I was entirely on passenger. They put me in a little early because I like to think they trusted me. It could have been necessity, too. One or the other. When the big fellows come around, I hauled 'em. I took Franklin Roosevelt from Parkersburg to Grafton. I hauled Truman a number of times. Those were regular trains, not specials. When Truman was President, he went in that private car, "The President" they called it. It belonged to the Pennsylvania Railroad and I don't know who started using it, but every president I hauled used it. Our B&O president used it until he got a car of his own.

I expect that in the last twenty years I worked there were only about three or four specials went over our division that I didn't haul. They'd call me and ask if I could do better than fifty miles an hour. I'd say sure. I never will forget one time; I was hauling all the company bosses in seven or eight private cars behind me. The last thing the superintendent said to me was, "You go just as fast as you can without turning us over." They had a telephone in the engine and before we got out five miles he came on the phone and said, "Hey, Clarence, you set that speed down a little bit, that's too much." They were raising hell already. I was on good track and I wasn't afraid of it.

I'd like to think I got those special jobs because I never quit studying. Studying right up to the week before I quit the railroad. For instance, we had to study superhead. When they put that on the steam locomotives we had a terrible time understanding what superhead was. I'd go to the master mechanic and we'd sit and talk about the locomotives. He'd make up hypothetical cases and want to know what I'd do. Air brakes. When I went into the air car, I could tell them about the air brakes right along with the rest of them. I knew what I was talking about. The air car was an instruction car about the size of a coach that was fitted up with all the different equipment. Everything new came out, that car got it.

Later I was secretary for the Brotherhood of Locomotive Engineers for my division. You had to send all your reports to the Grand Lodge. We couldn't have done without the union. We'd still be working for $1.25 a day. Perhaps not that bad, of course, but not much better. I know that the first time I got a $5 bill for running an engine for eight hours I thought that was just about the limit. I didn't think it could go much higher. Nowadays what they get, I don't know, but I'm sure it's something big. But the railroad wasn't about to give you anything unless you asked for it. We fought for everything we got and I was in on the fighting end most of the time.

I did think the B&O had pretty good officials. I got on all right with them and I shouldn't have because I was on the committee all the time. I had some tough fights over things like wages. A committeeman has to take up all the grievances from the men. We dealt with the superintendent, or that's who we started with. Sometimes we'd have to go all the way up to the top. They'd bring a private car out of Baltimore with three or four officials or we'd go there. Yet when I quit the railroad I had the highest compliment paid to me by a management man. The last day I worked I was in making out my quitting papers and the superintendent asked me what I was doing. I told him I was making out my final papers. "Well," he said, "you're in good health." I told him about my pension plan and if I didn't quit and went out and got hurt tomorrow, I wouldn't be eligible for anything. I couldn't afford to take the chance. He told me he didn't blame me and shook hands with me. Took me by the hand and said he wished me the best, and told me I was one of the best engineers on the railroad. He came up through the railroad. Started as an operator and worked up to dispatcher, and so forth. We had some fights, terrible fights over committee work. But we were good friends in spite of it. We quit best of friends.

Funny thing, when I left the railroad, I really left it. When they took my name plate off the caller's list I just turned and gave it to my daughter. I haven't been back since. It makes you sick to pass the railroad and see all the old landmarks knocked down. A friend of mine told me that part of the depot at Parkersburg was knocked down, and that building was just as old as the railroad.

Looking more like a young banker than a railroad fireman in the early 1900s.

115

Inverness, Florida, is a long way from the northern routes where Frank Lundy sorted the mails. When he retired, Frank headed south and doesn't want to know about Buffalo winters.

FRANK X. LUNDY
Inverness, Florida

They were the superpostmen, the clerks of the Railway Mail Service. Flipping letters into unmarked pigeonholes in a swaying Railway Post Office car at eighty-five miles an hour, men like Frank Lundy had to know the location of thousands of post offices. Frank had a mental map of delivery routes in every city and town on his run from New York to Chicago. The whole purpose of the Railway Mail was to speed the mails by sorting them in transit instead of letting them lie around a post office. And speed them they did! When the RPOs started to disappear in the 1960s, Frank was asked if he wanted to go into a post office. He said no thanks, and took a civil service job near his home in Staten Island, New York. Considering the mail service today, the post office might think about getting some of those RPO cars out of storage and speeding the mails again.

I was in the railroad wreck up in Corfu, New York, on December 29, 1965. That's between Buffalo and Rochester. A train coming the other way had logs on it; some of them fell off and lodged themselves underneath one of the rails. We came flying along and went right off the tracks. How I wasn't killed, I don't know. I was getting washed up at the time. We had a lavatory at one end of the mail car with a little basin that pulled down, a mirror and a toilet. There was also an ax, pry bar and a folding canvas pail in case you had to dig yourself out of a wreck. I was thrown behind the toilet bowl and wrenched my neck. I was stripped to the waist. It was four o'clock in the morning and 14 degrees above zero out there. I didn't feel a thing.

There was so much going on, and I think I was in shock or something. By the grace of the Lord I wasn't hurt badly, but the car was tilted about fourteen feet from the ground and I was at the high end. The mail sacks all fell down on the other guys at the low end and they buried Artie King. We had to crawl to get out and by then the firemen had put up ladders so we could climb down. I helped Artie and Louis Cohen get out. Louie started a fire with the registry stool. The clerk in charge, Sal Gabin, was hurt, so I was second in command.

The postal inspectors were right on the spot, I'll give them credit for that. This fat local postmaster came down and asked me, "How about the registered mail?" A big wreck and this fat-cat local is asking me about the registered mail! I got one postal inspector and asked him his name and looked at his credentials. I pointed out the fat cat to him, and went over and told that local guy, "Right now you're going to get some men and take the registered mail to your post office. You are now in the custody of that inspector." With that I hopped up on the bus with the rest of the people and I can still picture him calling back to me, "I don't know anything about this." I'm saying to myself, Fat boy, that mail is all yours.

I grew up in Manhattan. Yes, I was born on West 153rd Street between Eighth Avenue and McCombs Place. It was upper Harlem in the shadow of the Polo Grounds. It was a lovely section. We loved it there and I went to the Resurrection School. In those days going to high school was a luxury. Then I started attending night school at CCNY, taking civil engineering, and eventually I graduated from Mechanics Institute in New York City. I never completed college because of my hours. I was working days and sometimes nights. My brother, Dan, went into the mail service when he was 'bout twenty. He was five years older than I. He had about eight or nine years before I

went in. I took two examinations; in those days you had to place about 95 percent to get on a list. It was the Depression and you had guys walking the streets with college degrees. When these jobs came up, they'd stand in line. I took the test November 30, 1935, and I've still got the sheet with a 96.2 mark. I think there were some 180,000 who took the examinations all over the nation. I was on a list for architectural draftsmen with the government at the same time. But the Railway Mail Service was paying more dough than an architectural draftsman at the time. You started as a draftsman at $1,440 a year. Mail started at $1,800. Pretty good stuff, $360 difference at that time, and I was also on the list for post office clerk.

Like I said, it was the Depression and I'll tell you who we had working there in the mail. Guys like Louie Sacks, who had his master's from City College. Then he got a Ph.D. and I heard in the sixties he'd become an associate

The handle that's next to Frank (left) is part of the catcher arm that was used to grab the mail on the fly. With Frank in Syracuse in 1953 is Gil Parker.

professor out on the Coast. Frankie Zukor, he became a teacher of math. He was raised in the Hebrew Orphan Asylum. A lot of our guys had their substitute teaching licenses in those days. Bernie Kaplow, he taught math. None of them could make it teaching regularly because they just weren't appointing teachers. We had guys like Bob McCormick. He held a law degree. Murray Kirschenbaum, he finally got his license to practice law. It was men like that in those days. Smart guys. Wonderful group of men to work with.

Ninety percent of the men who worked for the Railway Mail in those days came from small towns where there was no work unless your father had a farm. Boys from up around Weedsport, Canastota, little towns in upstate New York. They resented our coming in from New York City and they also resented the Jewish fellows. It was one thing to be from New York and another to be Jewish! After a while they found out we were smart boys, no getting away from it. We topped the New York State list. We blended in later on and became buddy-buddy. In an RPO car it's like being on a ship. You're confined in that car and you'd better get along. There was another fellow, Doc Witherall, we had on the New York–Chicago run. On his time off he would preach the gospel, and he was also a chiropractor. When anybody would get hurt he would stretch them out on the newspaper table and go to work on them, no charge. He'd say, "Keep getting hurt, guys, I got to keep in practice." A fine fellow. They were all good men.

The Railway Mail Service was a great business. We griped and we groaned, but we'd get the work done. Many a Christmas I worked. Many a New Year's Day I spent out there because as a junior man you were just a sweat hog. Unless you could get a senior man to work for you, you

The "Railroad Mule Service." The crew of Train No. 39 running to Buffalo in 1950. The men are surrounded by the pigeonholes into which they sorted the mail. Frank's brother, Dan Lundy, is the fifth man from the left.

worked, and that was like trying to get a snowball out of hell. Even my brother wouldn't work for me, and if I couldn't get my own brother, who was I going to get? We didn't mind it, though; there was always a little break of fifteen or twenty minutes at the end of the line to sit down and chat with the guys.

We were known as the West Point of the Postal Department. More appropriately, Railway Mule Service. We'd eat on the fly. Take twenty minutes, push the mail out of the way and sit on the ledge. Some of the guys would come with frozen dinners. They'd put them right in the wash basin. Put a mail pouch over it and turn on the steam from the engine. Go away for five minutes, come back and they'd have their peas, chicken legs, whatever. Five guys would use the same tea ball. My buddy, Kaplow, was our chef with the tea. He'd insist on making the tea just so. He'd always be the last one to use the tea ball and he'd squeeze it with the spoon.

In 1939 I went to Penn Terminal and served my time down in what we called the salt mines, below the ground level. They had miles of tunnels down there. Freight elevators and chutes going down everywhere to take the mail to the trains. They had these four-wheeled cars that they'd pull with little motors. I was a distribution clerk and we made sure the mail was loaded on the train it was supposed to be. We acted as liaison between the post office and the railroads. I'd size up my platforms and see how much mail I had. We figured it in so many sacks to three feet, etc., and how many feet of mail we had would determine how many cars we needed. Storage cars were sixty-footer freight cars, or forty-footers. It got so you could do

that stuff in your sleep. It was up to the railroad to supply us with cars once we got the mail up on the platform. The railroads could be fined thousands of dollars for not providing a car or interfering with the transportation of mail.

To a lot of people, that's only a sentence, it doesn't mean a hoot. To an experienced trucker or railroad man, it was the most serious charge you could prefer against him. We were trained to believe that the public places confidence in that mail box on the corner, and if that confidence is lost, boy, you're in a bad state of affairs.

The first chance I had to go out on the road, I went. You put in less time, but you worked twice as hard. We got $2,000 more a year than the regular post office clerk. The way they worked it was that every six hours and twenty-five minutes you spent on the road was comparable to eight hours in a local post office. I often wondered if it was the speed of the train or what. How they picked out those figures I'll go to my grave trying to figure out. I worked for a while on the Boston–Albany run and then transferred back to New York and accepted a job in the Penn Terminal again until I could bid on the New York–Chicago RPO as a regular clerk. Everything ran on seniority. When your name came up, you got the job. No politics involved.

We had to know our schemes, postal laws and regulations. They would examine you on them every year the first ten years you worked. You studied 320 questions, and they could ask you a hundred. We had what we called our "pony" book. That was what we studied for the regulations. We used to go to Syracuse because the examiner there was a guy off the road and understood our problems. Whereas in New York you had five examiners and you didn't know who you'd get. Leo Kelly at Syracuse was an OK guy. You had to get 97 percent right. That is out of one hundred cards; you were allowed only three wrong.

I mentioned the schemes. A scheme is an area, say, the State of Indiana. The scheme would have maybe over a thousand cards in it to help sort the mail out while you were moving. The cards would list every post office and what railroad served it. They wanted you to memorize sixteen cards a day, but you'd do a hundred if you could. Just concentrate on it and use memory tricks, anything, so you'd get it down. Sometimes you wouldn't even be handling your own assignment. You might be working New York and they would hand you Pennsylvania to study. Boy, that was joy.

This was before zip codes, and you had to know the breaks if you were sorting a long street for delivery. Take Farragut Avenue in Brooklyn. That ran pretty long. Ran through three or four different stations of the post office and you were looking at number 456. You'd have to know which pile or bag to throw it in. They used to say you had to have a weak mind and a strong back to work Railway Mail, but when I think about it, I think it was just the opposite. You'd pound away on a scheme for months.

When I had the city of Buffalo, I got to know it like the back of my hand. I took an interest in the geography. You know the old story about the out-of-towner who comes in and goes to all the sights. I never went to the Statue of Liberty, but all those guys from Syracuse could tell you all about what's out there. I'd go to Buffalo and take all of the bus lines. Learn about the streets and different sections. Go up to the university, out to the Bidwell sections. Go out to the Lackawanna section by the steel mills. Walk around and learn it, talk to the people. I'd be working the mail and have this picture. I still remember it all, and you know how long ago that is.

I enjoyed it especially when somebody would call out an address in Syracuse and the guys living there wouldn't know it. I'd say, "Put it in University Station." How about that, they'd think, a guy from New York City telling us. Then they'd get the book out and look it up. Right again. I'd offer bets but got no takers.

We had to catch the mail on the road. I'm sure you've seen pictures of that operation. When we had the steam engines, most of the guys would wear handkerchiefs around their necks and you'd make sure you had your goggles on. You got a cinder in your eye and if you weren't wearing your goggles, you went to the hospital and didn't get anything if you were off the job. You'd face your back to the direction of the train and pull the catcher down. It had a handle on it and you'd catch the mail and pull it in. You'd have to look out every now and then to see your reference points. There might be a certain barn and you'd know it was only about thirty seconds from there. Every now and then the guys would catch the side of a freight car or something like that. They were mostly wooden then and you'd pull in a little lumber. If you missed a catch you'd make out a report. You'd say it was snowing, even in the middle of August, or raining so hard you couldn't see, or the sun was in your eyes, at night no less!

When we were working with steam engines, we had what they called the water pans between the rails. The engines would scoop up water for the boilers from them on the fly. They had one of those pans right before we got to Poughkeepsie. One day I was helping Walt Byrnes on the newspapers. I was supposed to close the doors before we went over those pans. Well, I forgot and left the back door open and we went flying over that thing at maybe sixty-five or seventy mph. He happened to be back by the rear door and he got some shower bath. He started cussing me out. I said, "Hey, you're from upstate and that's probably the first bath you had in a year. You're lucky I'm here." I was only a sub at the time and he didn't talk to me for the rest of the trip to Syracuse.

When Train 199 got into its famous holdup, at Johnson's Point in 1940, I wasn't aboard, but I knew two of the fellows who were. Johnson's Point is where the Bronx connects with Manhattan in the Marble Hill section. The train slows down there and there was usually a policeman up above the spot on a bridge. He'd wait until the train went around the bend and up the Hudson. According to the newspaper reports, that policeman was not on the bridge that particular night. The robbers had machine guns and they covered the engineer, conductor and brakeman. Made them stop the train. Then they put the gun into the mail car and said, "No nonsense, put up your hands!" Inside all the Railway Mail cars they had these grab bars. They ran parallel to the sides of the car. When you heard the air go on for the brakes, you would reach up, and if there was a crash, you'd be swinging on the bars instead of being thrown down the car. The holdup men handcuffed my friend Brooks Hall right to one of the bars.

Then they started shouting at Louie Wyler, who was the clerk in charge. Louie was facing the other way and was very hard of hearing. He was in World War I and something had happened to his hearing. He didn't see any of this until he finally turned around and he was looking down at this machine gun. He just about collapsed. The robbers grabbed a couple of sacks of mail, but fortunately they didn't take any registered mail, where you can have new cold cash that the Federal Reserve is sending to the local banks along the line. Well, they grabbed the sacks which usually contain parcel post and newspapers. Nobody got hurt and the train went on. We'd always kid Brooks later. Ask him where he kicked off the registered mail. "When are you going to go back and get it?" we'd ask.

In 1965 they started to decimate the lines and knock the mail cars off the railroads. The department head, Don Horton, offered me a field service job in the New York City area, supervising this and that and I said no thanks. After being out on the road and doing my job and not having anybody breathing down my neck, I figured I wasn't going to wind up in any post office and become a prisoner again and listen to some political nincompoop who didn't know his kiester from a tennis racket. We knew the laws, the ins and outs; transportation nationwide, we knew it. The whole bunch of us took pride in our work. We had to do everything. It was really a traveling post office. If a guy came up to the car and said, "I want a two-cent stamp," we had to give him one. You signed for stamps and you might not use them for six years. You still had to have them. The guys did everything. It was beautiful. Well, rather than do anything else I took my retirement, in 1968.

Although he's the youngest man in this book, Frank Bunker ran his share of steam engines. The Canadian railroads used steam longer than the American, and Frank spent over seven years in the right-hand seat.

FRANK J. BUNKER
Toronto, Ontario

The job has changed and Frank Bunker doesn't like it. Standardization of equipment, computerized operations and radio communications have all taken responsibility out of the hands of the engineer. With the long trains they run today, he still has to know what he's doing, but it's a different railroad. In the days of steam, an engineer might try to pick up some time by making a run for a siding ahead of another train. If he made it, fine; if not, he was in trouble. Might even spend a few weeks out of work. However, that was what brought these men to this work. It was the feeling that somebody wasn't looking over his shoulder while he was working, that he was in charge. Frank feels that a lot of the old-timers he worked with wouldn't want the job today. "They sure could get away with a hell of a lot more than they could now."

The old guys were great. They had a certain slant about things. The younger guys, they have a whole different point of view. In the old days there was so much more going on. They had so many stories, so many wild things happening. When you'd go on work trains, they used to give you two vans, one van for the engine crew to sleep in. We call 'em vans up here, but you call them cabooses. When you were sitting around while the cranes were working, the old hogger'd tell ya, "Go back and clean the van up," or something like that. You'd go back, and you'd soap all the floor and scrub the van out. Then one guy got the bright idea of pulling up after he took water in the tender, pulled the caboose up next to the spout and cracked the cupola window open and let the water run in for a while. Open the doors and that just cleaned everything. I remember one young guy got up there on the east end, pulled the spout down and the goddamn thing got wedged, the shut-off handle got stuck in under the window eave. Of course the force of the water, *bam!*, shut both doors. He's hollering like hell, trying to get somebody to come help turn the water off. The old van was damn near three quarters full of water by now. It was comical because wherever there was a leak around a door or a keyhole, water was shooting out in streams. The old hogger's lunch pail was floating on top inside, and it got kind of soggy. The kid was scared to go near the engine all the rest of the day.

I can remember some of the old guys I worked with. When you climbed up on the engine you'd never speak to the hogger until he spoke to you. I remember one looking me up and down and climbing up on the stoker housing to point up to the pressure gauge. "Here's where I want it. Not there or not there, right here." He put his finger right where he wanted it. "And don't let me hear them pops," he said, "either." Sometimes at night, working switchers, you felt sorry for the guys on the ground, brakemen working in sleet, rain and cold. There was a young fellow climbed up on our engine one night, oh God, it was cold. The old bugger running the engine said, "What do you do around here, son?" Hell, he'd been looking at that kid all night.

The kid says, "I'm the head-end man here. I'm the switchman."

That engineer looked him right in the eye, and he says, "Ya know, switchmen belong on the ground, not on the engine. Git!"

The kid looked at me, and I said, "Oh, goddamn, the guys's frozen."

"You shut up," the hogger said to me, and to the switch-

man, "and you git." So the poor kid, he had to climb back down the steps into the cold. Kids today, you told them that, they'd say, "You go to hell!" Not then you didn't. Then they could get away with a hell of a lot more than we can now. He'd sit there, that old engineer, he'd chew tobacco, and his favorite pastime was to try to hit the switch handles with tobacco juice.

It was a lot different then. If you were starting a job at nine o'clock, you thought nothing of being down there at eight. An hour before you were even getting paid on that job. Wipe her down, make sure of the coal and water, put the injector on, cut her real fine, and you'd get the old steam coming out of the sprinkler hose and wash her all down clean. If you were sitting around for five minutes with nothing to do, you always had a piece of waste in your pocket and you'd be wiping her down. The Canadian Pacific, they always were noted for their spit-and-polish when it came to the steamers. The nice maroon and black, trimmed in gold, and all that sort of thing. You could see your face in those boilers, and they'd polish the bell with Brasso. I guess everything changes with time.

That is not a steering wheel in front of Frank Bunker in this Canadian Pacific cab. Some CP engines used a wheel to move the reverse mechanism instead of a lever. Most engineers found it easier to use than the Johnson bar.

I was born too late, I know that. I'd like to have been retired about 1960. Things like kids throwing rocks at trains today. It's not even as bad this year as it's been in others. One guy in Chicago, a brick smashed the window and the glass went into his neck. He bled to death before they got him anywhere. Another guy got seventy-some-odd stitches from glass. I think that a lot of it was that in the old days the window was open, and you waved. The kids waved back and all that, but today the window is closed and half of the crews are no more interested in railroading than if they worked in a factory. I got to admit it, I wouldn't be on the railroad today if it hadn't been for the steamers. Used to spend hours around the tracks watching for this train or that.

I grew up in the east end of Toronto, and a guy I chummed around with, his old man was a captain on a lake boat. So when I was sixteen or so, I made a couple trips with him. I worked on the boats, I guess it was a year. I liked it, but it wasn't what I really wanted. You'd go into East Chicago and you'd sit there at that drawbridge watching the trains switching and running around all the steel mills. I wanted the railroads so much I quit the boats. I started railroading in '42 and fired for ten years before I was set up as an engineer. We used to have to make six trips on the stoker and six on a hand-fired engine before they'd let you go firing on your own. I got to know what I was doing because when I was working the ash pit I'd go in and help the guys lighting up the engines, which helps you learn how to fire. The whole thing with a hand-fired engine

Ex. CP engine No. 1057 is owned by the Ontario Rail Foundation, a nonprofit operation that runs steam excursion trains along the Georgian Bay in northern Ontario. Ontario Rail depends on volunteers and they have a good one sitting in the cab running their engine in this photograph.

is to handle the scoop right. Keep your fire even.

During the war I went overseas for two years as a dispatch rider on a motorcycle. Belgium, Holland, and then we went into Germany. Then they asked for volunteers for Burma. I could see by the way they had blasted Germany that Japan wasn't going to last long. We were going to come home here, get a month's leave and then go to Kentucky for a month's jungle-warfare training. Like I said, we figured it'd be over by then, so we volunteered. We were here at home when Japan gave up, so it was a good move. Then I went back on the railroad, ran steam for about seven years, and diesels from then until today. While I was away, the first diesels had come. The passenger units came in first, on the name trains, then the freight. Then the steam started to go. Toward the end they were letting the engines go downhill, not doing any more maintenance than needed. With the steam leaks in the winter, you couldn't see all the time. It was late '60 that the last one went out of here. With a few working another two or three years in scattered places.

Of all the steam engines we had I think I liked the Hudsons, the 2800s, the best. But mostly we had the 3100 and the 3101, which were the only two Northerns on the Canadian Pacific. They were on Trains No. 21 and 22. I never run the job with those engines, but I fired it steady. Them 3100s were good machines, but they really had just one speed. You'd give 'em so much throttle and then forget about it because you weren't going to get any more. We went out of here once and a guy got on and rode with us; he claimed he was the guy who designed them. He said that the whole trouble was the valves weren't set properly and they were just fighting themselves all the time. I remember, we used to go down on Train No. 22 and we'd pull into Cobourg and the Canadian National train, he'd be

right in there next to us. I think it was their Train No. 16 used to come in there, and he had one of their 6200s. Overnight sleeper train to Montreal, same as ours. Running on parallel tracks, sometimes we'd get out ahead of them, other times he'd get out first. But no matter what we'd do, we couldn't stay with him. He'd just walk away from our 3100s. Oh, we'd try but those engines had their own speed built in, as I said before.

I remember Old George Ward, he was a good old soul, and he was on there steady as engineer, like me as fireman. One night the 3100 was in for service, so we got the 2825, one of those new Hudsons from Montreal. We left ahead of 'em that night, and we were going over the road when the CN guy came by on his 6200. He gave us the old toot, too, and pulled the whole train by us. The flagman on the tail end, he gave us the old highball and a big salute. Old George, he walked over and he's standing behind me, and he said to me, "We've been looking at their hind end for a lot of trips. We've got the machine to do something about it tonight, so let's do it." So I says, "Go to it, George." He sat down and started to give her more throttle, and you could just feel that old girl nestle right down while we started after that CN train. Finally we caught up with the van and we gave the flagman a *toot, toot!* We went by that train and got up to the engine. He seen us coming, and it was funny, 'cause soon as he seen us he dropped her down. Our engines would take a lot more mauling than theirs would. We got the engine by him, and by this time we're going through Brighton, oh jeez, are we going! George looks at his watch, and, Christ!, we're ahead of time. So we had to wind the brake on her and we pretty nearly stopped at Wark. We killed the time there, then came down the hill into Trenton, stopped, got off and walked back. We used to lay there for an hour or two and then go back on 21. We ran into our master mechanic, Bob Grinton, and he says, "What were the pair of you buggers trying to do?"

George says, "What's the matter?"

He says, "What were you doing at Wark?"

George says, "Oh, I thought the tender box was running warm, so I slowed her up so we could climb down and take a look at it."

Bob looks at George, and says, "I was sitting in that first coach there, and I was cheering all the way!" They were a good engine, those 2800s, and they could really run if you wanted them to.

You know, you could get two engines, put them beside each other, you couldn't see a bit of difference. But get them on the road and you'd find out which one was the better engine in a hurry. The 3000s, the Jubilees, they were the high-wheel jobs, eighty-inch drivers. They were built for a lightweight train, to run between Toronto and Windsor on the Chicago train. Then they would really do the job, but when they started tacking sleepers on, things weren't so good. They could still run, though, once you got going. We were due out of here at ten P.M. but when Chicago or Detroit was playing hockey here, or if the Canadians were going to Chicago after a game, they used to hold our train for them. The teams had their own sleeper. We'd start out of here and then on the other side of Woodstock, we'd climb up a hill and then it was flat, straight, lovely track. Well, honest-to-God, out there them things would really go. I often wonder how fast we really did get going, because we had no speedometers. The New York Central steam engines that ran into here, their Hudsons, they had speedometers, and that's the only time I ever actually seen how fast we were going, unless you wanted to clock it with your watch. We used to go down through Burlington with them and I've seen them at ninety-nine miles an hour, a hundred a lot of times, and I knew we were running those 3000s just as fast out there. We used to have only fifty minutes from Toronto to the station at Hamilton, and besides that, a stop at old Sunnyside—which is gone—and, by God, nowadays the trains take an hour and ten minutes without the stop. Steam engines would really run. Those railroad magazines with their speed surveys always made me laugh. They would go by schedules and stuff, and they don't know how fast anybody was actually going out there.

I always figured that we're in a good position over here in Canada. Not just railroading, but everything. Over here we could sit back and watch you in the U.S.A., you'd come up with something new. You guys'd test it out and everything. Well, that's ideal. Then the Canadian roads'd go for it, and it would work. There was so much of that. The thing that used to amaze us here was those New York Central engines. You'd get up in the cab of their Hudsons and there'd be two valves for everything—backup valves, everything cramped in with extra stuff of all sorts. Of course by that time the tags were off everything and you'd say, "What the hell's this one or that one?" We'd turn a knob and pretty soon the water scoop on the tender would be going up and down. Something like that. We knew where everything we needed was, but it was those extra ones that'd throw you.

When I came back from overseas and went firing again down at Smiths Falls it was all freight-and-passenger runs, a good job. We used to run west to Trenton and then we'd cover what they called the K&P, which was the old Kingston and Penbrook, or "kick and push." That was some road! We ran a mixed train. We'd take a couple of freight cars and a passenger combine—baggage and passenger—and we'd jog along. I imagine twenty-five or thirty miles an hour'd be top speed. Everybody along the line, they all knew us. We'd let people off at their houses. At fishing places they'd catch a nice fat trout and hook it up to us in the engine. Everybody knew everybody and we used to stop for dinner, sit on a bridge, and fish. I never caught anything, but we'd sit there and nobody seemed to worry. The passengers would come out and sit too, and talk with us, enjoy themselves. I've seen them get down, get an axe out of the combine and help us chop a tree that'd fallen on the track. Nobody seemed to worry about much then. Nice people. The road's all gone now. There's trucks and cars going over where it was then.

Some great things that happened in those days, I'll tell you. One Halloween night we were coming down from the north with a 2300. There was a full moon. We were running as first Train No. 88, with second section 88 right behind us. We knew damn well he was right on our ass. So we were making a high dive to clear the line for No. 3, the *Dominion* going north. Jesus, we were coming as hard as she'd turn a wheel! Down through what we call the Humber—you come down a dip on a curve, and come up the other side. Just as we came around the curve, all of a sudden there must have been at least a dozen cattle on the tracks. Some kid had let them out, a Halloween trick. Well, what could we do? We hit them. Holy Christmas, one cow went underneath the train and broke loose the air-brake hose between the tender and the first car. Well, soon as we stopped, the tail-end brakeman, Mort Morris, he grabbed his flag and he was racing back like he was supposed to, because he figured the second-section train was making a dive just like we were and could be smashing into us in a few minutes. With no block signals, he had no way of knowing we were stopped. He'd have to flag him to a stop. Well, the head-end brakeman, he hits the ground too, and right away, *bing!*, he's got the air hose connected back for us. So we couple her up, get the air, whistle to start and away we go. Well, the tail-end men, they haven't a clue what the hell's happening up ahead. All they know is the air's gone, we hit something—hit a car maybe. Well, this brakeman was way back when he heard us whistling that we're leaving. Too late for him, the conductor back there, he didn't dare pull the air brake on because he knew we were trying to get the hell out of there. So, this poor brakeman, he started hoofing it down the track. He was walking along and he heard these moans. It was dark, remember. I guess he panicked and started to run. He don't know about any animal in the middle of the track and he hit it. Well, he fell down, got up and was feeling around for his damn lamp when he got into this cow. At that last straw, he said he just turned around and started running and he ran up that track all the way into Bolton. It was comical. It was sad about the cows, but he come in there and he was covered with blood. I see him today and he still laughs.

Things have changed a great deal on the railroads since the *Royal Blue* ran on his B&O. Today, on a platform in New York's Pennsylvania Station, Jervis Langdon stands in front of an endangered species, a passenger train.

JERVIS LANGDON, JR.
Elmira, New York

When Jervis Langdon was named Railroad Man of the Year in 1970, one of the panelists who voted for him said, "His candor and willingness to attack publicly the shortcomings of the industry are a refreshing contrast to many executives." Mr. Langdon probably inherited that candor from his great-uncle, Mark Twain, who wasn't afraid to attack shortcomings when he saw them. Twain spent his summers writing at the farm where the Langdons live today in Elmira, New York. The 1960s weren't pleasant times for high railroad executives. Mergers, bankruptcies and deteriorating passenger service were just some of the problems that men like Jervis Langdon had to face. The B&O, Rock Island and Penn Central had them all. When other people were giving up on the railroads Mr. Langdon was bringing new solutions to their problems. As another panelist put it, "At an age when most men are retiring, he has just begun to fight."

In the old days railroad people, particularly in train and engine service, were kind of a superior race. Even today this is often true. Sometimes it was smart to let the general chairman, who was a labor man, come up with the answer to a management-labor problem. Bill White used to run the Lackawanna and he was president of the New York Central for a while. He was a great friend of mine, and we used to talk about just that—how he could often trust the labor people to arrive at fair results. It wasn't always in favor of management, but then, management wasn't always right. In those days the trainmasters and division superintendents really ran the railroads. A lot of them were former train and engine service people. It was quite different than it is today.

The experience of Conrail, the first five years after they took over, shows how things have changed. There was all that government money, and some of the people running it had had no railroad employment at all. They moved in there without railroad experience. There's a language in this industry and you can tell in a minute if a person is a railroad man or not. These people didn't have it. What happened? By the carload, young consultants were brought in from business schools. This is one of the reasons why during the first five years Conrail had such a disastrous showing. Several of the Conrail general managers were good friends, and they told me that many of these kids, at high salaries, would come to see them with all the figures in the book, but no understanding of the real world; and it was worse than if they hadn't come at all.

These M.B.A.s did not seem able to come to grips with actual problems. Too much theory. Figures may point a direction, but when you put everything on the basis of what's been spit out by a computer, you can get fooled. There's a sixth sense about how to handle a railroad problem, and it doesn't come from getting a master's degree in business administration at Harvard or any other place. It comes from actually working on the railroad, rubbing your nose in the situations that actually happen, and having close working relations with the shippers paying the bills. This last is critical.

I worked for the Rock Island for a while. That was a highly marginal operation with the lowest traffic density of any railroad in the West, and no big industry on line. In and out of bankruptcy. We couldn't get operation supervision, even if we wanted it, from any college or university. We took young men who came up as brakemen and firemen, out of train and engine service, and promoted the best of them up to trainmaster and division superintendent. I

think, all in all, that it was a superior group of people.

One of the best of them, Bill Thompson, became general manager in record time. He did a magnificent job. And I really should commend the Harvard Business School because in those days George Baker, the dean, was a great friend of mine. In fact, George said he'd make a special deal if we'd ship some of our bright boys, two or three, up to that special executive training program of theirs. It was designed for people destined to be presidents or executive vice presidents—top jobs. Bill Thompson was up there at Harvard for three months, and he was elected president of his class! He'd never been to college. He is now a top operating officer at the Burlington Northern. I only mention this because a lot of people despair that the railroads are going down and the bright boys of the future are avoiding them and don't want any part of them. That just isn't so from my experiences with these fellows.

Even at this age, Jervis Langdon knew that he wanted a railroad career. Railroading was a father-and-son occupation, and the executive level was no exception. With him is his younger sister, Polly.

After I'd reached retirement age I was asked to be a trustee of the bankrupt Penn Central. The operating problems over there were made even worse when many of the supervisors, if they had a chance to get a job on another railroad, would grab it. The result was that we were badly short-handed, particularly in the engineering department. I said, "Let's go to the engineering schools and see if we can recruit about seventy or eighty kids to come into the operation." Everybody said that ours was a bankrupt railroad and that young fellows might be interested in the Santa Fe, or some rich railroad, but that they would not come over here. It turned out we couldn't keep those boys away. We had more applications for those jobs than we knew what to do with. Great kids! I met them all and while I don't say this was true of all of them, many had railroad backgrounds. A brother, father, uncle or grandfather. Some of them were fourth generation. You'll find that the railroads will never have any trouble recruiting boys into the business as long as there are railroad families around. The railroad business is in their blood and that's all they want to do.

For myself, I never thought of doing anything except work for the railroad. My father was in the Lackawanna Coal Company, which, in the early days, was part of the Lackawanna Railroad. Before that my grandfather was president of the Clearfield Bituminous Coal Company, which had its own railroads in Pennsylvania. My great-grandfather had several bituminous-coal properties, also in Pennsylvania. They all regarded themselves as closely identified with the railroad business. My uncle was the president of the Lehigh Valley Railroad, and when I was in school, I'd find out when he was going to be in Sayre, Pennsylvania, where the Lehigh's shops were. One way or another I'd manage to get down there and be with him the day or two he was in town. Sometimes I'd get a ride on an eastbound freight train and come back on another. I attended undergraduate school at Cornell and when I was graduated, I went to work for the Lehigh as a clerk.

I was very fond of the Lehigh. My first job was at 6 Broadway (the Produce Exchange Building in New York City) in the office of the foreign freight agent, checking the billing on trainloads of export grain coming down from Canada. Then I was transferred as a clerk to the office of the operating vice president at 143 Liberty Street. I lived at the corner of Thirtyninth and Lexington in a room with a classmate of mine at Cornell who was with the telephone company. We got $20 a week and ate our meals at Childs. You'd get a meal for sixty or seventy cents and the reason they were so cheap was because there was no meat. We'd live on that until my mother and father would come down on a weekend to see a play and they'd take us out to dinner, and we'd have a real meal.

My uncle told me, after I'd been at the Lehigh Valley for a year and a half, that if I wanted to get ahead faster it would be smart to go back to law school. I took time off, returned to Cornell for a law degree and then came back to the Lehigh as a law clerk. I went right into a lot of litigation in which the Lehigh was involved before the Inter-

Lieutenant Colonel Langdon (left) and Major Edward Allen in Assam, on the India/Burma border in 1942. Although not on duty as a pilot, Langdon says, "I made twenty-three trips over the Hump, often in the right-hand co-pilot's seat. We were a long way from Washington."

state Commerce Commission. There was so much work to be done, it was coming out of our ears. On the important ICC cases, I carried the chief counsel's briefcase and sometimes wrote the briefs. We were also involved in the New Jersey tax cases of that period. All the railroads there were being taxed at a rate which was four and a half times the rate of the next highest state. Jersey was living off the railroads, particularly Jersey City under the regime of its famous boss, Mayor Frank Hague. We worked on that for a long time and finally succeeded in enjoining the collection

of those taxes—temporarily, at least, in federal court. Then the New York Central asked me to come up to them at twice what I was making on the Lehigh and do essentially the same type of work before the ICC—rate cases.

I was old enough to realize that I shouldn't stay at the Lehigh. If anything, the dice were loaded against me because my uncle would make sure I didn't get any special favors. So I went to the Central and worked on many problems related to ICC regulation, freight rates, extending and abandoning lines, service orders, operating contracts, and so on. It seemed as though every aspect of the railroad business was subject to regulations, and a so-called commerce counsel, which was my title, had a chance to see and study and deal with almost every phase of the overall operation.

Next came the Chesapeake & Ohio, and again I was asked to do essentially the same thing for them, at twice what I was getting on the Central. I was very fond of the Central, but I couldn't get them to match what the C&O was offering. This was in the Great Depression, and the C&O was a rare thing at that time—a very prosperous railroad. I moved down to Richmond and tried commerce cases for them.

Then I was asked by the general counsel of the C&O, who was in Cleveland, to move out there and represent the railroad in the reorganization of the Erie. The C&O in those days had a majority stock interest, strangely enough, in the Erie, and one day in 1938 the Erie surprised everybody and plopped into bankruptcy. The C&O had made a large investment in the Erie, I think $70 million or $80 million. I worked on that Erie bankruptcy case for over two years and the war was coming along and traffic was begging to build up again. It was pretty easy to reorganize and the government wasn't wasting any time. Usually common-stock holders are wiped out in bankruptcy reorganizations, but we worked out a plan which allowed them to participate by getting new stock at a ratio of one share to five old shares. Working with the principal creditors (insurance companies and New York banks) we sold that plan to the ICC, and the C&O was delighted. The five shares were really worth nothing at the time of the bankruptcy but this one new share the common-stock holders got, with the increase in business, was worth something, and if they lost a little in the deal, they really came out pretty well, about fifty cents on the dollar.

Then the C&O asked me if I'd go in and understudy the head of the traffic department, so I became the assistant vice president of traffic. That was in early 1940 and I worked at that job through 1941. But I simply couldn't keep from volunteering when the war came along. I had learned how to fly in the thirties (fifty years later, I still fly) and tried hard to get in as a pilot but I couldn't pass the 20/20 eye test, or even come close. Instead the Air Force put me through officer's training school in Miami and then sent me to the China-Burma-India theater. I was there over two years.

One of my jobs was traffic manager for the "Hump" operation, flying supplies from India over the Himalayas to China. It was my responsibility to get the C-47s, C-46s and C-87s loaded with supplies for General Stilwell, and with bombs and gasoline for General Chennault's Fourteenth Air Force over in China. We had a large labor force that came from Cochin State in southwestern India to load the planes, and I had two or three officers at each of the fields. When cargoes got over to Kunming, in Yünnan, and the other fields in western China, I had to make arrangements with the Chinese to deliver the material further on in certain cases. At many of the fields we could make direct delivery, but certain Chennault units were based at forward strips beyond the round-trip range of our transports. When you had to have the Chinese make overland delivery by broken-down trucks you were lucky if fifty percent got through.

From my job as traffic manager I was moved over to head the planning for an expanded Hump operation. From an average of ten to twelve thousand tons a month, Washington wanted to go up to sixty or seventy thousand. I was told to find more airfields and make plans to double or triple the operation. I spent the better part of a year checking out potential fields for strips in eastern Bengal, and the plan we finally devised was actually adopted by the Air Transport Command. That's the one plan I've ever been in on that was carried out to the letter. You make plans all the time in business, but that military one was actually implemented and we felt very good about it.

Previously, my commanding general had been transferred to the Southwest Pacific Wing of the command, and I followed him later. There the operation was entirely different. We had seventy-five or eighty C-47s which were General MacArthur's air transport unit in the Southwest Pacific Theater. Whenever there was any need for air transportation of the ground forces, along with troop carrier units, we supplied it. We reported directly to MacArthur's headquarters, and as they moved toward Japan we followed them. We were doing that until the war ended. Although most of the flying was over the water of the South and Southwest Pacific, we never lost an airplane.

After the war I didn't go back to the C&O. I didn't have any idea what was going on back in this country, but I had gotten a couple of letters saying things weren't the way they had been on the railroad. The financier Robert R. Young had taken control and he had fired the president, George Brooke, whom I was devoted to, and also my former boss, Robert Tunstall, the general counsel. Four or five other close friends of mine had also left. I was offered and took a job as special counsel for all of the southern railroads. My job concerned any problem before the ICC where those railroads had a common interest. If, say, the Southern and Seaboard were fighting each other, I didn't have any part of that dispute. On the other hand, if the southern railroads as a group were fighting the northern railroads as a group (as they constantly were doing in respect to interterritorial freight divisions), I'd be deeply involved in the litigation. There is nothing like a divisions controversy to open your eyes to the pathetic condition of the railroad industry in its continuing inability to resolve its own internal disputes. The railroads, instead, run to the ICC with their dirty linen rather than set up machinery for arbitrating these purely industry problems.

A senior in law school at Cornell University, 1930.

Then in 1956 the Baltimore & Ohio wanted me to come

over as general counsel and I remained in that position until I was made president of the company in mid-1961. It was a bad moment to start, in a way, because in 1961 the B&O was heading for a deficit of $31 million and everybody thought it was going into bankruptcy! But the next year we were in the black and the next year after that (1963) even more in the black. Earlier, the C&O, my former employer, had come into the picture. They had acquired a lot of B&O stock and were applying for the legal authority to control us.

Back in the mid-fifties was the first time that we heard any mention of what later became the Penn Central merger; from that date on, merger talk was commonplace. On the B&O we had always said to ourselves that if we merged with anybody, we'd rather be with the C&O than anybody else. It was a railroad that looked and felt right to us. We said at the time that if there were going to be two systems in the East, the B&O should go with the C&O and we ought to include the New York Central. Then the Pennsylvania could go with the Norfolk & Western, including the Wabash & Nickel Plate, and so forth. Good competition, everything going for such a solution. Had those mergers actually taken place, if the mergers in the East had gone forward in that way, we would never have had a Penn Central and all that followed. The reason? Both big new railroad systems would have access to the all-important southern bituminous coal. The volume of high-grade coal originating in southwestern Virginia, southern West Virginia and eastern Kentucky would easily have supported the two eastern rail systems.

There's all kinds of stories as to why it didn't happen that way. I don't think anybody knows for sure. For one thing, Cyrus Eaton, then chairman of the C&O, was not enamored with the New York Central, to put it mildly. The justification for creating the Penn Central, in the words of the Pennsylvania Railroad people, was that instead of half of the east-west traffic using the Central's water-level route, all of it would. It was as simple as that. They said all the freight ought to be up on the water-level route and avoid the Pennsy's grades through the Alleghenies. Well, they made some mistakes in that. In the first place, the water-level route is sixty miles longer. In the second place, the winters up there are more severe, and finally, the grades aren't nearly the problem for the diesels that they were for the steam engines. I heard Mr. Jim Symes talk about a Penn Central merger in the early fifties at Harvard. We would go up there once a year for a confab with George Baker and I heard him talk about it at one of those sessions. Along with a lot of other people, I disagreed with the underlying basis for the merger, but the PRR persisted and dragged the New York Central along. New England politics forced the inclusion of the bankrupt New Haven; and labor was bought off with promises of lifetime jobs.

Well, as I said, the C&O came into the picture for me at the B&O, and I had reached the retirement age of sixty. I decided to leave because they were overruling projects which I had planned for the B&O, saying they weren't in the interest of the combined system. For instance, we had what we thought to be a wonderful plan for a coal transfer pier (along with storage and reclaiming facilities) in Baltimore which, in time, could have made that city a top coal exporter. The C&O vetoed the plan because they felt it would hurt the movement of export coal through their facilities at Hampton Roads. Maybe it would have hurt at first, but now, twenty years later, with twenty to thirty vessels backed up in the Bay waiting for loads, they're asking in Baltimore, Why wasn't this plan allowed to go forward? We had another B&O plan to do the same thing for lake cargo coal at Lorain, Ohio—coal going by lake vessel to destinations principally in Michigan and also Canada. Again the C&O objected, on the grounds that it would have hurt their dumping at Toledo.

I said the hell with it: I want to work with a company where, when you make a plan for the betterment of the company, it goes through. If at that time I had been looking at these projects from the view of the combined system, I think I would have approved them, for the coal transfer facilities we had on the drawing boards for both Baltimore and Lorain would have been more efficient than any C&O facility, and as such would have contributed in the long term to the unified system.

Then, Colonel Henry Crown, who had the major ownership interest in the Rock Island, wanted me to go out to the property, which had just entered a merger agreement with the Union Pacific. The Rock Island was a highly marginal operation and basically very weak, but acquiring it would give the Union Pacific what they had always wanted, access to Chicago and St. Louis. That was why they made their pass at it. It was a hell of a battle, with every railroad in the West in opposition. When these railroads get at each other's throats, no one wins. The only way to win a railroad-merger case is to deal with the opposition in advance. Often tough conditions have to be agreed to, concessions made, proposals modified in order to have some semblance of peace in the proceeding as it reaches the ICC for decision. It is wise to let the DOT and Department of Justice know what is going on. The Union Pacific was disinclined to give ground. Their attitude was, leave it to the lawyers. It took the ICC eleven years to "decide" the bitter controversy and when they did finally get around to it, there were so many conditions imposed that the Union Pacific walked away from the merger and the Rock Island had to go into bankruptcy. I don't blame the ICC as much as I do the western railroads for failure to hammer out an overall merger solution for the West.

This, of course, was long after I left, because when I was sixty-five, Judge John Fullam, who was in charge of the Penn Central bankruptcy, called me up and said, "I've got a good retirement job for you. Come down here and become a trustee for the Penn Central." My wife and I wanted to go back East, anyway, so back I came. That "retirement" job turned out to be a real struggle because the Penn Central was in awful shape. The root question was not "how" to reorganize the Penn Central but whether it "could" be reorganized on any basis. Liquidation, in other words, was a real threat. As a trustee, I wasn't really an employee of the Penn Central, I was an officer of the court. We were called upon several occasions to try and relate the circumstances that brought on the bankruptcy. My own view is that the single most important factor in the disaster was the loss of business, the continuing decline of volume. As simple as that. Ever since the Korean War the

PRR and NYC had been slipping in volume, while in the West and South railroad traffic was doubling and in certain cases tripling. Loss of volume in an inflationary economy is impossible to handle if the size of the plant and employment are frozen, and work rules for the labor force are beyond reach.

The man the trustees hired to run the railroad did not pan out and had to be let go. So in late 1973 I resigned as a trustee and became president and ran the operations until April of 1976, when Conrail came along. They took the railroad over, and that was the end of my railroad employment. However, since 1976 I've done a lot of work for Penn Central and the company is doing extremely well. They had enormous real estate holdings all over the country. Pipelines, all kinds of non-railroad assets that didn't go to Conrail, and they had carry-over losses from their former railroad operations which they used to offset their new income, and pay no income tax for several years.

I'm still on the board of Amtrak, but I don't expect to stay more than the end of the year [1981], along with the other two railroad directors. The Department of Transportation will be running the operation and will name the directors. It's all too bad. Alan Boyd has done a hell of a fine job as president. The Reagan Administration was really ready to roll it up, but Boyd has Congress pretty well behind him and they didn't want any part of that. I don't really know what is going to happen. The first decision must be, Do we want and need a rail passenger service, or don't we?

The way Congress runs a railroad, they choke you. Hold back on the money. For instance, they have it in the statute that you can't have dining-car service unless you break even. But you can't possibly make money on dining-car service unless you fudge the figures. You can't possibly charge what it costs to maintain and operate the dining cars, let alone cover the cost of food and the attendants. Dining-car service was always part of the public relations effort of the railroads, and in the case of such railroads as the B&O it really paid off. We ran that B&O passenger service, Washington to Chicago, despite the fact that we were losing money, because it was an added advantage to the B&O. For good will, and the way people spoke of us. There were a lot of people who were big shippers and they were impressed. When you added it all up, the bottom line was a plus, in my opinion.

I think the full-service passenger train as we ran them is gone forever in this country. Gone unless what they are doing in France and Japan can ever be made to pay off in this country. Somebody would have to fund it. The French have been successful and they don't have a lot of money. Yet they have been able to provide a fine level of service. So have the British, for that matter. They have trains that make ours look pretty bad, and they don't have any money either. We had great trains at one time. The Santa Fe had the *Super Chief,* and there was the *Capitol Limited* on our B&O. Wonderful train. And the *Commodore Vanderbilt* and the *Twentieth Century Limited* on the New York Central. When the *Century* left New York on every trip they gave her the railroad. A clear track. She moved out, often in several sections, and had the railroad without anything in her way all the way to Chicago.

I remember when business started to drop off on the B&O, we went out of our way to try further to improve the service. We put on special food, with salad bars, and many extras. We put on dome cars, and you could go through the Alleghenies, west of Cumberland, on a moonlit night and it was a great ride. We added stewardesses. It is a shame that service is gone, but nobody (except for the inevitable "deadheads") was using it. You got to a point where you couldn't continue an operation that was losing that kind of money. And instead of using our service, the big freight shippers were flying their own planes. Yes, there was a lot of sentiment and emotion involved. It was the same with the steam engines. We had to realize the diesel was a lifesaver. If we had to compete against the trucks with the steam engines, I doubt if the economics would have permitted a competitive operation. But there were many in management who were very reluctant to get rid of the steam engines. The Union Pacific was one of those railroads. As late as 1946 the PRR was buying new steam engines. The hard facts of business can be tough when you're dealing with emotions.

As a kid, I lived in the country up on a hill overlooking Elmira, New York. Down below were the old Delaware, Lackawanna & Western Railroad and the Erie Railroad. I remember I'd wake up in the night and hear those steam-engine whistles coming down the valley. I still hear them in my dreams.

When this car was new there were nearly a thousand men working for the Western Pacific in Portola. Today, the car is still running fine, but only a handful of men are working for the railroad.

WILLIAM E. TOUT
Portola, California

Golf, especially in the 1920s, was not a game you'd expect a railroad engineer to be playing. In the steam era the hours were long, and after getting a train over the road, a man just wanted to find the nearest bed. Layovers were usually spent playing cards or talking railroad. The hotel manager in Stockton, California, took Bill Tout out to play golf one day and he loved it. He'd never even seen a golf course before that, but as he put it, "Hit a golf ball right one time and you're hooked for life!" Obviously Bill was hooked because he's still at it every chance he gets. Everybody didn't take to it, however. He tells of one old engineer they took out to play. They weren't too far from the Western Pacific yards. The old-timer was paying more attention to the trains leaving the yard than to the golf ball. "We used to tell him, 'Come on, Tommy, let's play golf, the hell with the engines.'"

I think I'm the only hoghead who ever had his engine hit by an airplane. It was a Navy pilot who did it. Right after World War II, when they were mustering the pilots out, these two fellows, the Navy pilot and the guy who owned the plane, tried to hedge-hop my engine. But they didn't make it. The pilot hit the sand dome on top of the boiler and knocked a big hole in it. They tore a wheel off the plane, but managed to land it. When I got in, the roundhouse foreman was waiting for me. He said we'd have to keep it quiet, or the fliers would have to go to the pen and pay a big fine. I said, "Okay, but I don't know how I'm going to do it because I've got a hole in that sand dome big enough to throw a dog in." "Well," he said, "can you run the engine until I get you a new sand dome?" I told him I'd do it. Then the fellow who owned the plane—his name was Snap Applegate—I told him that we'd keep it quiet, but he'd better send down three or four bottles of Scotch whiskey to the roundhouse foreman for keeping his mouth shut. Applegate said, "What the hell's wrong with him? He must be crazy. We'll send him three or four cases!" I never heard tell of anything like that happening any place else.

I lost my father when I was nine months old. He was working for the Great Northern as a fireman when an engine blew up and killed both the engineer and my father. We lived in Anaconda, Montana, at the time. My brother was an engineer on the Union Pacific, so I guess railroading was in my blood. I'd see them guys up there blowing that whistle, riding along in those big locomotives and I thought to myself, maybe I can take on some of that good life. My mother didn't think too much of it, but it was good money and I decided on the railroad for a career. It looked a lot better than working in a factory. I was about seventeen years old at the time.

In 1918 I started with the Union Pacific. At that time you could get a job pretty easy because World War I was on and I was too young to register. A lot of the regular men were gone to war. My first job was engine dispatching. I stayed with that until I got on my feet, and after a year and a half I went firing. I worked all over the Union Pacific lines. Montana, Idaho, Wyoming. I think they had more engines than a lot of other railroads got boxcars. It was on a Thanksgiving eve, in Kemmerer, Wyoming, that I finally got fed up. The fireman on the train just ahead of us froze his hands taking coal on the engine. I said to myself, By God, that ain't going to happen to me! So I moved to California. I got married, settled down. I got a job on the Western Pacific.

It was so different. You felt like you were free. On the Union Pacific they were always looking for ways to fire you, and out here on the Western Pacific they were looking for ways to keep you going.

I remember, we were plowing snow out on the north line, and we'd been out there eighty-one hours. They used the rotary plows up there and I was the engineer on the plow for three or four seasons in the 1950s. There was a stationary steam engine in the plow to spin the rotary, and you'd have an engine pushing the plow into the snow. There was a man on the wheel, an engineer and a fireman in the plow. You didn't come under the sixteen-hour law on that job. It was considered a special. Well, we got in after that eighty-one hours and we were dead. We stopped in front of the yardmaster's office and this trainmaster, McSweeney, asked us where we were going. We told him we were going to the bar. The hind-end brakeman came up and asked McSweeney where we'd gone. He told him and said, "Take this twenty-dollar bill down there and lay it on the mahogany and tell those guys to lap it up." The Western Pacific officials appreciated it when you did a good job for them.

When I first came out here to San Francisco I caught this passenger train in the canyon. This engineer, his name was Sam Shaddock, we got halfway down there and he said, "All right, kid, there she is." I asked him what the hell he was talking about. "Get over here, you can run her." I never was so scared in all my life. After three or four miles I said, "There ain't nothing to it, is there, Sam?"

We burned oil on the Western Pacific, and that made firing an engine a whole different job. I remember firing a coal job on the Union Pacific, a passenger train between Pocatello, Idaho, and Lima, Montana. It was about four hours and twenty-five minutes going up and you shoveled sixteen tons of coal. Firing oil burners wasn't as much work, but you still had to think about what you were doing. Those 400s that we had on the Western Pacific, the big passenger engines, I think they held about 12,000 gallons of oil. They'd be loaded up with oil at Oakland and they'd go to Winnemucca, Nevada, on that fuel.

You filled the tenders from stand pipes that looked just like the water pipes, but smaller. After the oil was in the tender, you had to keep it heated so it would run up to the engine. It worked by gravity. There were heaters right in the tender and you could keep that oil at whatever temperature you wanted. Some of those engines, you had to have the oil pretty hot before it got in there; others, the engine would do much better if it was colder. It's like a human body. Some people will be freezing all the time and others will say that it's just fine. The oil would go from the tender into the atomizer, where the steam would break

Looking more like a golf pro than a locomotive engineer, this is Bill sometime in the early 1930s. It's hard to tell from his expression if he's happy with the way he's hitting them.

the oil into a fine mist and it would burn in the air. You had a firing valve that controlled the amount of oil you were putting in. Some locomotives had double burners and others had just one. Depended on the size of the firebox.

If you were doing things right, you'd have a clean firebox. You didn't have the heavy smoke and the cinders you had with a coal burner, but you did have trouble with the soot. Used to have to sand those engines out to keep the flues clean. You had a bucket of sand right there in the cab and you'd heave it into the firebox. The draft would suck the sand through the flues and clean out all that soot. I remember one time I was coming up the canyon on one of the articulated engines—Mallet—and I had two student firemen with me. The engine wasn't steaming worth a damn and you never seen a blacker crew. We stopped at Blairsden, California, to take water and these kids said they'd run out of sand and couldn't get any more. Would I mind if they gathered up some of the ballast and gravel down on the roadbed to sand her out a little? I said, "I don't care what the hell you do. Go to it and maybe we can get some steam in her and get over the road." When we started out, they threw that gravel and rock in there. Next I saw some people running. The rocks were coming through the stack and you could hear them—*clink, clink!* There's quite a force in there, especially when you're getting started. When we got to the next stop, the road foreman of engines asked me what the hell took place in Blairsden. I said that I didn't know of anything happening, why? He told me that we had broken all the windows out of the station. Hell of a thing.

Some of them engines were beautiful and some of them were hell. I remember one engine over on the Union Pacific. It was the 2545. There was one spot, in the Nugget Canyon, where they couldn't run that engine through. You'd get in there and she'd go off the tracks. They had civil engineers down there, everything, and couldn't figure it out. I don't know if they ever discovered what the problem was. Outside of that, she was a good engine. They could run it through the passing track at that spot, go right along, but on the main line she'd drop right off the track.

Those 400s that I mentioned were made by Lima and as good as any we had. The only thing, they'd slip quite a bit. You had to use a lot of sand on the rails to get them going. They came here during World War II. They were government engines and all the railroads got some. The government made one design and each railroad took as many as it could get. They needed the power for the war and they opened the window back in Washington. I think those engines paid for themselves pretty fast. They were built to move and they did. I liked the Mallets for hauling freight. You could go further for water with them and you could handle long trains better with them. We'd pull, maybe, seventy-four cars. That was all one engine could handle.

After that, they'd put a helper on the back of the train. We used to use helper engines on pretty near every freight train in this district. We had two pretty stiff grades. You usually knew how heavy your train was, but if you didn't, that train would tell you how much you had behind you when you hit the first hill.

I think if there was one engine I really liked the best, it would be engine No. 26. She's now down in Los Angeles in Griffith Park. I had her on a helper-engine job. She was just a hog, but I liked everything about that engine. She was an easy rider, good steamer and I think she had the best valve motion of any engine I ever saw. Once in a while you would get a lemon. There was one engine I didn't like at all. The 178. That engine would just get on my nerves. It just wasn't any good, and I couldn't do the things with it that I could do with the others. Just like buying a new shirt you don't like. No matter how hard you try to like it, it never looks good. Finally you just want to throw it away. You couldn't throw a locomotive away, but you could stay away from it if you could.

The first diesels we got here were the switch engines. We'd had demonstrators here before that, but the first ones that really worked on the railroad were the switchers. Then we got them all. I'll say this for them, they were more decent to run, easier to run, let's put it that way. You just pushed a button. An old lady could do the same thing. On a steam engine, you had to know your business, listen to your exhaust. Know all the things that went into running them. You had to put your knowledge to work with them. Diesels, you just got up on them, had a nice seat box and everything, punched the button, and that was the end of the party. I'd say, if I had to pick one of them, that the 700s were the best diesels they had on the Western Pacific. They were General Motors types, but the diesel I really liked better than any of them they didn't even buy. That was a Fairbanks Moorse we had on trial for a while. She was worth five of the General Motors as far as I was concerned, but an official in charge said he didn't even want a report on her. I think there was some business going on with General Motors at the time and no matter what the engine would have done, it wasn't going to make it.

I think if I had my choice, I could handle a train better with a steam engine. Especially starting and stopping passenger trains. They had a different brake valve on the diesels. The only thing I could say, it was like was riding on a pogo stick. You didn't get the smooth braking you did with the steam engine. You had to be careful with the diesels. I don't know why they came out with the new-fangled thing in the first place. You had to know what your train was going to do, so you made a running test when you were leaving town. That test would tell you just about how your train was going to handle when you applied the brakes. You also had to know where the slack was in your train. I'd always stop with the train stretched out. Some engineers would shut the engine down and bunch the train. I didn't go for that and always ran up with the throttle open. Not full capacity, of course, but enough to keep the train stretched out. That way there was no slack between the cars when the train started; the back car would start at the same time the engine started. I don't know how much you rode on those trains, but if you had that slack running in and out, you'd get a rough ride.

If you think of a train like a string, you keep it stretched, it's hard to break. Get some slack in it and then pull it, it'll snap. In freight, it depended on how your train was made up. Passenger cars all weighed about the same; freight cars could be empty and that would change things around a bit. If you had a lot of full loads on the hind end and a lot of empties on the head end, you'd keep it bunched. If it was the other way around, the empties on the hind end, you'd keep it stretched. If you got a bunch of tank cars and they weren't fully loaded, they'd get to slopping back and forth and you could feel your whole train moving back and forth. The fruit trains were the best trains to pull. They had those Santa Fe refrigerator cars, and it was a freight train that handled just like a passenger train. They kept those cars in beautiful shape and the piston travel on the brakes was at a standard travel. That made a big difference in how a train handled. These other freight cars, you'd get one with a piston travel of six inches, the next one would be sixteen inches. Each car would handle differently. But the railroads kept those refrigerator cars in good shape because they wanted the fruit trains to move fast. You wouldn't have the tonnage on those trains like you would with the others, either. We had seven, eight of those trains coming out of here every day. They'd start the last of August and run until November.

We pulled a lot of stock trains, too. There used to be a lot of hogs came from Iowa, going to San Francisco. We used to take a lot of sheep out to the desert, and they shipped a lot of cattle out of the desert in the fall down to the lower country. They could only keep those animals on the train for twenty-four hours and then they'd have to unload them. Stop the train and they'd have these men who would unload them into stock pens, feed them and then put them back on the train and away you'd go. Those trains stank. You could get lousy just going by one of those trains on a motorcycle.

There was one of these Basque ladies that run the hotel at Gerlach, Nevada, where we used to tie up. Her husband was a sheepherder. You talk about a fleabag, that was it. They had a little restaurant over there. The food was good, I'll say that, but the hotel was the damnedest old crumb joint you ever saw. All railroad people, a few sheepherders and a couple of drunks mixed up with us. We knew all the crews and associated with them. It was very friendly on the WP. On some railroads, it was so big and there was so much business, I guess you wouldn't get to

If just about everybody in town worked for the railroad, the place for a group of school chums to have their picture taken was on a locomotive. Bill's wife, LaVinna, is standing (middle) on the pilot.

know that many people. Those stock trains stopped running about twenty years ago. I don't think they even have any stock cars anymore. Gave all that business to the trucks. Gave a lot of business in general to the trucks. All the railroads want to do now is load the cars on the West Coast and never have to stop until they get them to New York. They're like the gamblers in Las Vegas who want to just take the cream off the top.

There aren't any locals anymore. They did away with all that. At one time a freight had to clear a passenger train by twenty minutes. If you didn't, you'd hear about it. They'd always be preaching to you about keeping the trains on time. Later on they'd put the same passenger train in the hole if they could see a move where they could help themselves with a freight train. Later they started to try to get rid of the passenger business altogether. They'd let the trains come in late, and dirty. They'd never clean them. Yet there was a time when you had more officials than passengers riding on the *Zephyr*. They'd take a man right off in those days if he wasn't handling it just so. They'd tell him, "Get back in freight if you want to work here." I've heard it said that the *Zephyr* was the best train in America, and I put about twenty years in that Feather River Canyon, some of it on that train. I'll say this, it went through some of the prettiest country. You'd come up through there, especially on a moonlit night in the fall when all the colors were on, and you can't imagine how beautiful it was. I'd just sit there and listen to her bark, and look at all those

I quit the railroad in 1964. I said to myself, If I'm going to have any leisure time, I'd better take it now. Play golf, do any damned thing I want to. I did a good job for them, I think. It was a good-paying job. They told me it beat a pick and shovel all to hell.

This train shed is behind the former Central of Georgia Station in Savannah, Georgia. Built at the time of the Civil War, the station was taken over by the city of Savannah when train service ended, and has become a visitors' center.

HOKE S. ROLISON
Savannah, Georgia

The Nancy Hanks II *made her last run on April 30, 1971. Named after a bay mare who set a world's trotting record in 1882, who was in turn named after Abraham Lincoln's mother, the train ran between Atlanta and Savannah. Hoke Rolison brought her into Savannah on that last night. He still has the train orders and one of the plaques that were on the side of each coach. The plaque came off with a hammer and chisel when he realized their next stop would be the junkyard. It now hangs on the wall, a reminder of what once was a great train. There's a song:*

> *Some folks say that* Nancy *can't run;*
> *But stop let me tell what the* Nancy *done.*
> *She left Atlanta at half past one*
> *And got to Savannah at the settin' of the sun.*
> *The* Nancy *run so fast*
> *She burnt the wind and scorched the grass.*

I still have the first ticket I ever made. It's in pretty bad shape, but I'm glad I saved it. I had a brother working on the railroad at the same time, already an engineer. To qualify, you had to ride the road a few days on your own time. The day I arrived, my brother was to take this engine up to Augusta and they worked out a scheme for me to go out as the fireman. That was January 29, 1937. Firing for my brother on my first run; I found that old ticket the other day in the drawer. My brother had told me that they were going to hire some men, and if I wanted a job, to come on down. It was the worst part of the Depression.

When my parents got to me, the seventh son, they had just about run out of names. We had an old governor and senator from Georgia, name of Hoke Smith, and I guess he was one of my dad's favorite people. Anyhow, they hung that on me in 1906, the year I was born. The Seaboard Air Line Railroad went up through the area where we lived and I used to see those fellows get out in those old overalls and that big oil can and get to putting oil around. The fireman would be up there getting water and I just thought that was something great. Just amazed a country boy to see that kind of thing going on.

We had a pretty good-size farm, about 270 acres. I had five brothers in World War I. The oldest one and myself were the only ones who didn't go. It was a pretty rugged life

There is no mistaking what these two gentlemen do for a living. Freddy Peay (left) and Hoke Rolison are wearing the uniform of their trade at Meldrim, Georgia, in 1941.

on the farm and I don't think we had gotten over the Civil War. There were hard times after the war and things had never really gotten better. I can remember seeing a lot of crippled old men. There wasn't hardly anybody who hadn't gone and been killed or crippled up in that war. My grandfather had a hand that was out of shape. He got shot through his wrist; somehow they never got it straightened out, and it just stayed like that.

Railroads used to have passenger trains through the rural areas, and of course they dropped off the mail to the post office and supplies to the depot, things like that. When they did away with those passenger trains, a lot of times they did away with the post office and the town lost its identity altogether. The little town I was raised in, Ohoopee, in Toombs County, used to be a pretty good little village, quite a lot of business. We had a sawmill, cotton gin, turpentine works and a number of little industries employing quite a few people. Didn't pay them anything to speak of, but they did have some sort of job. When they did away with the post office, it became just a side place in the road. Now the old farm and everything has changed hands. The old people passed away and there wasn't any of us left to work up there. We go up to the old cemetery a

couple of times a year and work up there. Keep it up. It goes back to the early 1800s—my grandfather and grandmother are there. The house is still there but it's not taken care of anymore. I sort of hate to look at it, since it's gone down so bad. The whole family just sort of left.

I left too, and joined the Army in 1928. I was in Hawaii nearly three years, and when I came back, it was just about as bad as when I left, so I re-enlisted and stayed in the service until—I guess it was 1936. I finally got out when things were getting a little better. When I went down to the railroad this old superintendent asked me what I had been doing. I told him that I'd been in the service for a few years. He told me, "Those damn servicemen aren't worth a hoot and they aren't worth a damn." I asked him if he wouldn't give a fellow a try. It turned out he was just kidding me about things, and he finally said okay and signed me up. I went to the doctor and got straightened out and went to work. My brother showed me a lot of shortcuts to take, but I wouldn't have wanted to fire for him regular. He showed me how to build your fire and how to get ready to go out on the road. Of course we had to ride the road, like I said, for about ten days or two weeks before we could qualify, and they didn't pay you a thing. Now I think they pay those boys about $10 a day when they are students. They have good jobs today.

When I started, in 1937, it was a pretty good year, but in 1938 things fell off. I made it through pretty well working extra and taking all of the outlying jobs. You had to leave town to get any kind of job, you know. In 1938 they needed some switch engineers and this old road foreman, he came around and asked me if I was a switch engineer. I told him that while firing, I run one every day around there. He took me out and we messed around awhile. You didn't have to pass any written examination or anything. The old switch engine was a pretty good job. You would work eight or ten hours and then you were home.

About 1940 I fell into regular work and I got married in January of that year. I was promoted to main-line work in '41. From then until the end of 1971 I had a job of some kind. For my last four years I was on the streamliner, the *Nancy Hanks II*, that ran to Atlanta. Well, in April of 1971 they did away with the passenger service and I went back into freight service for the rest of the year. I guess about the turn of the century they had an old steam train called the *Nancy Hanks*—and that's why this was the *Nancy Hanks II*. It was a dandy train for a long while, but you know how the railroads tried to get out of the passenger service; they used to tell us that the mail car paid the expenses of the train. Then the Post Office did away with the mail car, and finally the railroad even got rid of the express and the baggage car. Everything was just day coaches. If you had luggage, you'd have to handle your own. I guess at that time they were paving over the whole country and if people wanted to go someplace, they jumped in their car. Gas was at a reasonable price them.

It was April 30, 1971, when the *Nancy Hanks II* stopped running. It was an awful sad time, like the end of an era. I guess for over a hundred years, passenger trains had been running in and out of that station here, maybe longer than that. There are some brickwork underpasses underneath the railroad just west of the station that date back to well before the Civil War—1830 I think they say it is. The smokestack over at the old roundhouse was built by slave labor in the 1830s. They tore down the old Union Station we used to have here. The Seaboard, the Atlantic Coastline and the Southern Railroad all used it. It could have been a landmark for hundreds of years if they would have preserved it, but this interstate highway had to come in through that station. It must have been a gimmick of some kind to sell that fine thing to make way for the interstate. Of course, I know the railroads wanted out of it because they had established this new station three miles beyond where this one was. Everything had to back into that old downtown station. That took a lot of wasted time and they wanted to get away from that. Now Amtrak trains can head on in and head on out and it makes it a lot better for them, but I don't think it was right to tear down the old station. It was all marble work and it was beautiful.

But we let so many nice things get destroyed that railroad stations are just one of many. They didn't even save any steam engines except that little old one down in the historical area. We had some real nice engines on the Central of Georgia. We had the old Mikes, they were an all-around engine. We had what they called a Mountain, we used them in freight service, too, but they were mostly for passenger service. They had some old Mohawks, too. Jack Simpson's daddy got killed on one of them. It blew up on him, I think it was No. 770 or No. 771. I saw the engine when they brought it back to Macon. A bad-looking sight. I really don't know what happened, I used to hear about those firemen and engineers on the Macon road talking about running with low water. Some of those old engineers, the least amount of water you could see in the gauge, that was all right. They were real happy about it. Some of those men thrived on that low water, but it scared me. They'd

say you had hotter steam and you could do more with it, but I wanted to do it with a bit more water. Later our engines were equipped with a feed water pump; the water ran through a heating unit until it almost boiled before it went in the boiler. That was a big saving, putting hot water in there instead of cold and I guess it accomplished what those guys were trying to do with their low water.

None of us had any regular engines. At one time, you know, you had your own engine, your own fireman. That was your man, that fireman was. That was before the firemen were organized. If an engineer liked you, you had a job with him. Of course, you might have to go out to his house and cut his lawn the day you was off or something like that to keep on the job. Maybe they wanted some of the brass on the engine polished. That happened before my time, and I'm glad of it. I never did think it was the thing to do. They used to have the same sort of thing in the old army. You were a "dog robber," they used to call you, if you were an orderly for the captain. If he had an automobile, you'd take it down and wash it.

There was a big difference in the men you'd work with. Some of them had to be perfectionists but everything just didn't go right at all times. They'd be getting upset and do some cussing at you. Other men, some of them were just the nicest old guys you'd ever want to know. I remember one engineer who never got out of sorts. He didn't care if he had one hundred pounds of steam or two hundred. Didn't bug him at all. Some of those fellows, if you had the old shovel working, they would get over there and fire for miles and miles and let you run the engine. I think they were just doing it for exercise and being good guys too. I know I had different fellows firing for me and I would get down there and fire sometimes as much as they would,

Hoke Rolison and the *Nancy* in 1969. Reduced to four cars in that year, she had only two more years to run between Savannah and Atlanta before service ended.

just to keep in shape. There were some pretty rough days.

I don't know if you've heard this story, it's an old railroad story. This engineer told his fireman, "You see this point right in front of me here, I want you to keep that needle on that gauge pointed straight toward that point." Well, they got going and the needle started coming back, and back, and finally it was pointing towards the fireman's side. The fireman's working as hard as he can, all the while, and finally he got up and walked over to the engineer and said, "If you want that needle pointing toward you, you'd better come over and sit on my side, we'd better swap seats."

When the diesels came, there was one good thing: when they got old, the railroad would send them back to the factory for a new engine and everything. The factory would send them back to you good as new. It took months to work those old steam engines over. Our big steam-locomotive shop was in Macon and they run them in for class five or six repairs that included everything. They had crews working day and night on those things. Of course when I first came they didn't have automatic stokers, but I guess around the early forties they started equipping them with the stokers. They started with the heavy freight engines and a few years later everything had the stokers. That made firing a better job. Even running them was easier because you weren't afraid of breaking a man's back.

During the war we worked a lot of hours here, with a lot of oil coming out of Louisiana. Most of it went through Augusta and up into Carolina. We had troop trains and general cargo of all kinds. There were a lot of military movements, and even after the war we had a lot of military movements for a year or longer. Fort Benning on the west side of the state would make a complete division movement to Europe, for instance, and we would handle most all of that. We ran all the way in the dark without a block signal until the last few years I worked. Then we had about twenty miles of signals out of Macon down to a little place called Gordon. I never had any real wrecks—I guess we had a few on the railroad—but I didn't have nothing like a head-on collision.

A few odd things would happen. One night there was a train ahead of us, and we didn't know about it. He was a local freight and was waylaid and running late. He went into a siding on a curve and we were behind him, as I said. Now, we had to meet with a train a couple of stations beyond and we were running late on top of that. So I went barreling around this curve. When a train goes into a siding he is supposed to turn the red markers on the side of the caboose onto green. This boy didn't think about it, didn't know somebody was behind him that close, and he forgot to turn his markers. So I come around this carve and there are those two big red markers looking at me. I didn't know if he was on the main line or what. I jammed on the brakes and was going to jump before we hit that train, but we went right on past the hind end. Safe, but a shock, and it scared me pretty good. I stopped pretty close to his engine and this engineer seen me stop there and he walked over and asked me what the matter was. I told him about his markers and a few other things too. But we were just glad it worked out the way it did.

I remember another engineer, he was on the *Nancy* running opposite from me. One morning he was going up

the road and some cars were on a siding and there was a piece of farm equipment on the end car with a big red lens on it. The way that thing was sitting, this red lens looked just like the switch target. Well, they got real close to it, and the fireman suddenly hollered, "Red switch! Red switch!" He jumped up and went running back through the engine. The engineer, he jammed the brakes in emergency, and he lit out through the engine too. They thought they were going to go right into the siding and hit those cars and they didn't want to be up front when they hit. Well, they got back to the baggage car and looked out and they were going alongside of those freight cars. He said the train stopped about two or three cars beyond the end of that siding and he felt pretty stupid sitting out on the main line with the brakes in emergency for a piece of farm equipment on a flatcar parked on a siding.

Up North, all of those big railroads, they have so many signals. I guess eventually we'll have them all the way down here. They are using that CTC [Centralized Traffic Control] now. That is a beautiful way to operate a railroad. It can slow you down, run you through a siding and nobody even has to stop for anything. They've got these long, long sidings and you're running there while the other fellow goes by and then you come back out onto the main line. It makes a real nice operation. Down near Macon, we couldn't run too fast because it was real crooked, but we used to get late on the *Nancy* and they wanted you to run a good schedule. On good track, we would run sixty or seventy and I imagine we would run some of those old steam engines up to eighty miles an hour. Used to click them mile posts pretty fast when we were late.

I've enjoyed my railroad career. We had some good days and some rough ones all mixed together, but somehow I think I'm glad it's behind me. There's a lot of pressure. But some funny things happened on the railroad too. I remember one time this guy was firing for me on a stoker job; it was a solid oil train. A tank-car train was hard to handle. Sometimes you would get a little slop in the tanks and it'd cause the train to surge and handle funny. We were having a hard time trying to spot the tender under the water tank and I kept having to back the train up. I'd go right on by it every time. With steam every fellow had his little way of doing things and I'd seen those old guys when I first started, they would reach up, set their brake, pull off a few pounds on that gauge, and stop right where they wanted to. This old fireman was comical. He came over to me and said, "Look here, when you get down to the next water tank and have to back up, shut off that stoker for me, will you?" I told him to get his tail over to his side of the cab. He knew I was going to miss that stop.

A lone survivor of the steam age can be seen in what once was a busy yard in New Haven. The coal tipple stands there today not because of nostalgia, but because the railroad felt it would cost too much to tear it down.

LEONARD B. DORMAN
West Haven, Connecticut

Leonard Dorman is in his nineties, but he doesn't act it or look it. Since his wife died he's moved into an apartment in West Haven, Connecticut, where he still loves to talk railroading. One of his favorite stories is about the time he was at his granddaughter's wedding reception and there was a problem with the exhaust fan in the restaurant's kitchen. The fire department evacuated the building when people started dropping from the fumes. First a fireman and the policeman came over with an anxious look and asked Leonard how he was feeling. He said he was fine. A few days later at a union meeting for the retired New Haven Railroad men, one of his friends asked him why he didn't get sick. Another fellow, who had fired for Leonard, spoke up and said, "How the hell would he get sick? Len ate smoke and gas for over sixty years."

You should have seen some of those guys out there! They called me one night to New Haven to go over to New London, Connecticut, to qualify a man on the switcher over there. I went over on the *State of Maine Express*, New York to Portland. Rode in the coach. The train stopped at Sound View station on a hill. It had about twelve or thirteen cars with sleepers on the rear. The conductor came looking for me. Hell of a nice fellow, used to know him well and he knew I was on that train. His father used to be an engineer and his brother fired for me. He said to me, "Christ, Len, that guy is wicked up there. He's banging this train around."

I'd noticed. He was trying to start the train and couldn't get it going. He had a steam engine at that time. I told the conductor, "Don't let him get going. If he does get her going, pull the air. I'm going up on that engine."

I walked up and got up on the engine and said, "What the hell's the matter?"

The engineer said, "I can't start it. I tried and the slack ran out."

"Jesus," I said, "don't you know how to start an engine on a hill?"

I told him to get out of the seat and I put the brake on. I eased back and got my slack between each car a little bit at a time. Then I released all the brakes and started just a bit. Got each car going and took them right out. He was an old-time engineer, too. He'd have had everybody out of their bunks back there. Oh, we had some that were no good at all.

Any kind of business, you're going to get some bad ones. They had a fellow named Clinker King. I was firing one time and working a job with him. We're up there going down Berlin Hill and he shuts the engine off, puts the brake on, stops. Right there, he stops. Then he goes over in the woods to relieve himself and he leaves the water pump on. I said to myself, The hell with you. I left the pump on. He came back and he had a damn boiler full of water and not much steam. He's yelling, "Why didn't you shut the water off?"

I said, "You put it on, why the hell didn't you shut it off!" I used to have fights with him all the time.

He was going up another time, I wasn't on with him that day, and there was something ahead of him. He went down a hill and right into the tail end of the train ahead. So he's on the same job going up there a while after, and he's showing somebody what happened, and damn if he don't run into somebody again. I think he finally ended up in a switcher in the yard. He always claimed he was the only man who could fire one of them 3600 switch engines we had. They were sons-of-guns. Just wouldn't steam. You

put a fire in them, there was enough coal for twenty years. They used to call that a Clinker King fire.

We had some good men, too. More good than bad. I had this Clarence Armitage and he was one of the slickest things you'd want to see. Nice fellow, everything you'd want in a man. I was firing for him one day and we had that dynamometer test car on behind us. It showed everything you were doing on the engine. How you were handling her, speed, everything. The guys riding that car told me that they'd been on hundreds of railroads and they never had a fellow that was as slick a runner as Clarence. We used to have a job going to Springfield, Massachusetts, freight both ways. We had a 3300, No. 3334. Jesus, she was the finest engine you've ever seen. Had a duplex stoker on her. You could set it up and never have to touch that engine all the way to New Haven. I'd fire to Hartford and then Clarence would fire to Springfield, sometimes all the

In the cab of Train No. 6, the *Bunker Hill*, Leonard Dorman makes his last trip into the New Haven station, April 1961. Amtrak is still running a train it likes to call the *Bunker Hill*.

way back to New Haven. They called me one day and told me we were going to have a 3000 on the job. A hand-fired bomb. I told them to book me off the job. A couple days later they told me that engine was going to be on there regularly. I decided if I wanted to eat, I better go to work, so I took it. They wanted the great old 3334 for the *Maine Bullet*. But old Clarence, he wanted to fire same as he did before. I said, "No, that's too much work." Darned if he didn't. Fired clear to Springfield. He was active, a real good man.

I worked with Western Union doing line work before I went on the railroad. Our headquarters were in Burlington, Vermont. We used to work in New York, New Hampshire, Maine, Vermont, and down into Massachusetts. I went with them in 1908, I think it was. The New Haven Railroad had taken control of the Boston & Maine at that time and they had a lot of covered bridges. They were putting in new bridges and we were moving the wires. We were working at Greenfield, Massachusetts, and it was March and a rotten day. Slush and all. We used to bring our lunch, even if half the time you had to thaw it out to eat it. We were wet and cold, so I told the guys I was with, "The hell with it, let's walk back and go out to a restaurant and get something decent to eat for a change." We had something to eat and then we went to the station to get warm. The boss, man named McPartland, stormed up and he asked us what we were doing there. I told him we'd come up to get something to eat and to get dried out. He started hollering and he said something else and I said something and pretty soon I said, "Go to hell." I got on a train and went back to Brattleboro, got my stuff and came home to Westfield, Massachusetts.

In those days you could get a job any place you wanted. My father worked on the railroad in Westfield as a machinist. He asked me what I was going to do and if I wanted to go firing. I told him I did. I got this guy I went to school with, Art Cleary was his name, we were pals. I said, "C'mon, Art, we're going firing." There were six or seven of us that came down that day to New Haven. I was lucky because I only had to fire for seven years. I got set up as an engineer in 1919. They didn't set up more men until 1923, and those few weren't up for more than a month when they put them back firing again. They didn't set up more until 1939 because business was so bad.

A friend of mine, Jimmy Murphy, went firing in 1914. Went out and rode the jobs and got signers. Got all broke in, but he didn't go on the board. That meant you were available for jobs. Your name went on a list, and when you got to the top you got the next job going out. His father had a farm and he went home because they needed him there. They were cutting ice and putting it in for the summer. He didn't come back until 1916 and by the time he was due for the board, about twenty men went on ahead of him. Jimmy didn't get set up until 1939. Fired all that time. We didn't get too much money firing in them days. When I did it I think it was $1.25 a day, ten-hour day and no overtime. Seven days a week. It meant a lot when you were promoted to engineer.

I fired a job out of Northampton, Massachusetts, for a while. We went to Hopewell, New York. The job was called "the Dingbat." We'd come down the Canal Line to Plainville, Connecticut, and they'd put a helper on you to get you over the Terryville Tunnel grade. Then you'd come down into Waterbury and you'd branch off and head west through Sandy Hook, Connecticut. We used to meet the other train on this run, and the passing siding was out on stilts with a swamp underneath it. Rotten! What a place to put up and wait! We'd be there about four o'clock in the morning and the damn mosquitoes were that big. They'd just eat you up.

There were some big hills over there and we needed a helper engine to get up. And they had recording clocks on those mountains coming down, too. You had to use just so much time coming down those grades and the clocks were connected to the main office in New Haven. They'd show how fast you went. Go too fast and they'd call you to come in the office and talk about it. They also had recording clocks on the high Hudson River bridge at Poughkeepsie. That bridge limit was fourteen miles per hour and they meant it. When I was working for Western Union I was over there and walked across that bridge. It was something impressive. Later I was riding with an engineer, Frank Walsh, and we went over the Poughkeepsie Bridge to Maybrook yard. On the way back we're coming down the hill and I says to him, "Frank, you're going pretty fast." He told me he was all right. Well, he wasn't. He had to go to the superintendent's office and I think he was out of service awhile. There were some clever engineers on that Western Division. With steam engines and with the diesels, too. They got so they could go right down that hill and just make that speed. They'd hold the train brake on and keep the engine brake off, and the train would stretch out nice as you please while it slowed down.

Like I said, I got set up in 1919. I just had the Canal Line. That's what we called it. There used to be a canal

from New Haven to Northampton. When they built the railroad they followed or built over the canal. Only a little of that railroad line is in use today, but I did a lot of my firing there and let me tell you, that was a busy railroad. All your stuff from Maine came over the Boston & Maine and they gave it to the New Haven at Northampton. Then they ran down to New Haven and New York or wherever they were going. All freight. You talk about busy! Stuff coming down from Maine. We'd have potatoes. Whole trainloads of just potatoes. If it was very cold, they'd have guys right in the cars, one to every three or four, to tend fires in them. Had to keep the potatoes from freezing.

When it started getting warmer they didn't need the fires and they'd start to throw the wood off the cars. That was wonderful wood, all hardwood. I used to take it home and burn it in the furnace. I lived in Northampton then. Potatoes, you never had to buy them. Get them out of the cars. Didn't have to buy Christmas trees, either. Before Christmas there'd be solid trains of Christmas trees coming down from New England. One year they got them

Except for the two unhappy grandchildren, everyone seems to be

140

having a good time wishing Leonard well on his last run. Family, friends, officials and even the family priest have turned out for the event.

down to East Bridgeport and for some reason they didn't get them out in time. So they burned up carload after carload because they weren't any good anymore. Christmas had come and gone. East Bridgeport was a big yard then. They had seven switches in there on each track. The whole railroad was busy in those days.

During Prohibition they used to run excursions to Montreal. We called that train "the Bootlegger." The company put a bulletin out telling us not to call it that. They wanted to think that those travelers were going up to see the sights or some damn thing. We used to have four or five sections going up to Montreal. You should have seen those trains. Coming back they were even worse. They were a mess. I used to catch them once in a while, and what sights they were! They ruined the cars. Windows broken, seats broken. Same thing on New Year's Eve. The railroad used to run specials down to New York City for that blast. Even before they got on the train those people would be drunk. By the time they got to Grand Central many of them couldn't get off. What the hell they were going to New York for, I'll never know. I never went up to Times Square or nothing with that crew. I'd just go over to the office and have my New Year's there. They'd have to load them survivors back on at three A.M. They used to run a lot of special trains, all sorts of them, in those days!

I stayed at the Railroad YMCA for nine years when I was working out of New Haven. When I first came down here another fellow and myself had a couple of rooms on State Street right across from the engine house. But it was cold and then I was all alone and finally I said, "Hell, I'm going down to the Y." That's all that was in that Y in those days, railroad fellows. Everybody was getting called from there and it was such a handy place to live. It was nice being around all the railroad fellows because you had the same things to talk about.

I ran everything they had: steam, diesel and the motors—that's what we call the electrics. I liked the steam. I liked the diesels. Warm, comfortable. You had a nice seat and you had two engines most of the time. If one let you down, you could always get in with the other one. You very seldom had a single engine out on the road. I ran about all the steam engines they had. I liked the 3300s as good all-around locomotives for freight or passenger. We used them on the New Haven–Worcester jobs.

The 1400s were nice jobs; they were the streamliners that pulled the New Haven's home trains. When we first got them, a fellow from the factory would ride along. They'd fuss over them when they were new. I remember one time, the regular man was off, and I caught a job with a 1400. The fireman was Jerry Conners and he says, "Hey, Lennie, you're running her a little different."

I said, "Like what, Jerry? This is a steam engine, isn't it? I been running steam engines ever since I been on the railroad. Why the hell would I run this one any different?" In fact, the fellow that was with us from the factory said I did all right but that fireman wanted me to work it a little harder. I said, "Jerry, we're making the time, ain't we?" I ran it the same as I would a 3200 or a 1300 or anything else.

The 1400s were fancy but they were steam engines like all the rest. I was coming down in a 1400 one day with the *Merchant's Limited* before they got speedometers. I was

getting into North Haven so fast that I shut her off and drifted all the way into New Haven. Nobody said a damn word. Then they put the speedometers on them and you had to watch it.

I had a close call when I was firing. We were on a local freight just north of South Deerfield. A fellow named Henry Hosmer was my engineer and he blew his whistle at some kids playing on the track. They got off and climbed up on the bank. He had stopped the train in case they didn't move. Then, as Henry started up again, this little girl about two years old suddenly runs down and gets on the track again. God Almighty! Them old engines, they had running boards on the side, along the boiler. I tore right out of that cab, ran along the running board and

Superintendent Frank Moran climbs up to shake hands after Len's forty-nine years of engine service with the New Haven.

jumped off the front end. I picked her up and gave her a slap on the rear end and told her to go home. Trains can't stop fast like autos and I guess we'd have cut her in two if I hadn't jumped out. The train crew saw it all happen and they told New Haven about it. I still got the letter that the Railroad sent me commending me for doing that.

I remember another time we were going up the Williamsburg, Massachusetts, branch one day in a jitney. That was a gasoline rail car. There's a school right by the station and there was a couple of kids fighting. I blew the horn and one of the kids started running up the tracks. He must have been six or seven years old. Every time I blew that whistle the kid would take off some more. I had a lot of road supervisors sitting right in the front beside me and I thought they were going to die laughing. That poor kid, every time I blew the whistle he'd put on more speed.

I got a lot of nice work running those gasoline cars, but I never could understand how the manufacturers got away with one big fault in them. You pumped up the air brakes by running the engine over a certain speed. You didn't pump no air, you had no brakes. One day I'm going down Holyoke Hill toward the Connecticut River and I put the brake on—and I've got no air! When it came to me what the matter was, I put her in neutral and opened up the throttle. Otherwise I'd have gone down into the river.

I never did run the Budd rail diesel cars. Never qualified on them, but they were a damn dangerous thing too. If you put the brakes on and your wheels locked, then the brakes released so you wouldn't slide the wheels. Now you didn't have any brakes at all. That's a nice thing, isn't it? They had a bad wreck on the B&M when one Budd car went into the tail end of a train. Killed two or three. They changed them after that.

It was 1942 when a fellow named O'Connor, who used to take care of the bids in the superintendent's office, told me that they wanted me to take a job as instructor on some new electric freight motors we were getting. They were brand-new, the 150s. They were made by General Electric and they were streamlined locomotives. The older motors were shaped like square boxes, if you ever saw them. That was a beautiful job. I got paid my engineer's rate, my expenses, and everything else. I spent about two years on it and qualified a lot of men on those motors. They were slippery engines and you had to be careful getting them going. They were powerful, too, and the blowers made a hell of a lot of noise. I remember one time a conductor was walking through the engine past those blowers and he got sucked up against the wire mesh that was round them and couldn't get loose. He was yelling bloody murder for a while until we saw him back there. He was a hell of a sight.

Next the company sent me a note that I had been appointed road foreman of engines. I refused it at first. I didn't want to be road foreman because everyone said all you did was clean fires, that is, show firemen how to keep a clean fire. I told the officials that I didn't want that job because I liked what I was doing. If you're a road foreman, you got no home or nothing. Always on the road. Well, they told me to take it for a while, and if I didn't like it, they would let me go back to what I was doing. Figured I had nothing to lose, so I tried it. I wasn't sorry afterwards because I got acquainted with a lot of fellows on the railroad that I would never have met otherwise. That was 1943 and it lasted until 1949. I was instructing engineers and firemen on the new diesels between New Haven and Maybrook, New York. No fires to clean. Then I went back on the main line running until I hit my seventy-first birthday. The last job I had out of here on the main line, I'd leave New Haven at nine o'clock in the morning. Get into Boston at eleven forty-five. Then I'd leave Boston at four in the afternoon and be back here at seven. Nice job.

Them young fellows put me back in the yard. They had meetings and the result was that the company agreed you had to quit at seventy. I was already over the limit, and so

He was just a young fireman when this picture was taken in 1915: Leonard; his wife, Ruth; and (left to right) their children, Ruth, Marjorie and Walter.

I quit. I took a job as a guard. The young fellows have their Brotherhood meetings down here at the K. of C., third Sunday of every month, but I don't go inside. I don't know enough of those fellows. Anyway, they've all got beards and that sort of thing. The guys who went firing after I got off the railroad, they're engineers now and have the Boston runs. In my time we had to have forty years' seniority rights to hold a Boston job. I couldn't even get a switcher here in New Haven until I had twenty years' experience.

They have a dinner for us every year. First Sunday in November, for all the retired men. It's a wonderful meeting, and you talk with some of those fellows you haven't seen in three or four years. Fellows that worked with me, fired for me. I guess it worked out all right. We're still living, anyway. I'll be ninety years old this year and I didn't think I'd live this long.

I liked railroading, especially on steam engines. Nobody else talking, telling you what to do. You were your own boss. You had to run that engine. How was your water? How was the air? How was the pressure? Everything was up to you. Nobody telling you this and that. No sir, you were the one responsible for that engine and that job. You were the man.

The station in Sayre, Pennsylvania, has survived, but the railroad that built it was not as fortunate. Passenger service on the Lehigh Valley ended in 1961 and the railroad ceased to exist in 1976 when it was absorbed into Conrail.

CLYDE S. REDFIELD
Winter Park, Florida

On a snowy day in 1958, Clyde Redfield eased train No. 11, the Star, *up to the platform in Buffalo and ended forty-six years on the Lehigh Valley Railroad. If anybody was born to run a steam locomotive, it was Clyde Redfield. Some of his first memories are of Lehigh camelback locomotives pounding past his grandparents' house in upstate New York. Twenty years later he was up on the deck of the same locomotives trying to keep up a head of steam. When you go to his retirement home in Winter Park, Florida, there is little doubt about what he did for a living. On the table there are models of locomotives, photographs on the wall, paintings, even a train house number. He may be retired from the Lehigh Valley but Clyde's spirit is still up in the cab of the* Star.

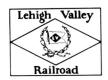

I'll tell you this much, I don't think there are many questions about steam locomotives that I can't answer. I made my first trip for money on November 30, 1912, and went out on my last trip on November 30, 1958. I grew up in the town of Farmington, Ontario County, in western New York, and I was a railroad man ever since I was two years old; we played railroad in the neighborhood. We would take our tricycles on the dirt road by the farmhouse where we lived, and the right-hand rut was the eastbound track, and the other rut was the westbound track. We'd get going against the traffic and have a fight over it. We ran our little railroad like the real ones.

I was supposed to have been a farmer like the rest of the family, since my ancestors had all been farmers through many generations. My father thought my brother and I were going to be farmers too, and gave us thirty acres. We set out an apple orchard on it, with 1,042 apple trees that had gotten to be ten or twelve years old and were just starting to bear fruit when the temperature went down to around 36 degrees below zero for two or three nights. The trunks froze through, the limbs split, and they never was any good after that. I sold my half to my brother and got out of apples. We never made any money to speak of and I decided I didn't want to be a farmer, anyway. I was crazy about railroads.

When I first started we had those camelbacks. "Mother Hubbards," we called them and they was good engines. When they first put the *Black Diamond* on, they had a camelback with the big high wheels; they ran like a scared cat. They had a two-door firebox. When you put coal in the right door, you shoveled right-handed. When you put it in the other one, you had to shovel left-handed. You had to be as good with left as with right. I used to go out to the old barn lot and shovel wheat, first over one way and then back over the other way with the other hand, so I could do pretty good when I first went firing on the road at Manchester, not far from home in Farmington. In fact, on a day when there wasn't anything going on around the farm and I could get away, I'd go down there to the yard and get on with one of those men from Sayre, Pennsylvania, that had a through run to the Niagara Bridge. I'd fire that Hubbard engine right to the bridge, helping the fireman all the way. You know, starting out in those days you had to work three weeks for nothing. Work on the track cleaning fires, work in the yard, and then make three road trips with a crew who would sign your paper if they thought you could do the job. The papers would be sent in and then you were put on the firemen's extra list. You established your sen-

iority date with the first day's pay you made. You got $3.12 for firing a locomotive in the yard for twelve hours. Three or four years afterwards, we got the eight-hour day and for a time they cut your pay to $2.60 a day. I was married and bringing up kids, and that was still big money for a working man in those times.

I started working towards being an engineer as soon as I could. We had a school down at Washburn's garage for our third-year exam. I'd make diagrams that I could hang on the wall so that I could point out this and that on the engine to the rest of the men. I was kind of the teacher of the class. I guess my interest lay in the locomotive end of things. When I had a chance to, I would go to the Lehigh Valley shops at Sayre, and study the workings of the engines being rebuilt. I'd even climb down through the dome when they'd removed the flues, so I could study the boiler braces, crown bolts and the boiler construction. When we took the examination, Charles Page, the examiner, came to Manchester with a special car. We took the written examination of about three hundred questions over two days, and then Mr. Page would go over all the questions with each student to make sure that you really knew what you were talking about, and hadn't just memorized the answers. After we were finished, Mr. Page said, "Mr. Redfield, I have examined many men for engineer on the Lehigh Valley Railroad, but you're the first one to answer every question one hundred percent. Now, you know, no one knows it all, so would you be satisfied if I gave you a mark of 99 and 99/100 percent?" I was so pleased that I told him certainly, fast enough.

For all of that, I fired for a long time, twelve years altogether. I was kind of sore about that. They were short of engineers, but they couldn't get firemen at all; it was W.W.I so the railroad was using men who could have been running engines as firemen. They had to. Finally, though, I made it. I worked at Manchester, my home terminal when I was in freight service. I'd run freight between Manchester and the bridge—that's the Suspension Bridge at Niagara Falls. I liked the passenger jobs better than I did the freight jobs and so I took it upon myself to deadhead on my own time to Buffalo to come out when the layover was in Buffalo. When they changed the layover to Sayre, I'd deadhead to Sayre to run the jobs out of there. The passenger crews went right through Manchester so I had to deadhead if I wanted those runs. I'd bed in the *Star* eastbound, and the *Maple Leaf* westbound. The *Star* went over the Ithaca branch, and the *Maple Leaf* over the main line, Van Etten Junction to Geneva Junction.

In those days there were the Buffalo engineers, and the Manchester engineers, and there was a little feeling be-

Even diesel haters like this engine. Clyde Redfield stands next to Alco's finest, the PA passenger engine in Buffalo. In fact, it has been called "the honorary steam locomotive" by some rail historians.

The sign was made by the shop crew in the Lehigh's Sayre engine shops. On his last run, friends gathered along the line.

tween then. The Buffalo men thought they were a little superior to everyone else and whenever any brand-new engines came on the division, the Buffalo men got them and we got the old ones in Manchester. So, when I went to Buffalo to run a couple of those main-line passenger jobs, I didn't know just how things were going to work out. I would be working with a Buffalo fireman and I was afraid the feelings wouldn't be too good. But who should I get for a fireman, but Dan Oakes, an old friend of mine. Well, he put his arm around me and took good care of me; he was a good scout. Dan, he lives near Manchester. When I'm up north in the summer, I go down to see Dan. We go out for dinner and railroad a little and make a couple of fast runs. He was with me a long time on those passenger jobs.

In the early days there were passenger trains every hour, back and forth each way on the Lehigh, but by the time I had seniority, there were only three main-line passenger runs left each way. That's why I had to have forty years' seniority in order to hold down one of them. Before that I was an engineer on the branch line run that came from Rochester out to Rochester Junction to meet the main line. They finally took those trains off and put on buses. I was the engineer on that last passenger run out of the Court Street depot at Rochester. When I retired in November 1958, they took off all the passenger runs on the whole Lehigh Valley Railroad, and that's where it is today. It was a shame. I don't think they tried as hard as they could to save the passenger service and the great trains like the *Black Diamond,* the *Maple Leaf* and the *Asa Packer.*

I don't think they had many diesels on the Lehigh before World War II, but they arrived fast when they did come. They rode nicer than a steam engine, but they are dirtier than you might think. You can put on a clean shirt, go out on one of those diesels, and when you get to the end of the run, the inside of your collar will be greasy from the fumes. When the exhaust-pipe gases are leaking into the engine, the tears will run right out of your eyes, and you can't do nothing about it. It's terrible, and I understand that today a lot of engineers are afraid of lung cancer.

A lot of things happen to a diesel that you can't fix when you're on the road. In fact, you can't carry any metal screwdriver, hammer or any metal tool to do anything with, and it's a good thing you can't. You'd get electrocuted. Most of the wiring and things in cabinets are sealed up where you can't get at them, and you wouldn't know what to do anyhow. Another thing, the air is coupled in with the electrical part of the locomotive. The switches that change the current are changed by air. If the temperature gets down to zero and that lubrication gets kind of hard and stiff, they won't change. It's not all fun out there when the diesels start acting up.

One day on the *Diamond* going down, the engine was bothering all the way from Buffalo, and when finally we got to within fifteen miles of Sayre, we didn't have any more power than you would have in an automobile with the motor idling. It was downhill, just enough to keep us coasting about eighteen miles an hour. We didn't dare stop, nothing we could do, and we figured we'd better leave well enough alone. Well, all of the officials were out there when we rolled in and they cut the engine out of the train. They couldn't find out what was wrong, and even the experts from the factory couldn't tell what was the matter with the darn thing until they took it back to the shops.

On a steam engine, you could get off and walk around and twist a valve here or poke in there, and you could see what was broke, or if it was a hot box, or whatever was wrong. One day while I was firing, the reverse rod broke on the valve gear. We were working pickup freight, dropping and picking up cars along the way. We couldn't reverse her from the cab, so every time we wanted to reverse, I'd pry up the valve gear with a shaker bar and block it up with a piece of wood so we could run in reverse. We got our work done and got that engine in. If the engine wasn't steaming, as a rule you could look in the firebox and see if the flues were plugged up or not, or what else was wrong. I was brought up on the steam engine and I loved them, and I loved to learn about them. The diesels, you could open them up and let them go, that's about all you did to them.

Those big T steam engines the Lehigh had (they bought the last in 1932), what wonderful engines they were! In

The original one horsepower car. Clyde (left) and his brother Frank put the horse in back so they couldn't see him.

my mind, they were just about the best-looking locomotives of the steam-engine days. On ours, or anyone's railroad. There were, of course, engines that were streamlined, or painted pretty colors, but as an engineer, I took a fancy to those 4-8-4 Ts. They had two big air compressors on the front end, and that big tank with six-wheel trucks. In freight service, one of my best runs was from the Suspension Bridge to Manchester, a distance of one hundred and four miles. With those T engines, and those big tenders, we could make the run with those fast trains without stopping anywhere for water. With all other engines, a stop was always required. Another thing I liked was the steam-operated water pump for putting the water into the boiler. That made it so much easier to control the water supply. Also, in freezing weather, it was a lot easier to supply the boiler with the water pump, put the heater on the injector, and leave it there. Before the coming of these engines, locomotives were equipped with mechanical lubricators, but the Ts were the latest design and even the hub liners and the chafing plate between the engine and tender were mechanically lubricated. After all, they were the newest, and more powerful than earlier ones. I think that in the judgment of company officials, the T engines were superior to any others in our system.

The steam engine was always fascinating to me. Just think that you take water, use just enough fuel to boil that water, make steam at 250-pound pressure, and use it to propel that huge machine, and the train it pulls. It was wonderful, with the engineer and fireman working together on it, a real team. After the engine had made so many miles, it was put through the shop and rebuilt and when it came out it looked brand new. They kept rebuilding and modernizing the engines and, unless they got totally wrecked or were just too small to pull anything, they lasted for years and years.

During World War II, they appointed me road foreman of engines, located at Sayre. We were supposed to ride with the crews, especially on troop trains. They wanted us to be on the engine to help out if something broke or went haywire, to help fix it up. One day an air pipe broke off a cylinder, and steam was shooting all over the place. We stopped for water and, you know, we fixed that darn thing with some fence wire. Got it back together and it stayed closed. All of those little things you could do with a piece of fence wire! If an engineer got into trouble, you'd get a statement from him, and you could recommend discipline. I never recommended much discipline myself. I didn't believe in too much of that. Causing hard feelings would only lead to more things going wrong. There was a lot of friction with the mechanical department which didn't want anything that would fall back and be blamed on them. I just never liked the job. I was away from home, our son was over in the war, and Mabel was home alone. The general manager tried to get me not to resign, but I wanted to get my hand back on the throttle. I was on that job about a year and a half. When I got off, it was good to go back home again.

The men I worked with on the railroad were good scouts. Some were pretty rough, but most of them did a day's work. Some of them drank a little, and I had firemen that were that way too. If you ran into a man like that, the rule was, you were supposed to turn him in. I never turned in a man in my life. I just did his work for him, and my own, and got over the road as best I could. Just try not to work with the man again in the future. I remember one time with a fireman who was really a mess. Could just about walk. I got the train to the Suspension Bridge, firing the engine and running it, both. I put the brakeman on the seat to blow the whistle at the crossings. That fireman got canned a short time after, but it didn't have nothing to do with that trip. Things like that on the railroad usually took care of themselves in time.

Right today, I've been a little luckier than most. I'm the oldest man in age, and the second-oldest man in seniority of the Buffalo Division that's still alive. I'm going pretty good, yes; my legs bother me a bit, but I don't know of

Mabel and Clyde Redfield on their wedding day, October 7, 1916.

anything else. I was lucky—I was very lucky and I'm very thankful. I'll tell you one other thing, I was always kind of a religious man. I never went out on a trip without calling on the Deity. Each trip was in some way different from the others; you had decisions to make and you'd always learn something new. I loved to run those locomotives and, I guess you might say, I'm still an engineer in my thoughts. My wife and I can look back on sixty-two years together. She packed my lunch and saw me off to work. The Good Lord has been kind to us and I hope, if there are railroads in the next world, that the tracks are smooth and the engines are all good steamers.

From this angle, the concourse of Grand Central Terminal looks as it did when trains like the *Commodore Vanderbilt* were still running. Move the camera a few feet either way, and the commercial realities of today would intrude.

WILLIAM J. HALEY
Mt. Kisco, New York

They look down from the clock high over Forty-second Street as they have since Grand Central Terminal was finished in 1913: Hercules, Mercury and Minerva, representing Strength, Speed and Progress. The commuters who use the famous station might suggest that these personalities might be replaced by slower and less powerful gods, considering the state of the railroads today. Bill Haley commutes every day from his home in Mount Kisco and he knows what it's like to ride those trains. He also knows the problems that a railroad faces when money is hard to find. It's very easy to complain and find fault, but that isn't going to solve the problems of the American railroads. People like Bill Haley still have faith in the system and the people who are trying to make it better. If that spirit can be maintained, Hercules and his friends may be looking down on happier commuters in the near future.

A stationmaster in the United States is a great deal different from a stationmaster in Europe. In Europe he runs the railroad as well as the terminal—that is, the section of the railroad he's involved with. In fact, I think that some countries have apartments over the station for the stationmaster. Occasionally one will drop in when he's in this country. We had one from Berne, Switzerland. He gave us a rundown on what he does. I would gather that he's a pretty important guy in the town structure. They try to split up our duties more in this country.

There are fifty-eight people involved with the stationmaster's office. There are also sixty in the building service, also the information booths, upper and lower, baggage room, lost and found, company mail room, parcel check room, stationmaster's and assistant stationmaster's offices, ladies' room and the ushers. That's the total force. There are tenants in all the halls of the building. At one time there was a terminal manager's staff for that. The stationmaster's office is called on now to assist the real estate department by showing areas that might be for rent. For instance, there is a tennis club here, and a racquet-ball club being built. These tenants are some of the things that have come along as the railroads have changed.

At one point, I'm sure you know, they were thinking of ripping Grand Central down. "Save Grand Central!" People were handing out leaflets about that all over the place. I've got one right here. We who worked here had mixed feelings. The majority of our people worked for Conrail or Penn Central and those railroads paid our wages. It was those railroads that were planning on building over Grand Central and we weren't going to bite the hand that was feeding us. We wanted Grand Central to continue in its present form, but we still had to realize that the railroads were in very bad financial shape at that time and had to get revenue from wherever they could get it. I guess you could say that I'm glad it didn't come to that.

What changes they've had to make, we had to adjust to. You know that the Off-Track Betting office is the old New Haven Railroad ticket office. They have a very good business, very good. Have from the start. We had an emergency here one day. I'll never forget it. It was during a work stoppage. There was some labor trouble here and apparently one of the disgruntled employees set off a pepper bomb in the terminal. That's something like mace and makes your eyes water. We got the city in here with their emergency services and the sergeant in charge didn't know what it was. He decided to evacuate the terminal.

On top of the world. With a couple of buddies, Bill Haley (right rear) checks the view on Sugar Loaf Mountain in the Adirondacks in 1935. Bill is an avid camper and hiker to this day.

That was the first time we ever did that. We got everybody out of the terminal except the gang in line at OTB. When they finally found the pepper bomb, it was up on top of the OTB area. Now, those guys in line were the closest to that thing and they had their handkerchiefs over their faces, but they wouldn't leave. Like I said, they've always had a good business.

I was born and brought up in Yonkers. My father was a civil engineer for the old New York Central. He worked for the New York Central in another era. At the time, he was the Central's representative when it was building the various buildings over the tracks. The Commodore, Biltmore, Roosevelt, all those buildings. He was seventy years old when he retired. First railroad job I had was during school days, working as a timekeeper for a track gang over on the West Side. That was back in the thirties and I didn't think too much of it. We were working down in the cut where the tracks run and, Good Lord, people were throwing everything, even bedsprings, out of those apartments. Every once in a while they'd yell "Duck!" and a bag of garbage would come down on us.

I started full-time with the railroad in December of 1940 as an extra mail and baggage porter. Every year they put a group of young people to work, extra, during the Christmas rush. We worked from December 1 until December 24, and then we were laid off. Then I was rehired on January 7, 1941, as a mail-car loader on Track 14. That area was then the mail facility in the terminal. In 1943 I became a separator. That's a job where you organized the mail into the various RPOs (Railroad Post Office cars) by destination. In other words, you had graduated from someone who was a local car loader to one who knew a group of cars and the mails that were carried in those cars. On the New Haven trains at that time, for instance, Train 56 had a storage car and an RPO car. Train 4 had a storage car for Danbury which was taken off at Norwalk, for the Danbury-Pittsfield Division, and two RPO cars, one for Boston and one for the short-line towns. Then a storage car in back of that. Behind that was a baggage car. There was some mail in that car, but mostly express and baggage. Train 362, she carried a Mount Vernon storage car, a New Rochelle storage car, a Port Chester storage car, and a car for points between. That was a big one. That train made morning deliveries. While they were going out on the New Haven Railroad, over on the New York Central tracks, other mail cars were also carrying mails for the North and West.

It was some business, let me tell you. When they lost that mail, they lost a $10 million business, just out of Grand Central alone. Number 21 had an RPO. That went to upper New York State. We tested that one out one

night. We mailed a
letter here in the terminal
fifteen minutes before departure,
and that piece of mail made early-morning
delivery in Tupper Lake, New York. That's way
up in the Adirondacks on a line that's not even running anymore. I doubt you're going to find that kind of service now.

Just before the war I had gained clerical rights and I was working in the General Baggage Clerk's office, only to be drafted early in 1945. It was during the Battle of the Bulge. I think I was one of the very, very few who were drafted from the railroad. They considered the railroad an essential industry and tried not to pull the men away unless they absolutely had to. I was assigned to a service unit in the Fort Service Command serving the Southeast. We were stationed at Camp Gordon in Georgia and were a separation and redistribution center. Things like that. One thing I remember from those war years, before I left for the service, we had an air-raid drill in the terminal. I can recall turning out all the lights in our section of the baggage room which was on the Forty-fifth Street side. It was the most eerie feeling when I turned out that last switch. You were in total darkness up there. I couldn't move because it was so pitch-black.

The baggage wing of the station was torn down and now that's the Pan Am Building. The Pan Am lobby is where the old baggage driveway used to be. It was there, right after the war, that we received the bodies being shipped back to be buried in the various national cemeteries around the country. I think for the better part of a year we had people in the baggage department handling those remains, receiving them from the piers, dispatching them to the various trains going to the Midwest, upper New York State, New England. It wasn't a very pleasant reminder of the war.

Of course, when I got back in '46, my seniority went on and I came back on the afternoon turn as a New York Central baggage dispatcher. We dispatched all the baggage to the trains, from four o'clock to twelve o'clock. You asked about lost baggage. You'd be surprised. That is something that would amaze you. We didn't lose as much as you would think, not with the amount we were handling. Not

nearly as much as you experience on the airplanes today. Everything went into sectors in the baggage car depending on the destination. You knew what was coming off and what was going on. It was a good system.

In 1949 I received an appointment as a special foreman on the mails, and worked the night shift. Night was when the bulk of the mail moved. I worked on that for four years and then went on as assistant station baggagemaster on the night tour. Midnight. At that time we worked with the Postal Transportation Service.

I can recall baggage being stacked twenty feet high, especially at the beginning and end of the summer, for summer camps and resorts. The railroads lost all that business when they started using buses and trucks. Those camp moves were a tremendous production. We had people in the stationmaster's group who were here for a solid week. They lived right in the Biltmore and would meet a camp group at a certain point in the terminal and take them right down to the train. It was their responsibility to set the train up for that group. When the long-distance trains were phased out, the big camp moves went too.

It's sad to remember those liners, or the fleet, as they called them in those days. People in crowds coming and going from those trains. Business was wonderful. A train like the *Century* had a couple of hundred people on it. You had at least ten cars on that train and it usually ran upwards of sixteen when really busy. She'd be right over on Track 34. Right up to the end of Track 34 and that electric motor sticking out beyond the platform. Every night it was like that, and that was just one train. There were twenty-seven trains leaving out of this terminal in those days. That was just the long-haul trains—not counting the commuter service.

Many an evening I was covering the head end of the *Century*. She carried mail, baggage and a few pieces of express. There was a good deal of hoopla with that train, depending on who was traveling that night. They would have the press down there taking pictures if a movie star was riding, or a big politician. Of course, they would have the *Century* carpet rolled down. Nobody, but nobody, ran over that carpet with a baggage cart. No sir! You had to use the elevator to get up to the head end. They'd have a delegation of railroad people out there every night to see it off. The passenger agents were always around, too. They knew everybody. They were like the supersalesmen of the railroad. I just saw one a while ago, Charlie Andrews. He's now a warden in a nature preserve. His bailiwick was theatrical moves. He knew all the theatrical agents. Each agent had his specialty. Jack Sweeney was another one. He had athletic teams like the Yankees, and the emerging NFL football teams at that time. They'd have several cars reserved for the team. Jack would have the tickets and he'd handle everything through the traveling secretary for that particular team. It would be a regular ritual. He'd parade down, put the team on the train, shake hands with the traveling secretary. "Trust you have a good trip and if you need anything, just wire us." Off they went. Now they charter planes for that sort of thing.

In those days the train was the only way to go, and those passenger agents were quite a deal. One of those agents would handle a family like the Fords. They'd call him and tell him they wanted to come east on Train 48 and he'd get their reservations. Get them a suite on the train, set things up in the dining car, take care of the baggage. Even get them hotel rooms and take care of things in town for them. They would ask for the agent and knew them and counted on them to get things done. The big problem was when one of the agents retired. He had to decide who he was going to give his people to. You had to handle those folks very carefully. The redcaps had their people, too. They'd take care of somebody all the way from the taxi to the train. When he was coming back on the train they'd be there to take care of him going the other way.

When those long-haul trains disappeared, a lot of jobs disappeared too. The six hundred men we had in the baggage department when I was there are now down to ten. During the peak of the railroad business we had, maybe, three hundred and fifty to four hundred redcaps working over the twenty-four hours. There are four out there now, two to a shift.

We lost that mail contract in 1968 and I was transferred

They just don't take photographs like this anymore. Little boys probably wouldn't put up with the clothes. Bill and his mother, Rose, and sister, Cathryn, in the 1920s.

to the stationmaster's staff at that point as an assistant; in 1980 I became the general stationmaster. I'm in the process of breaking in the assistant stationmaster to take over when I retire. I'm kind of "on hold" at this point until we see what's going to happen around here. We have a five-year contract with Conrail and they are going to be giving up the passenger service when that runs out in the next few years. We don't know if the MTA or Amtrak is going to take over. That's the big question. Whoever gets it is going to have to spend some money. We are now running a commuter railroad at this terminal. We have nearly five hundred commuter trains in and out of here every day and just a few Amtrak trains. Equipment, that's our biggest problem right now. Money and equipment. The tracks are in pretty good shape because they've been working on them. Now they have to go after the rolling stock. On the upper Hudson we're running equipment that should have been retired a long time ago. The diesel locomotives we have there are old-timers from the New Haven. They are a real problem and are always breaking down. They're looking forward to electrification on the Harlem Division from North White Plains to Brewster. Then they could use the multiple-unit cars all over the plant. Electrification is going to be expensive and a long process. A number of the stations are going to have to be relocated. Some of them are on curves and they have to be on a straightaway because of the high-level platforms on the cars. It's a political football because a lot of those towns own their stations.

Then there's the new equipment, like the SPV 2000, to replace those smelly Budd rail cars that they use between Brewster and Dover Plains on the Danbury branch, and things like that. One problem with the new equipment, a lot of people think, is that they are getting too sophisticated with it. In steam-engine days they never had the problems they have today. Steam just kept on running. The engines and the cars. All this new equipment we're getting has problems we never had with the old commuter cars. No-close or no-open doors, no-work lights, no-go air conditioning, stuff that's always breaking down. I've commuted my whole working life, so I've seen it all. When I first moved to Mount Kisco we had the steamers and they were really good. I've heard it said that when a steamer broke down it took some searching to find out what was wrong and only a nickel to fix it. The new equipment, it's easy to spot what's wrong but it costs a million to fix. The best I think we had was when I was coming in from Yonkers on those old Mutts. That's what we call the MUs or multiple unit electrics. I don't remember the damn things ever breaking down. They didn't have air conditioning but they did have fans. You'd just raise or lower the windows. They just kept going for years and years.

Very few of the people I commute with know what my job is. I feel it's better that way because those that do know frequently call my house at night about little asinine things: they were standing on the station platform and saw a loose bolt here or something else there. Little insignificant things. However, you're always on the alert. You never know when you're going to get a good tip that something is unusual. I keep my eyes and ears open when I'm riding. After a while you're able to pick up the mood of the passengers. We had the revolts here a year ago this sum-

Yes, he does ride his own trains. Bill checks his watch at the Mount Kisco station. Commuting to Manhattan every day, Bill is of the opinion that the railroads do have a future. We agree.

mer. That was the worst I've ever seen it. Angry people were coming in here, twenty and thirty at a clip. That's why we have that security pen out there in front of the office. Several of my people have been assaulted. I can remember, myself, being in on an evacuation of a rear-ender. We were helping the injured passengers out of the train and this one guy coming off the train says, "Do you work for Penn Central?" I said, "Yeah, can I help you?" With that, he took a swing at me. Well, you have to realize that they're so frustrated and they take out their frustrations on the first thing that hits their eye. This is the only place they've got, the stationmaster's office. Summer of '80, that was the worst. They were climbing the walls every morning and every night.

I'll tell you, though, on the whole the commuters are very patient. They seem to be able to cope with everything, the great majority of them. I think they realize that we are trying to improve things. The conductors are the ones who really get it. They are in the actual front lines, the trenches. I don't think there's one of them that hasn't had somebody take a poke at him. However, when all else fails, the conductors send the bad cases to the stationmaster's office.

We've got our share of problems in the terminal itself.

One of the big ones is around the phone booths. Purse snatchers, pickpockets, friends of mankind like that. Holidays are bad. When you have a lot of tourists you have a serious problem. Tourists are distracted by novel sights and are easy pickings for these local types who make quite a profession out of crime. The railroad has its own security force to deal with such people and they aren't sitting on their hands. If you've noticed, they've got cameras throughout the terminal on the upper and lower levels and they have a base at the police desk to keep an eye on things. There's been a lot of publicity about the bag ladies and derelicts, or, as they like to call themselves, the displaced persons. We try and maintain a live and let-live policy with them as long as they don't cause any problems with the commuters or a hazardous condition for themselves.

We have met with the people who run the various shelters throughout the city and we try to send them for help if we can. The New York *Times* did an article on two people I'm very familiar with. Gave their life history, how they came to be in this area, things like that. Very interesting, but I think the two they picked out have mental problems. They aren't all there. The displaced persons have been around for years. I can remember years back, we'd cut through the steam tunnels on a rainy night. We'd use them for shortcuts going from Fiftieth street to Forty-second street. The huge Consolidated Edison steam pipes are down there and it's pretty hot. In the winter, you'd see a few of them sleeping in those tunnels. We didn't know any of them, but they knew us. I saw one coming down the sidewalk a while back and she said, "Good morning, Mr. Stationmaster, I trust you have a good afternoon." I said, "Thank you," and kept on walking. I even got a Christmas card one year. It was from "Your friends, the displaced persons." I saved that card. It's quite a memento.

The question has been put to us often: How are the railroad people today, as opposed to the ones of yesterday? No matter how you answer that, it causes an argument. I usually say that in my forty-odd years with the railroad, I have met just as many people who try to do a good job now as back then. We have some very competent young people who are trying to do, and are doing, a very fine job. Unfortunately, they are discouraged at times by what goes on today. I try to tell them that it happened years ago too. It wasn't all rosy back then, like some people would want you to think. We have some young industrial engineers in our operations planning department, for instance, who never cease to amaze me, both with their intelligence and perseverance. They are giving 110 percent, which is what good railroad people have always done. I compare them with the so-called old-timers that people are always talking about. I worked with those people. All in all, the average railroad man, I think, deep inside, still maintains that old spirit.

152